The Persecution of the Prophetess of God
and of the Followers of Jesus of Nazareth

The Persecution of the Prophetess of God and of the Followers of Jesus of Nazareth

The History of the Cruelty of Church and State

What you read here
is merely the tip of the iceberg

Compiled by Matthias Holzbauer

Gabriele
Publishing House

The Free Universal Spirit
Is the Teaching of the Love for God and Neighbor
Toward People, Nature and Animals

The Persecution of the Prophetess of God
and of the Followers of Jesus of Nazareth.
The History of the Cruelty
of Church and State
1st Edition, March 2020

© Gabriele-Verlag Das Wort GmbH
Max-Braun-Str. 2, 97828 Marktheidenfeld, Germany
www.gabriele-verlag.com
www.gabriele-publishing-house.com

Original German Title:
Die Verfolgung der Prophetin Gottes
und der Nachfolger des Jesus von Nazareth
Die Geschichte der Grausamkeit
von Kirche und Staat

The German edition is the work of reference for all
questions regarding the meaning of the contents.

Translation authorized by
Gabriele-Verlag Das Wort GmbH

All Rights Reserved

Printed by: KlarDruck GmbH, Marktheidenfeld, Germany
Order No. S 471en
ISBN 978-3-96446-034-9

Cover Foto Montage: © Igor Zh./Shutterstock.com / © Fabianodp./Shutterstock.com

You will be amazed:
such a thick book –
only about persecution.

But that's how it was for 40 years:
persecution after persecution.

That's how it was in the Middle Ages,
That's how it is today.
Read the introduction

Table of Contents:

For Orientation: the Background 9
The Eternal Word, the One God
from Abraham to Gabriele. The Prophets
of God Clarify: The Baal System 12

Do Dictatorial Religions Endanger
Our Democracy? 40

1. Introduction 68

2. The Helping Hand of the Christ
of God Is Spurned 73

3. The Defamations Begin (1981-1984) 79

4. The First Enterprises of the Original Christians
Are Fought Against or Hindered (1984) 141

5. The Smear Campaign of the Churches
Against a Commercial Project
in Würzburg (1985) 161

6. The Expulsion of the Friends of Christ
from Hettstadt (1985-1996) 202

7. Attacks by the Church Against
a Natural-Medicine Clinic (1986-1997) 258

8.	The Modern Inquisitor Wolfgang Behnk (1991-99)	289
9.	9. An Original Christian School? That Cannot Be Allowed! (1986-2011)	341
10.	"End-Time Apostles" or: God Gave Warning in Time (1985-2000)	370
11.	State and Justice Department Under the Thumb of the Church	396
12.	The Effects of the Defamations	454
12.1.	Disturb the Activities of Their Community of Faith!	456
12.2.	Deprive Them of Their Livelihood!	466
12.3.	Isolate and Discriminate Every Single One of Them!	528
13.	Despite Hostilities and Chicanery: The Kingdom of Peace Is Emerging	543
Appendix – Reader's Letters		615

For Orientation: The Background

"The Persecution of the Prophetess of God and of the Followers of Jesus of Nazareth. The History of the Cruelty of Church and State" – what is this book about?

It is about Gabriele, the prophetess and emissary of God in our time. She received from God, the primordially eternal One, the mission to bring the teachings of the Kingdom of God to this Earth, to the extent that they can be passed on with the words of human beings.
She accomplished this mission. In just a few decades, her tireless efforts have resulted in a worldwide work that goes out via radio and television stations. The results are freely accessible to everyone – in word, picture and sound in many languages – in the Tent of God Among the People, the Ark of the Covenant of the Free Spirit, with the Sophia Library.

Against what resistance did all this have to be achieved? How much suffering was connected to this superhuman achievement? How much mental cruelty from her tormentors did the prophetess of God have to endure? That is what this book is about.

For decades, the cassock wearers of today, the priestmen of the church institutions proceeded with untruths and suspicions, with permanent incitement against the word from heaven, against the bearer of the word, Gabriele, and against all those who, with her, work for a life according to the Sermon on the Mount of Jesus of Nazareth.

The events described in this book are part of a millennia-long fight by the priestmen of all times, who are attendant on the idol Baal, against the bearers of the word of God. They slandered and mocked the prophets of God of the Israelites; they instigated the cruel torture and murder of Jesus, the Christ, and with sword and pyre, they wiped out the numerous movements that followed the stream of early Christianity during the Middle Ages.

A murder of the human being Gabriele by priest-believing followers and dependents was prevented by the fact that, via transmitters, the Kingdom of God announced to the servants of Baal the cosmic march of the seven Cherubim against the "god" Baal and his violent criminals.

The Middle Ages are not the past, and this book substantiates this with a wealth of verifiable facts. A past that has not been dealt with is present. How present the Middle Ages still are in some people's minds can be seen, for example, in an E-mail message that was received by the Original Christians in November 2017: "Too bad there's no longer an Inquisition. I'd be there if they torched you lot."

The Inquisition of the Middle Ages has merely put on a "more modern" garment. Murder has often been replaced by character assassination. Today, as well, the state has provided the Church with a forum, and the Church has carried out what it wants.

Behind the fight of the cassock wearers against the Free Spirit is the system of the old serpent, which is exposed in a TV broadcast under the topic "The Eternal Word, the One God from Abraham to Gabriele. The Prophets of God Clarify: The Baal System."

Modern Inquisition continues to have an effect into our time, as another TV program under the title "Do Dictatorial Religions Endanger Our Democracy?" explains.

These two broadcasts provide some background information, the knowledge of which helps to better understand the events described below. Therefore, they are presented at the beginning of this book.

Martkheidenfeld, November 2017

The Eternal Word,
the One God from Abraham to Gabriele
The Prophets of God Clarify: The Baal System

From time immemorial, prophets of God have lived and worked among the people. Many know the names of God's great prophets, who, over the last 4000 years, brought the eternal word of God to humankind: Abraham, Moses, Elijah, Isaiah, also Amos, Jeremiah, Ezekiel, Hosea, Daniel and many others, up to Jesus of Nazareth, the greatest prophet. And after Jesus of Nazareth, there were many prophets, illuminated men and women – the names of whom only the fewest are still known today. Today, a great prophetess of God is living among us again, Gabriele, the prophetess and emissary of God.

Where do God's prophets come from and why did and do prophets of God live among us again and again?

God's prophets and prophetesses are high spirit beings from the Kingdom of God, men and women, who tried and try to awaken the awareness of the One God in the hearts of the people, the God of love, of peace and of unity. All prophets of God, men and women, bore and bear witness to the Kingdom of God, to the eternal Being; they bore and bear witness to the one God of love, who is the Father of all His children. Through His prophets, the loving Father calls to those of His children who left the eternal homeland.

At the beginning of God's creation of the Being, a high spirit being, joined by others, did not want to join the ranks of the other spirit beings to be in unity, in the equality of the filiation of the Father-Mother-God, but wanted to be like God, themselves. These spirit beings wanted to rule according to their principle of inequality, of above and below, of "Divide, bind and rule!" With this, they opposed the divine principle of unity, of kindness, love and meekness, which is: "Link and be!"

Right from the beginning, the rebellious ones were in disagreement with one another. However, from their differences in desires and concepts directed against God, they chose Baal as their common head ruler. Baal is their "god." Baal embodies their principle of hegemony. In short, we call it the Baal system. The Baal system fights against the divine attributes of filiation, of Kindness, Love and Meekness, which are the foundation of eternal life, created by the true, eternal God of the pure Being.

Ever since the Fall-beings turned away from God, the Eternal, beside the pure Being of the true, eternal God, there is the Baal system, the principle of "Divide, bind and rule." As time passed, its adherents – the rebellious beings – removed themselves more and more from the pure Being of the Kingdom of God, because the Baal system led to ever greater densification among its followers and their dwelling places.

Step by step, the Fall-worlds formed, until finally the lowest level emerged as the material cosmos, which also includes the Earth. Since then, the Baal system, the principle of "Divide, bind and rule," exists on the Earth.

Rulers were established according to this principle. Whom do they serve? According to this principle, religions formed. Whom do they worship? Whom do they serve?

According to His law of freedom, God, the Eternal, allowed His rebellious children to do as they liked. In His mercy and justice, He even gave them a quantum of His divine light-ether to take along, without which the Fall-beings wouldn't even have been able to exist. The light-ether contains the essence of the law of God. Thus, the Fall-beings had the possibility to accomplish their own creation according to their ideas.

But at the same time – since the beginning of the Fall – God, the Eternal, informed His fallen children about the consequences of their actions and called them to turn back and change their ways. From the beginning – over unimaginable periods of time until today – it was and is the highest spirit beings from the Zenith, from the Sanctum of God, who fulfill this task on behalf of the All-Highest. This is the justice of God, because the Fall also originated from a spirit being out of the Sanctum.

From time immemorial, the highest spirit beings have been working on the Earth as the prophets of God, as His emissaries of love for God and neighbor. From time immemorial, they shed light on the Baal system and its servants in ritual garb, bringing to the people the message from the Kingdom of God, the law of love for God and neighbor, the call of the eternal homeland to all fallen children.

From the very beginning of the Fall until today, the Baal system has been fighting against the Kingdom of God, against His messengers, His prophets and His message of love for God and neighbor. And for 2000 years, its wrath has been primarily directed against Christ, because He again brought the filiation attributes of Kindness, Love and Meekness to the Earth, and through His deed on Golgotha,

became the Savior and Redeemer of all fallen beings.
The Baal system appears again and again in varying garb. But it is always the same system, it is always the cults and cult priests, always the "Divide, bind and rule." This is how Baal can be recognized. God has no system, no religions and no priests. God is the life; He is the "Link and be."
As Jesus of Nazareth, His Son, the Christ of God, the Co-Regent of heaven, described the Baal system in clear words, when He spoke to the religious representatives of His time, the caste of priests back then, saying:

You are of your father the devil, and your will is to do your father's desires. He was a murderer from the beginning, and does not stand in the truth, because there is no truth in him. When he lies, he speaks out of his own character, for he is a liar and the father of lies.

And Jesus of Nazareth also found clear words for the priests themselves. He called them serpents and brood of vipers, and said:
Woe to you, scribes and Pharisees, hypocrites! For you are like whitewashed tombs, which outwardly appear beautiful, but within are full of dead people's bones and all uncleanness.

All this can be read in the Bibles of the churches. In many examples, what Jesus of Nazareth further thought of the Baal system has also been passed down there. He pilloried the disdain of the life from God and His divine commandments, the torture and killing of animals and the bloody sacrificial cult of the caste of priests of His time, which, using a whip, He drove out of the temple where the blood of the animals for sacrifice flowed profusely, using the following words that have been passed down:
My house shall be a house of prayer, but you have made of it a den of robbers!

Instead, like all prophets of God, Jesus of Nazareth, brought the message from the Kingdom of God, His law of love and freedom. Jesus of Nazareth indicated again and again that He was part of a current of all the prophets who bring the one message from the Kingdom of God, among other things, with the words passed down:
I have not come to abolish the law and the prophets, but to fulfill them.

And 2000 years ago, Jesus clearly described what the law, the content of the common message of all the prophets of God is, namely, the law of the Kingdom of God. To the question of a Pharisee regarding the most important law, Jesus of Nazareth gave the following answer:

You shall love the Lord your God with all your heart and with all your soul and with all your mind. This is the great and first commandment. And a second is like it: You shall love your neighbor as yourself. On these two commandments depend all the Law and the Prophets.

All the words to this effect, can also be read in the passed down scriptures of the churches, in the books of part-truths, as the Christ of God once labeled them in our time.

Apparently, there was a reason why Jesus of Nazareth frequently indicated that He and the prophets come and teach from the same current that comes from above. Apparently, even back then, the words and actions from the pot of lies of Baal's sacrificial cult were falsely attributed to the old prophets by the sons of the liar – to express it with the words of Jesus of Nazareth – just as this has befallen all true prophets of God until today.

But Christ, in Jesus of Nazareth, irrefutably bore witness to the fact that all prophets of God taught and lived according to the law of God, according to the commandments of God, just as they were given by God, the Eternal, through the prophet

Moses, and were lived and deepened by Jesus of Nazareth. All of God's prophets rose up against the sons of Baal, against every priestly cult of Baal in every garb. All the prophets spoke out against the cruel pagan cult of blood sacrifices and the slaughtering of animals.

What is actually reported today about the old prophets?
Abraham lived on the Earth about 4000 years ago. From the divine revelations of our time through Gabriele, we know that Abraham is the law-prince of the divine Earnestness, a Cherub before the throne of God. God, the Eternal, is the primordial God, the primordial Being of love.
Through Abraham, the knowledge about the One God came to the Earth and since then, it has been retained. Abraham followed the call of the One God and left his homeland to open up a land far away for a people that follows the One true God and lives the laws of the Kingdom of God on the Earth. We later frequently encounter this vision of the promised land in the traditional scriptures and today, again in the promise of the Kingdom of Peace of Jesus, the Christ.

Today, in the books of the churches, it is implied that Abraham, the great prophet of God, was pre-

pared to murder his son on the altar at God's request. The idea that God, the Eternal, could demand such a thing stemmed from the Baal cult, not from the One God, the Creator of all Being. God, the Eternal, the primordial love, is the primordial life, not death. God, the Eternal, does not demand any sacrificial death. Why should He, who created all life, destroy life?
To offer up our all-too-human aspects to God, the loving Father, on the inner altar and to leave them there, that is what pleases God, not murder and manslaughter on bloody sacrificial altars in the demonic spirit of the Baal cult.

Just as questionable is the veracity of another tradition: that when God abstained from the sacrifice of the child, Abraham sacrificed an animal in place of his son. It's true that Abraham had grown up in a cultural circle of polytheism and grew up in the sacrificial cult of the ruling system of Baal. But even though Abraham may have been still captive under this old, years-long influence at the beginning of his calling, this would have changed, at the latest, after his training by God to be a prophet.
After the calling of the human being, Abraham, to be a prophet, Abraham, the bearer of divine Earnestness, was trained directly by God in the principles of the law of the Kingdom of God, as also

took place with the other great prophets of God: with Moses, the bearer of divine Order, with Elijah, the bearer of divine Will, and with Isaiah, the bearer of divine Wisdom.
But the scriptures passed down remain silent about this. Why don't we find any words regarding this? It has been passed down from many other prophets of antiquity that especially the disdain for life and the violation of animals is a particular abomination to God, and that this central feature of the Baal system in all its garbs was massively pilloried by the prophets over and over again. Among other things, the following words from the prophet Hosea have been passed down:
They offer sacrifices as gifts to me. They eat the meat of the animals they bring. But the Lord is not pleased with any of this.

And the prophet Isaiah said: *He who slaughters an ox is like one who kills a man; he who sacrifices a lamb, like one who breaks a dog's neck.*

Again and again Isaiah denounced the slaughter and sacrifice in the spirit of Baal and similar words from the prophets Amos and Jeremiah have also been passed down in the Bibles of the churches.
Despite this clear attitude of all prophets against Baal, against his priests and their sacrificial cult, we

read absurdities about the great prophet Moses, the bearer of divine Order before God's throne, in the scriptures passed down. He, through whom God led a people into freedom and to whom God gave His eternally valid Ten Commandments – excerpts from the law of love of the Kingdom of God, of the primordial love and of the primordial life – this great prophet of God, of all people, supposedly instituted a caste of priests. He supposedly vested them with extensive authority and, as the will of God, he supposedly gave them instructions for disgusting rites and ceremonies, in which innocent animals, creatures of God, were tortured to death in the cruelest ways, cut into pieces on the altar and then burned, for – as it says – *a pleasing odor for the Lord,* so that afterward the priests could then devour the choicest parts of the animal carcasses.

Of the prophet Elijah, in whom the bearer of divine Will was incarnated, it was not only rumored that he bet against the priests of Baal and defeated them in sacrificing a bull, but supposedly he also gave the instruction to kill all priests. All these things are a part of the insignia of the Baal system, of the God of cruelty: violence to, and murder of, human beings and animals. And in the same breath, it is reported that during his whole life, Elijah opposed the priests of Baal who do such things.

Regarding Isaiah, the bearer of divine Wisdom, his time on Earth is reported truthfully, that Isaiah denounced idolatry, the sacrifice, the lust to murder animals in the sacrificial cult of the priests and of the people. Isaiah demanded compassion and helpfulness instead of idolatry. The prophet Isaiah announced the coming of the Messiah, of the Redeemer, which was fulfilled in the Christ of God, in Jesus of Nazareth and His deed of sacrifice on Golgotha.

He brought the vision, the prophecy of the coming Kingdom of Peace, of the Kingdom of God on Earth. Many people know that no animals will be sacrificed anymore in the emergent Kingdom of Peace, because there will be no priests in the Kingdom of Peace, but solely the Christ of God, who spoke for the animals.

If God speaks through Isaiah about peace for human beings, animals and nature in the coming Kingdom of Peace and announces the coming of the Messiah, of the Prince of Peace, was God then mistaken with the other prophets, through whom He allegedly demanded murder and manslaughter of human beings and animals, or is God, the Eternal, even changeable?

Even in the traditional scriptures, to which the caste of priests also refers, are the words: *I, the Lord, do not change.*

The scribes of our time, the theologians, call these contradictory scriptures "Priestly Sources," which were often written down by priests only many centuries after the death of the respective prophet.

It is certain that no prophet belonged to the caste of priests, no prophet, who came from God, founded a religion or was devoted to a religion – to say nothing of belonging to one. Christ, in Jesus of Nazareth, did not belong to a caste of priests, either. He came from the people; He remained among the people; He was free of religion, like all prophets before and after Him, until today, as well as all His followers.

Why, then, are the prophets that God sent to the people mentioned at all in the scriptures of the caste of priests, in the scriptures of the religions? Because the entire caste of priests appropriated the prophets, in order to attribute their own style to the prophets. The caste of priests of yesterday and today talks about the prophets, but in reality, they talk about themselves, because what they talk about never came from the prophets.

The priests imputed to the prophets the Baal system's ritual slaughter and butchering. One wonders whether the millennia-long evil merely used the great prophets to ensure its Old Testament consumption of meat? And that, because until today, the sacrificial meat-cult of the priests of Baal of yesterday is the meat-cult, the cult of the palate of today. The Baal of yesterday is the Baal of today.

If the caste of priests of yesterday and today would live what the prophets actually said, there would be neither priests nor religions nor churches.

2000 years ago the Baal system was in an extreme uproar when the greatest prophet, Christ, the Son of God, the Eternal, came to the Earth. The servants of the Baal system responded to His message of peace from the Kingdom of God, His call to follow Him, and to set off with Him on the path back to the eternal homeland, with stalking, lies, slander and character assassination all the way to murder, because they saw their demonic hegemony threatened.

Rightly so, as history tells us. Christ, the Son of the All-Highest and Co-Regent of heaven, overcame the Baal system with the power of love, the law of the Kingdom of God. On Golgotha, He became the Savior and Redeemer of all souls and human beings and of the entire creation of Being. From

His divine part-power of the primordial power, He transferred an energy-filled support to each soul. Through this, He irrevocably ensured the filiation attributes of Kindness, Love and Meekness, which are retained in the innermost part of each soul and of each ensouled human being. Right from the beginning, the Baal system with its "Divide, bind and rule" wanted to extinguish these filiation attributes.

Christ Himself personifies these filiation attributes from God's love. As Jesus of Nazareth, He lived them as an example and taught them in His Sermon on the Mount. He showed the people the way to again develop these divine attributes and to follow Him.

After the resurrection of the Christ of God and His return to the Kingdom of God, many people began to live in early Christian communities according to His teachings. But the Baal system did not give up. Baal soon insinuated himself into the early Christian communities and increasingly gained the upper hand. Under Emperor Constantine and his followers, the Baal system became the solely tolerated state religion under the false label of "Christian." From then on, the Baal system raged even more strongly against Christ.

All the followers of Jesus of Nazareth were persecuted, the prophets of God who came to the Earth again and again, also after Jesus of Nazareth, were the most mercilessly and cruelly persecuted. Many were murdered, always with the means of their time, because they all stood up for Christ, the Son of God, who exposed the Baal system and thwarted their demonic plans.

The Seraph of divine Wisdom also had to endure this fate many times; since Jesus of Nazareth, she has incarnated as the prophetess of God in various countries and cultures, and today, lives among us in Gabriele, as the prophetess and emissary of God.

For nearly 2000 years, under a false name, the Baal system has left a broad trail of blood throughout history with its massacres. This is Baal, who calls himself Christian. There is nothing Christian about him. Anyone who knows the teachings of Jesus of Nazareth recognizes this. None of this has anything to do with Christ, the teacher of peace of the love for God and neighbor. Why, then, all these crimes and most vile deeds under the term Christian?
Because the Christ of God Himself personified, lived as an example and protected the filiation at-

tributes, Kindness, Love and Meekness. It is Him, His name that the Baal system wants to drag through the mud.

That is the credo of Baal, whom Jesus of Nazareth described as a liar and murderer right from the beginning.

Even though the Baal system appears under a false label, yet, it can be recognized, especially when it helps itself to the name of the Christ of God, because then, we have to merely measure the words and actions of its servants against the words and actions of Jesus of Nazareth, to expose it.
In our present time, Christ Himself has done this with mighty words of revelation through Gabriele, the prophetess and emissary of God.

Out of His authority as the Son of the All-Highest and Co-Regent of the Universe, Christ raises His voice as plaintiff for the millions of people who fell victim to the crimes committed by the power conglomerates under the abuse of His sublime name Christ.
In the words of the Christ of God, the millennia-long abuse of His name and of His teaching of peace from the Kingdom of God becomes apparent, and those who hide behind it, and are subject to their

own judgment according to the law of cause and effect, have been exposed and denounced.
In many places, this abuse of His name, which Christ brings charges against, can be recognized: Neither Jesus, the Christ, nor any prophet of God ever founded a church or a sacrificial cult, or ever instituted priests, pastors, dogmas, ceremonies, relics, sacraments or alleged saints.

Who, then, invented churches, sacrificial cults, dogmas, ceremonies, relics, sacraments and alleged saints?

All the prophets of God – with Jesus of Nazareth leading the way – spoke out against the Baal cult of sacrifice, against the killing of human beings and animals. In the first early Christian communities, there were no butchers and no meat eaters, no hunters and no soldiers.
Who is it that today justifies the killing of people and the wholesale slaughter of animals?

It is striking how much His name was and is mocked and scorned by such and many other patterns of behavior, which Christ denounces in His great revelation.
Why don't the religions commit such misdeeds under their own name, instead of under the name

of Christ? Because Jesus of Nazareth, the Son of God, protected the core of being in every soul.
And why, then, are there so many splinter religions under the name of Christ? Who is it who develops such religions? Who is the ruler?

Let's read about this in the Vatican's dogmas that are still valid today:
We declare, state and define that it is absolutely necessary for salvation that every human creature be subject to the Roman Pontiff. His authority is divine!
This is how the infallible dogma of Pope Boniface VIII in the Bull Unam Sanctam from the year 1302 reads in the Vatican, and which is still valid until today.
God, the Eternal, knows no subjugation.

Who is it that makes the pope "divine"? Who is it, who, from the very beginning of the Fall until today, demands that other rulers in the world bow before him? Who is the head ruler?
In His great revelation and in clear words, Christ charges against the blasphemy that lies in such and similarly presumptuous doctrines and demands.
Jesus, the Christ, said: *I have said nothing in secret.* Who is it that speaks of the mysteries of God? Which God has secrets?

Who is it that calls himself the representative of Christ on Earth and needs the Vatican secret archive? Which Christ is hidden in the Vatican archives? Who knows a murderous Christ? It was not Jesus of Nazareth. Who, then, is hidden in the secret archives of the Vatican?

Is everything that is hidden in the secret archives the past? If the Crusades, Inquisition, the burning of witches, the persecution of heretics, religious wars and much more that lie in the secret archives are the past – that is, expiated, everything made amends for, the treasures of the robbed people and nations given back as far as possible – then all the documents could be made available to everyone. So, why are the archives kept locked up? Who has the key to the Vatican archives?

Christ, the Son of God, does not have a key to a secret archive; Christ has the key to the kingdom of heaven.
How misdeeds – if they have not been atoned for – can still be effective after centuries, indeed, millennia, can be recognized by the example of Emperor Charlemagne, who today is called "the Great" by some. About 1200 years ago, Charlemagne wrought havoc all over Europe with violence, war and terror in nearly 50 campaigns, in

which he decimated entire nations under the insignia of the Catholic institution. He acquired his name back then, the "butcher of Saxons," due to the unimaginable brutality and cruelty with which he raged against the people of Saxony, placing them – as many others, too – before the choice: "death or Catholic."
In our time, the city of Aachen in Germany presents the Charlemagne Prize every year. Many Excellencies and dignitaries from all over Europe, who use the name of Christ in the names of their institutions, have without scruples let themselves be honored with this prize that bears the name of the cruel butcher Charlemagne.
Whom these Excellencies and dignitaries truly serve becomes apparent through the award recipient of the year 2016, the head of the Vatican. To make it even clearer, the prize was not given to the recipient in Aachen, as is usually done, but the secular powerful had to make a pilgrimage to Rome again, to pay homage to the pope, exactly like 1200 years ago, when Emperor Charlemagne had to kneel before the pope in Rome back then.
Still much more takes place for which the name of the Christ of God is abused:

Jesus, the Christ, taught the Ten Commandments and the Sermon on the Mount and lived them as an example for us. He said: *Every one then who hears these words of mine and does them will be like a wise man.*

Who teaches: *Faith alone is enough?*

Who appoints dead people to be so called saints, to whom people should pray in continuous prayers and whose bones they should venerate?

From Jesus, the Christ, we know that there is only one Holy One, the Father in heaven. He said: *And when you pray, do not heap up empty phrases as the Gentiles do, for they think that they will be heard for their many words. Do not be like them, for your Father knows what you need before you ask Him.*

If God knows what we need, for what, then, the prayers to the alleged saints, who, in turn, are supposed to bring about something as intercessors to God? – What? – These are merely a few examples of the many that Christ holds up in His charge to those who abuse His name.

God, the Free Spirit, leaves to each one his freedom. That is why each person has the freedom to believe whatever he wants. For some people all these cults and rituals acts may be in order. But why don't those who affirm all this, use their own name for it, instead of Christ's name? Since in their own Bibles it says that Jesus, the Christ, taught and lived the exact opposite?

40 years ago, when the Baal system realized that the Christ of God had again come to Earth through the prophetic word of God's prophetess, Gabriele, there was a great uproar again. Danger lurked for them in Würzburg, the residence on Earth of God's prophetess. From there, in the prophetic word, Christ, the Son of God, again brought to the people the loving Father, the Spirit of love and freedom, and, as 2000 years ago in Jesus of Nazareth, He called all people to follow Him, Christ, free of religion and without any coercion, without priests and pastors, without dogmas, rites and ceremonies.

As Christ explains in His mighty revelation, in 1979 He, Christ, had directly extended a helping hand to the heads of both large religious conglomerates, including the pope.

Via the prophetic word through Gabriele, Brother Emanuel – this is how the Cherub of divine Wisdom introduced himself to the people – directed many questions to the churchmen on behalf of Christ. He took the Bibles of the churchmen, which he called a book of "part-truths," and the statements contained in it from Jesus of Nazareth. He compared these statements to the doctrines and the behavior of the churchmen and asked them, again and again, who had taught the churchmen, who call themselves Christian, to act against the words of Jesus, the Christ.

Thus, the Cherub of divine Wisdom asked, among other things:
Who founded the organization "Church" and who condones the state within a state?
Who crowned the heads of the churches and who gave them titles?
Who said: Take the tithe and build splendid churches and let yourselves be paid by the people according to your titles?

The Cherub of divine Wisdom cited a wonderful statement by Jesus of Nazareth that is still contained in the Bible:
Come to me, all who labor and are heavy-laden, and I will give you rest.
But what does the ecclesiastical organization say? You who pay, come all to me and give, if possible, even more. If you are not a paying Christian, then you are not a church Christian either, because you are excluded from the one true grace. ...
The institution with its leaders relies on the Bible and does not live it! What does our brother, on Earth called "Holy Father," have to say about this? What a presumption, "Holy Father"! Did Jesus advise this to you, dear brother, or does this unima-

ginable offence against the sole Holiness come from the dogma factory?

After many questions and admonishments, the Cherub of divine Wisdom announced to the church leaders the desire of the Christ of God that all may fraternize and strive for perfection in the true brotherhood and community of Jesus Christ. The church leaders did not feel that the Cherub of divine Wisdom and the Christ of God were worthy of an answer.

Today, after nearly 40 years, in His great revelation, the Christ of God Himself gives the church leaders the answer they had refused Him.

To the Baal system, the community in Christ, of which the Prince of Wisdom spoke, is the greatest danger, because freedom, unity, peace and love for God and neighbor in Christ signifies the end of the Baal system, the end of "Divide, bind and rule," the end of the Fall.

While Christ again reached out to the bishops and offered the pope a direct conversation back then – to which, in turn, no reaction followed – the religious conglomerates of power were already secretly organizing their persecution authorities. With great sums of money and with a lot of personnel, they activated their persecution officials and established new Inquisition offices, in order to silence Christ.

At first, the priestmen tried to appropriate the prophetess of God into their institution, just as they had handled others during the Middle Ages. When this didn't work, the system reacted to Gabriele according to its tradition: with persecution, character assassination, threats to her livelihood, to the extent that the respective worldly power allows this. Today, murder is no longer part of it. Perhaps, therefore, the words of the head Lutheran inquisitor to some of his victims: *In the Middle Ages we would have dealt with you much differently.*
But otherwise, the inquisitors in cassocks were mostly given a free hand by the powerful in state and society, many of whom have the insignia of the Baal institution on their flags.

Also in our present time, the inquisitors are waging their campaign against Christ, the Son of the All-Highest, and Gabriele, the prophetess and emissary of God, under the abuse of the name of the Redeemer of all souls and ensouled human beings. Today, too, they try to mock and deride Him, the Son of God.

They still believe that they can defeat Him, He, who already defeated them 2000 years ago. They believe that they can silence His word.
But that is no longer possible. Through Gabriele, the prophetess and emissary of God, His word is worldwide today. Millions upon millions of people hear and read it daily.

The Spirit of truth promised by Jesus of Nazareth has come in the prophetic word of the great teaching prophetess and emissary of God, Gabriele, and has led the people into all the truth. It also exposed the Baal system. More and more people are recognizing the whore of Babylon and are turning away from her according to the words spoken by the Seer of Patmos about 2000 years ago:
Come out of her, My people, lest you take part in her sins, lest you share in her plagues.

The Baal system is at its end. More and more people are turning away and following the call of the Christ of God, the Redeemer of all souls and ensouled people into freedom. It is the one word of the One God, which Christ and all the prophets of God proclaimed, and proclaim, from Abraham to Gabriele.
The "Let there be" in the inceptive messianic, sophianic age of the love for God and neighbor makes

everything apparent. The "Let there be" is the will of the Creator-God, of the Transformer, who makes all things new, a new heaven and a new Earth, with the incipient Kingdom of Peace of Jesus Christ. Christ Himself has again announced His coming in the Spirit in the words, I come soon.

Dear readers, may aspects of this explanation as well as the words of the Christ of God in His great revelation, indicated at various points today, be a help for your own decision. Each one has the freedom to decide himself what he wants to believe. But he may not abuse the name of another for what he has decided for. Surely everyone will agree with us on this point.

July 2017,
Gert Hetzel

Do Dictatorial Religions Endanger Our Democracy?

Dear readers,

I am a pacifist and a staunch democrat and I stand by the teachings of Jesus of Nazareth. As a democrat, I want to address a topic today that concerns all democrats. It is about the influencing and weakening of our democratic constitutional state by totalitarian regimes. We Germans know from experience the danger that issues from totalitarian regimes, from dictatorial regimes and their aggressive ideologies of absoluteness and world domination.

Here, we sit up and take notice when we read that for all fundamental questions of social coexistence and public welfare in Germany, and before every important decision, extensive activities are started that have their origin abroad – namely, at the Vatican regime in Rome. They culminate in the personal statements of the pope and a large number of conversations between high-ranking German decision-makers, and the ruler in Rome – to the exclusion of the public.

Such behavior is, in itself, already unusual for a democracy. We are experiencing an outcry in the

USA, where contacts abroad in connection with democratic decisions are being investigated under the word "treason."

All this is exacerbated if this foreign regime has, like hardly any other in the history of the world, trampled the right of freedom and human rights underfoot; if, by referring to its ideology, it has instigated or condoned – hundred-thousandfold persecution, torture and murder, Crusades, Inquisition, witch-hunting, genocide and much more; and if through this, it has millions of people on its conscience.

No one will dispute that this description is applicable to the history of the Vatican regime with its ideology, which it calls its "faith."

And what is it like today? Has the Vatican regime dissociated itself from its totalitarian and murderous past? Has it discarded the structures and policies that were the basis for its misdeeds? Or simply asked: Does the Catholic regime in Rome today profess to democratic principles, to the fundamental right of freedom and of human rights, as they are written, for instance, in the Human Rights Charter of the United Nations and in the European Human Rights Convention? To come straight to the point: The Vatican has signed neither of these. If we now continue to pursue the question of how the Vatican regime deals with the terms of the democratic basic principles of the right of freedom and of human rights, then I can present a few verifiable facts. But please draw your own conclusions. Please understand my remarks as follows: The questions are presented for you to think about them, because especially with these statements, everyone is asked to decide for himself.

Indications on the relationship of the Vatican regime to democracy can be found, for example, in the so-called Fundamental Law of the Vatican City State from Nov. 26, 2000. Right in Article 1, sentence 1, it states: The Supreme Pontiff, Sovereign of the Vatican City State, has the fullness of legislative, executive and judicial powers. Powers – this word, in the name of Christ?

Besides, it can't be expressed more clearly: No trace of democracy, but full, total, absolute autocracy of the pope. And because he apparently seems to stand above everything, the usual attempt by dictatorships to maintain at least the appearance of a liberal democracy is not even made.

By the way, anyone who thinks that the designation of the Vatican as a state is a joke is wrong. It's true that the Vatican really doesn't consist of more than a rambling palace with adjacent buildings and gardens on an area of barely 0,44 square kilometers within the city of Rome, with only one owner, the pope, and a "population" of about 400-500 rotating "citizens," almost exclusively men. Nevertheless, many countries worldwide take the Vatican's claim seriously and grant the Vatican regime many diplomatic and other such privileges as those of a state. Thereby, the Vatican regime operates as the "Holy See," over which the pope likewise presides as absolute ruler.

Thus, according to the criteria of international law, what the pope rules over is not a state, but nevertheless, a powerful worldwide economic and personnel network. Much has already been written about its immeasurable wealth. How far its arm and influence actually reach is described in a report that was compiled in the USA in 2013 for the Obama administration. There it says about the Vatican regime:

Despite the disparity in size, governance, and history, we are both global powers, with global interests and influence. From many points of view, the Holy See is unique to the world in its ability to pursue its own agenda. The Vatican, with its diplomatic relations counting 180 countries is second only to the United States.

"To pursue its own agenda" means: to assert its own power interests.

How this Vatican regime basically defines its relationship to the rest of the world – independent of the public image of its respective current officeholder – is shown by a look into other Vatican documents, for example, in the "Teaching of the Catholic Church as Contained in Her Documents" by Josef Neuner and Heinrich Roos, where the Bull "Unam Sanctam" by Pope Boniface VIII is printed under number 342 and culminates in the sentence:
... *We declare, state and define that it is absolutely necessary for the salvation of all men that they submit to the Roman pontiff.*

Until today, this sentence is marked as an "infallible" precept of faith of the Roman Catholic Church.

In another official textbook "The Christian Faith," by Josef Neuner and Jacques Dupuis under Margin Note No. 1005, one can also read what is in store for anyone who does not submit to the Vatican regime's claim to absoluteness as well as to being the sole true Church of salvation. It says there:
The ... Roman Church firmly believes, professes and preaches that no one remaining outside the Catholic Church, not only pagans, but also Jews, heretics or schismatics, can become partakers of eternal life, but they will go to the eternal fire prepared for the

devil and his angels, unless before the end of their life they are joined to it [the Church].

However, the Vatican threatens the eternal fires of hell not only for life after death, but to very concretely make sure that disbelievers – according to its interpretation – land there more quickly. In the aforementioned collection of dogmas by Neuner and Roos, this sounds like the following under number 352:

The Church, by virtue of her divine institution has the duty of most conscientiously maintaining the treasure of divine faith unimpaired and complete and of watching with the utmost zeal over the salvation of souls. She must therefore with painstaking care remove and eradicate anything that is contrary to faith or in any way harmful to the salvation of souls.

You can find many other similar regulations, unchanged until today, in all the Vatican's program of collections of binding regulations, for example, in the Corpus Juris, in the Catechism, in dogmas and decrees.

Does this alarm you as much as it does me? Such and many similar regulations are not merely non-binding sentences in old books. If you know the bloody trail that the Church of Rome has left behind in history, then you know that this aggressive doctrine of force – designated as the Catholic faith and valid unchanged – has become bitter reality for millions of victims. Among other things, this prompted the well-known international church historian, Karlheinz Deschner to draw the following conclusion, already in 1986:

After intensely studying the history of Christianity, I know of no organization in antiquity, in the Middle Ages and during the present times, including and especially the 20th century, that at the same time is so long, so continuously and so terribly burdened with crime as is the Christian Church, particularly the Roman Catholic Church.

(Die beleidigte Kirche, Freiburg 1986, p. 42 f.) Whereby Deschner himself was taken in by the church's fraudulent labeling with the name "Christian"!

What kind of regime is this that produces such rotten fruit, not to mention the moral competence of its rulers? Can we expect from the absolute ruler of a regime, which, already according to its program, is authoritarian and totalitarian, to respect the achievements of a liberal democracy, democratic principles, such as the integrity of the life of all people, freedom, freedom of religion and all other human rights? Decide for yourself! There are more facts concerning this.

Perhaps you think that a regime that has stubbornly defended medieval concepts for over 1000 years will change with a new man at the top? Because the public appearance has changed? That is not even possible, because the Vatican regime's totalitarian axioms and claims to absoluteness until now cannot be changed at all. They stem primarily from popes and saints; and according to Vatican dogma, popes cannot err; according to Vatican doctrine, they are infallible, when they speak "ex cathedra."

The inalterability does not apply merely theoretically, it is also confirmed by practice. Unaltered today as before, wherever the Vatican can assert its influence, the fundamental right of freedom and human rights are ignored. This is most clearly visible in the Vatican itself, but also in Germany, the influence of the Vatican regime is evident everywhere, in the equal rights of men and women, in the prohibition of discrimination, in the right to form coalitions, in the right to freedom of religion and in many other rights.

That nothing substantially changes where exactly such an impression is externally awakened, is most clearly visible with the so-called abuse scandal under the Vatican's umbrella that has occupied the public for more than ten years. It is about the entanglements of the Vatican regime in at least

200,000 cases estimated worldwide, in which clergymen of the Church in Rome raped children and youths or committed some other offenses against them.

After the old Pope Joseph Ratzinger resigned, who for decades, as prefect of the Inquisition, was responsible for these cases, which were likewise hushed up for decades, the new pope – in an effective publicity move – promised consistent clarification and processing of such cases. What actually happened is described as follows by the respected Neue Züricher Zeitung (Newspaper) on January 20, 2017, with reference to the book "Lussuria" by the Italian journalist, Emiliano Fittipaldi: *No pope has so volubly condemned pedophilia as has Francis. But also under him, the Catholic Church de facto still protects the culprits in its own ranks.*

A book published in 2010 – "The Case of the Pope" – likewise deals with the worldwide child abuse crimes of the Catholic clergy. It also investigates the responsibility of the Vatican, as well as of the former Pope Ratzinger for these crimes. The book was written by the well-known British Senior Advocate and head of the largest British law office representing human rights, Geoffrey Robertson. During the course of his investigations, Robertson

determined again and again that the Vatican regime was able to successfully protect the clerical perpetrators from public prosecution for decades. Finally, he reached the following conclusion:
The Holy See, a pseudo-state, has established a foreign law jurisdiction in other friendly states pursuant to which, in utter secrecy, it has dealt with sex abusers in a manner incompatible with, and in some respects contrary to, the law of the nation in which it operates, and has withheld evidence of their guilt from law enforcement authorities.

One of the "friendly states" that Robertson refers to is Germany. Several hundred cases became known here; the unknown cases are presumably much higher. The Vatican knows the cases because they have to be reported to the Vatican. There, until today, they are under the so-called papal secret.
Secret, well and good. But did Jesus, the Christ, teach any such thing? Did He teach a rule of silence and secret archives? Anyone who breaks this rule of silence, including the victim, is threatened with excommunication, which, according to the Margin Note no. 1005 in the book by Neuner and Dupuis mentioned before, and according to Vatican doctrine, can lead to eternal damnation for the victim – not for the criminal.
Robertson's statement has never been disputed.

Of course, this raises the question: How far does the power of this foreign state, the Vatican, extend in Germany? To what extent has it exhausted its "unique ability to pursue its own agenda" in the world, as it says in the afore-mentioned report to the US government? That is, to assert the interests of a totalitarian organized regime against the law of a parliamentarian constitutional state in such a way that even dangerous criminals are withdrawn from the control and arrest by our parliamentarian constitutional state? I ask this as a staunch and troubled democrat.

That the Vatican, an undemocratic state, maintains many activities in Germany is known.
Does it thereby respect the sovereignty of the German state and does it unconditionally keep the laws that apply to all Germans and the Constitution? Read the facts and then decide for yourself:
Regarding the tax law, the labor law, the coalition law, the right to freedom of religion and conscience of others, the prohibition of discrimination, criminal law and many other areas, the Vatican and its registered adherents make use of an abundance of exceptions and privileges, by referring to their agenda, called "faith."
Referring to this "agenda of faith," whose content and scope is determined solely by the ruler in the

Vatican, this foreign regime exerts its influence without control on our liberal constitutional state with its government, democratically elected by the people. For example, this foreign regime determines who is appointed to certain German professorships at German universities; it controls the religion classes in schools, it determines cardinals and bishops, who are paid not by the foreign regime, but by German taxpayers.

That is the principle: In all these points, the democratically elected government in Germany willingly submits to the absolutist foreign regime. The German taxpayer has to pay, no matter what faith he has.

Often the Vatican regime refers to agreements from the time when Germany was still completely repressed by the dictatorial Nazi regime.
From devised, centuries-old, alleged claims, which supposedly can never fall under the statute of limitations, the Catholic regime collects hundreds of millions from the German state, while itself, using the statute of limitations as objection, is unmoved and turns a deaf ear to the German victims of its clerical child abusers, when they request a modest compensation for the soul murder committed on them.

In manifold ways, the system controlled by the Vatican in Rome annually deprives the actually sovereign, democratic German state of billions upon billions in money. It claims subsidies and material benefits of nearly 10 billion Euros, and more billions flow to it by way of its service organizations and commercial enterprises, which, in many areas, are favored by the state.

With the billions that all German taxpayers have to come up with – also those who have never had anything to do with the Vatican's Catholic construct or no longer want to have anything to do with it – the partisans of this foreign organization worth thousands of billions lead a life in luxury and affluence, with monthly salaries, at government cost, of up to 15,000 Euros plus housing and a company car. At the same time, more and more German citizens are falling through the economic and social network and living at the minimum subsistence level; every fourth German child is meanwhile threatened with poverty. Ever more people are even threatened with becoming the "working poor," that is, poverty despite full employment.

These are merely a few and only the most obvious effects of an undemocratic foreign regime on the democratic constitutional state of Germany and all its citizens.

The regime in Rome also maintains a close network of thousands of subordinates in Germany, who are directly committed to the pope in Rome or to his bishops. In Germany, for instance, by referring to their "faith" and their "secret," these men take the right to disregard otherwise self-evident civic duties. Thus, invoking their status as priests granted by the Vatican regime, for example, the right at their discretion not to report imminent criminal acts or not to cooperate in their clarification. In part, they evade control by the state also by referring to their own special status similar to a state, for example, in the case of data privacy, which comes very close to the meaning of the term "state within a state."

This includes numerous processes in which the Vatican directly, and with privilege, exerts influence on state decisions, for example, in the area of public media organizations, but also in the discrimination and persecution of other religious orientations – via the state counterpart to the clerical Inquisition – and even in the education of judges.

Do you know of another totalitarian foreign power, which just as extensively, or at all, intervenes in the democratic German constitutional state?
But the influence of the Vatican network goes even much farther. According to specifications from

Rome, it controls countless facilities, clinics, kindergartens, and places of instruction and education. There, from earliest childhood, children and youths are influenced according to the Vatican doctrine by co-workers, who, partly through an oath of loyalty, were also sworn to the totalitarian Vatican regime. Such minions and functionaries also sit in German governmental organs everywhere, in governments and parliaments up to the highest ranks. There, according to their oath of office, they are actually obligated to the well-being of the German people and not to the Vatican regime. However, in its rules of faith, the Vatican regime obligates them to violate this oath of office when the "faith" dictated from Rome, the Vatican agenda, demands this.

But the Vatican doesn't demand this only from its office holders. When in doubt, all Catholic civil servants always have to decide in favor of the Vatican regime, even when this violates their oath of office. No one can escape this dogma who was once registered as a member in the books of this organization, which are not subject to the control of the constitutional state, either – not even by leaving the Church. The Vatican Church does not recognize the withdrawal of a person from the Church. The Vatican regime asserts an eternal claim of possession on every registered person, even beyond death.

Therefore, this absolute demand for obedience applies to every Catholic politician, every member of government, every official and every judge. In the final analysis, they all have to obey the order of the ruler in the Vatican, even when this order contradicts the statute and law of the German state.

This universal claim to absoluteness and submission is laid down and can be read in the Vatican regime's comprehensive body of rules, among others, in the Catechism under No. 2242 and in other regulations. Also in this case, the already known drastic threats of punishment, including eternal hell, apply to disobedience.

What do you think: Whom will a Catholic decision-maker or judge follow when the Vatican's agenda demands that he decide contrary to statute and law? The law and his oath of office to the constitution – or the dictate from Rome, out of fear for the salvation of his soul?

Actually, that was merely a small excerpt from the great number of encroachments by a totalitarian regime in Rome on the liberal democracy of Germany. But it justifies the following question: Is not this claim to absoluteness and submission by a potentate from Rome already an infiltration of democracy? Is it not a violation of the sovereignty and of the will of the German electorate? Everyone is meant to be forced to believe what the ruler in Rome prescribes, because he is infallible. And everyone has to follow his instructions. If the person does not do this, then he is threatened from there with the worst consequences, not only for this life, but even for the salvation of his soul, for his eternal life.

Is this not an incredible presumption and outrageous threat for those who don't let themselves be ensnared by the fairytales with which the Catholic construct passes itself off as the only saving grace? But how do convinced adherents of the Vatican regime – out of fear for the salvation of their soul – react? What do you think?

Therefore, does the white head in the white robe in Rome decide what applies in our democracy? Shouldn't the people vote and decide whether they want to be led by foreign dictatorial power-constructs?

One should be aware every day of how the construct works, which operates with the fairytale of being the only saving grace. And one should constantly ask: How is all this compatible with the right of freedom and of human rights, with a parliamentary democracy and above all, with a liberal democratic Constitution?

And how is it compatible with the teachings of Jesus of Nazareth, in whose name they practice all this? And if we continue to think about this:
Can anyone, who is dependent on a non-democratic regime like this one, even be a representative of the people in a democratic constitutional state or even a representative of a democratic state?
How do you see this? It's about our democracy, and everyone is asked to decide for himself.

In your reflections about the threat to democracy by the regime in Rome, please leave God, the Eternal, and His Son, the Christ of God, out of it, because the Vatican regime has nothing at all in common with them.
That for its Catholic construct, the Vatican regime abuses the name of Jesus, the Christ, of the Son of the eternal God, of the greatest prophet and Redeemer of all ensouled human beings and souls, of the teacher of peace and freedom and of love for God and neighbor, is, namely, the greatest fraudulent labeling in the history of humankind.
Christ has nothing to do with a regime and the disastrous machinations, with which the Catholic construct has been covering the Earth for about 1700 years, spreading hardship, misfortune, persecution, murder, war, eradication and genocide. The greatest crime, the greatest infamy, consists

of the fact that the Catholic regime has committed all these misdeeds under the abuse of the name of the true Christ of God, following which the victims and their souls turned away from Christ.

Presently, this infamy is being exposed worldwide, as well as who stands behind the Vatican regime. The woman from the heavens announced in the Revelation of John, the so-called Apocalypse, whom we still want to talk about, and several sons of the true God clarify.

I also want to contribute to clarification here. Again, the following applies: I present the facts, you decide!
Already with a first glance into the Church's own scriptures, you will realize that the Vatican and its priestmen can have nothing to do with Jesus, the Christ. Even though today it is scientifically acknowledged that the reports in the scriptures were often changed and falsified in their meaning by priests, you will not find a word anywhere saying that Christ appointed priests or a pope. Just the opposite of this is reported there:
Serpents, brood of vipers and sons of the father from below, who is a liar and murderer right from the beginning, and the like, is what Jesus of Nazareth called the administrators of religion of His

time. Jesus, the Christ, taught "God in us, in the innermost part of each person." God does not need any intercessors and administrators of religion.
And what claim do the priests themselves raise?
Regardless of the alarming share of offenders against children and youths, the general self-image of the men in long robes is shocking. Here are only several quotes from priests: In 2012, the resigned Pope Ratzinger described priests using a statement by John of Ars:
Oh, how great is the priest! (...) God obeys him: he utters a few words and the Lord descends from heaven at his voice, to be contained within a small host (...) After God, the priest is everything! ... Only in heaven will he fully realize what he is.

Even greater is the hubris that speaks from the words of the General Vicar of Toulouse, Jean-Baptiste Caussette, in an old book of religious exercises for Catholic priests:
I do not flatter you with pious exaggeration when I call you gods.
And: *In the government of the world, I do not stand somewhat below the cherubs and seraphs, but above them, for they are merely the servants of God ... while we are his assistants.*
If priests think it's due to them as gods to sexually abuse children, who, then, is the god, whose as-

sistants they are? – It can only be the "god" Baal. The true God, the Eternal, is omnipresent. He needs no assistants.

If a normal citizen were plagued with such notions of omnipotence, he would be taken to a mental health facility of the state. But under the umbrella of a totalitarian system in Rome, men in long robes, who see themselves as gods raised above every human right and law, indulge, mostly unpunished, in their impulses in the midst of our democratic community.

It is certain that Jesus, the Christ, never founded a religion, just as little as a prophet of God ever did before and after Him. That would also be absurd: Every religion means separation.
Unity prevails in the Kingdom of God; God has no religion. And that is also how it should be on Earth, as Jesus taught in the Lord's Prayer, the prayer of unity, in which all so-called Christians pray: *Your will be done, on Earth as in heaven.*
Nor did Jesus teach about a "Holy Father," but the opposite: *And call no man your Father on earth, for you have one Father, who is in heaven.*
Who is it then, that puts himself above the word of the Christ of God and has himself venerated as "Holy Father"?

Nor did Jesus teach about "saints." According to the Baal system, "saints" are gods to whom one should pray. Saints are thus a product of the Baal "god." And what have the saints achieved, what have the prayers to the saints achieved? The unavoidable climate disaster; the Earth is being destroyed more and more; hardship, suffering, misery, war and death prevail everywhere.

Jesus did not teach any rites, ceremonies, sacraments; nor is He still hanging on the cross, because He is risen. In the Vatican regime, the crucified One is hanging everywhere in the churches. On Good Friday, He is covered up and on Easter Sunday they hang Him up again – why? Because they have crucified the teachings of Jesus of Nazareth. Therefore, what kind of Christ is in the priests?
They hung the true Christ on the cross, believing they can still keep Him there.
For the priests, is the resurrected Christ in them, or are they with the Baal "god," with the demonic, which still wants to do in Jesus, the Christ? The church doctrines have nothing in common with Jesus, the Christ.

About 150 years ago, the Russian author Dostoyevsky already gave an extensive answer to this in his story "The Grand Inquisitor." In it, the

Catholic Grand Inquisitor confronts Christ who has reappeared: *Why have You now come to hinder us? ... We have corrected Your work and have founded it upon miracle, mystery and authority.*

And what the Church's mystery consists of – a word that we constantly encounter with the Vatican regime – the Grand Inquisitor frankly expresses toward Christ: *We are not working with You, but with him – when we took from him ... what you did reject with scorn, that last gift he offered you, showing you all the kingdom of the earth.*

The Grand Inquisitor means the meeting of Jesus of Nazareth with Satan, which is reported in the scriptures, when Satan offered Him all the riches and treasures of the world and was spurned by Jesus.

Dostoyevsky's Grand Inquisitor not only says with whom the Vatican Church is, but also that it accepted Satan's offer and where its seat is to be found: *We took from him Rome and the sword of Caesar, and proclaimed ourselves the sole rulers of the earth.*

Just a story?

And what does reality look like? Who proclaims himself the ruler of the Earth today in the words:

... it is absolutely necessary for the salvation of all men that they submit to the Roman pontiff.

These are the words from the Vatican in Rome.

Until not so long ago, who let himself be rendered homage with the following words when ascending the throne:

... *know that you are the father of princes and kings, the ruler of the world, the vicar of our Savior Jesus Christ on earth...* .

These are the words of the Vatican regime to the pope in Rome.

To whom do the beautiful and mighty of the world, the pilgrim synodals, make pilgrimages, to receive a blessing and to kiss the ring?

To the pope in the Vatican in Rome.

And who said yes to the offer: all the treasures of this world? What is one of the richest organizations of this world with thousands of billions in assets and treasures of this world?

The regime in Rome.

Not only Dostoyevsky describes the Vatican regime in Rome. We read similar things already in a much older scripture, in the previously mentioned Revelation of John, the last book of the Bible, the so-called Apocalypse. It contains the prophetic vision of the Seer of Patmos, who nearly 2000 years ago prophesied the future of the world and the downfall of the adversary's regime, which he describes as the whore of Babylon:

The Seer of Patmos describes the whore of Babylon as a city with which the kings of the Earth committed fornication, a city which rules over the kings of the Earth.

Again the question: Who corresponds to this image today, who raises this universal claim to power today? The Vatican regime in Rome.

The Seer of Patmos also symbolically saw the whore of Babylon as a woman who bears the word "mystery" on her forehead and is drunken with the blood of the murdered people, whom God sanctified and who had risen as witnesses for Jesus.

Which regime constantly carries the word mystery before itself and which regime has been persecuting and killing prophets and people for 1700 years, because they speak up for Jesus, the Christ? If you like, you can read more in the Revelation of John about how the regime described as the whore of Babylon wreaked havoc, and then compare the vision of the Seer of Patmos with the history of the Vatican regime in the city of Rome.
Then, if you like, draw your own conclusions.

The advice in the Revelation of the Seer of Patmos is clear:

Come out of her, my people, lest you take part in her sins, lest you share in her plagues!

In the vision of the Seer of Patmos, the downfall of the whore of Babylon is initiated through the works of the woman from the heavens, whom he describes as: *clothed with the sun, with the moon under her feet, and on her head a crown of twelve golden stars.*

The one who believes the eternal word of the one God through the mouth of prophets and is not befogged by the Baal-construct's lies of mercy with its wrathful and vengeful idols of eternal damnation and hell, recognizes in the words of the Seer of Patmos, in the woman from the heavens, the Seraph of the divine Wisdom, Sophia.
By way of Sophia, the world knows today that through the Cherubim before God's throne, His law-princes, the Fall of the whore of Babylon has been initiated. With the whore of Babylon falls her Baal construct, in whose spirit she committed her misdeeds under the false label "Christian."

Another word of explanation concerning the Baal system:
Baal is a cruel god-construct, a matted belief in idolatry, the main support of which is mystery. Baal

always purports the mystery. Inherent in a mystery is always the lie or even the crime. Baal is the manifested untruth, the lie and lust to kill, harlotry and fornication in the face of the true God, who is the love for God and neighbor. Baal is the one whom Jesus of Nazareth called the father from below, who is a liar and murderer right from the beginning. If his doctrine did not have to hide behind the mystery, but were the truth, then his servants would not have had to kill millions of people, including the prophets. This holds true until today for the priestly guild of all times, where the precursor of massacre is murder by lying or character assassination.

The priestly guild in the Baal current. ... Where do you stand, now that you not only know how the foreign undemocratic Vatican regime has free rein in our democratic state, but also by which unholy spirit this regime is driven?

As a democrat I feel deceived by this, for democrats have chosen democracy and not the influence of a totalitarian system.
The Baal current is still making trouble, more than ever, it is fornicating with the mighty of this world, as the Seer of Patmos called it. But its end is approaching.

When you constantly hear and read about scandals – quite recently, again about drug and sex orgies in Rome in the former rooms of the Vatican Inquisition – then you know how far Baal has already fallen.
And we also know from the Cherub of divine Wisdom: The whore of Babylon is falling.

Dear readers, if the facts presented have helped to reveal the "mystery" of the Baal system, then you also know the answer to the question in our title: Do Dictatorial Religions Threaten our Democracy? You determine it, just as it should be in every functioning democracy: Decide yourself, and draw your own conclusions. Make your choice, where preserving your democratic rights are concerned.

July 2017
Gert Hetzel

1. Introduction

Throughout the ages, the caste of priests with its dogmas, rituals, ceremonies and ritual acts – and in the past, all too often with brute force – has bound people to itself, thus preventing them from finding their way to the Free Spirit, God in us. He, God, the Eternal, did not found a religion or appoint any priests. He, the All-One, is the Father-Mother-God, the Creator of all life. He is the eternal love that dwells in each one of us. Therefore, He does not need any mediators or even "representatives" on Earth – He can be found in us, in the soul of human beings.

Out of love for His human children, God, the Eternal, sent His messengers, His prophets, again and again – high beings from the Kingdom of God, who taught the people the law of God, the love for God and neighbor, and enlightened them about the Free Spirit, God in us. God does not have the language of human beings. In order to be able to speak to the people, He, the Eternal All-One, needs an interpreter, a speaking instrument. Because the adversaries of God want to prevent people from hearing the voice of God, they attack the speaking instrument. God's emissaries have always been persecuted and fought against by the respective ruling caste of priests using all conceivable means. Just as the priestmen mocked and slandered the prophets of God of the Israelites, incited the people against them and had many of them cruelly murdered, so did they also have Jesus of Nazareth, the greatest prophet of God, cruelly tortured to death on the cross. And so, with lies and slander, with fire and sword, they also proceeded against all those who drew on the spiritual revolution of the first Christians and began to shape their lives together according to the Sermon on the Mount of Jesus of Nazareth.

However, the voice of the Eternal, of the Free Spirit, does not let Itself be silenced.

Today, in our time, God, the All-One, gives His eternal word from the divine Wisdom for all people, in a fullness as never before in the history of humankind: through Gabriele, His prophetess and emissary in our time.
The eternal word, the word of the Free Spirit through Gabriele, flows from God's infinite love for all His children. Christ, the Son of God and Co-Regent of the Kingdom of God, goes after every single child, every sheep – including the sheep that turn against Him, just as Jesus of Nazareth

spoke in the following sense: I leave ninety-nine righteous ones standing and go after the one stray sheep. Through Gabriele, the Spirit of God guides people and souls to the eternal law of love for God and neighbor, to peace and freedom, to the true life, which is unity. But He also points out who, through the distortion and perversion of His simple teachings by abusing the name "Christian," has been leading His human children astray for nearly two millennia.

In the early years of the worldwide work of the Christ of God, which was built up through Gabriele, the Kingdom of God therefore turned directly to the church authorities, in order to hold up to them the mirror of their remoteness from God and, at the same time, to reach out to them and offer them a direct conversation with the Christ of God. The church officials thus had the unique opportunity to recognize the millennia-old false path of the caste of priests, their own wrong attitudes and thus, the misleading of humankind. Under the direct guidance of Christ, they could have changed many things for the good and initiated the process of making amends.

Anyone who wants to read these letters to the pope in Rome, as well as to the Catholic and Lutheran bishops of the German-speaking countries, could turn to the Vatican's secret archives. Perhaps you, dear reader, will then find out the names of all the Vatican "sect commissioners" working there. This will doubtless be found in the 85 kilometers of shelves in the secret archives.

Instead of taking the hand of the Christ of God, however, the cassock wearers of the present day did like the cults of priests of all times: They vilified the eternal word of God.

The institutional representatives initially reacted to the offers of conversation from the Kingdom of God with silence – they did not even deem it necessary to respond to the letters. However, about a year later, in December 1981, when the followers of Jesus of Nazareth published the letters together with a revelation of the Cherub of the divine Wisdom, they unleashed an unimaginable smear campaign against the work of the Christ of God and against His prophetess, Gabriele. This is comprehensively and extensively described and documented in this work.

This documentation contains the essential facts and records; however, it is not able to come even close to conveying what Gabriele, the emissary of God, had to endure for decades through the church persecution campaigns in terms of mental cruelty, injustice, character assassination, ridicule and defamation of the eternal word of God and of her person – while, at the same time, out of love for God, for her fellow people, and for creation, she built up the work of the Christ of God, which has meanwhile become worldwide.

From Abraham to Gabriele, it is the eternal word, the one stream, the one love, God – and from Abraham to Gabriele, it is the adversaries of God, the cassock wearers, who persecute His emissaries, the prophets, and His word of love and unity.

2. The Helping Hand of the Christ of God Is Spurned

The Lord's offer shall be held open for many months. This had been declared by the Cherub of divine Wisdom before the throne of God, called Brother Emanuel on Earth, at the end of his letter to the pope in Rome in November 1980.

In this letter, conveyed through Gabriele, the prophetess and emissary of God in our time, the Cherub of divine Wisdom had made the offer to the pope that Christ Himself, the Co-Regent of the Kingdom of God, wanted to speak to the head of the Catholic Church through the word of His prophetess, *in order to still save from this secularized church what can be saved.* The voice of the Lord wanted to become alive and lead the way within the church institutions.

However, the churches, as stated, responded neither to the letter from the Cherub of divine Wisdom of September 1979, nor to the letter of November 1980 to the head of the Catholic Church, nor to the offer made in January 1981 to all the bishops of the two major denominations.

With this, it was now clear to the whole world: the churches, which wrongly call themselves "Christian," had not accepted the helping hand, the offer of the Christ of God, the gift of grace, as it was called in the letter to the pope.

This means that they had chosen to fight against the Christ of God and against His word of truth, of the love for God and neighbor, which is given to humankind today from the Kingdom of God, through the prophetess and emissary of God, Gabriele. With this, the churches remain in the tradition of the caste of priests, because it has always been the priests and scribes, the administrators of religion, who again and again in earlier times, persecuted the messengers sent by God, the Eternal, His prophets, literally, until blood was shed.

The Baal system, to which the cassock wearers belong, defends with all its might the priesthood of the external religion and especially the concept of an allegedly punishing God – a concept with which they can frighten people and bind them to their rituals and ceremonies. Baal is the cruel god construct – and the matted belief in the gods emanating from this construct is, at the same time, the main bearer of the "mystery," since the contradictory nature and monstrousness of the Baal construct has been concealed by the cassock wearers from time immemorial until today, by referring to the alleged "mystery of God."

But God, the Eternal, has no secrets from His human children. He is the truth, and He reveals the truth to His human children through His messengers.

If the Catholic construct were the truth, then it would not have had millions of people killed, nor the prophets, the bearers of the word of God.

The preliminary stage of murder is murder by lies, also called character assassination. With lies and slander, the priestmen repeatedly took action against the bearers of God's word – and they do this today, as well.

From a purely external point of view, it is also a highly unequal struggle today: Here, the powerful church institutions with their riches, their power and their influence on politicians, mass media and the people servile to them, built up over centuries of indoctrination, by inculcating people with the belief that they alone are the ones who represent God and His word on Earth. There, a handful of Christ-friends, who gather around the prophetic word, rich neither in money nor influence. Here, scholars and theologians, who pull out all stops on distortion, lies, calumny – there, the prophetess of God and her fellow companions, who are committed solely to the truth, as it is expressed in the Ten Commandments of God through Moses and in the Sermon on the Mount of Jesus, the Christ.

But Christ, the Redeemer of all souls and human beings, does not let Himself be stopped by the obduracy of the cassock wearers, as the Cherub of divine Wisdom announced in his revelation made public in December 1981:
The Lord of life is striving to teach humankind the steps to divine consciousness, so that the souls can rise after their path on Earth, and find their way back to the Father's house. Jesus Christ now calls His people to accept the true teaching and to follow Him, the only Good Shepherd.

The true teaching is the teaching of love for God and neighbor, the fulfillment of the Ten Commandments of God and the Sermon on the Mount of Jesus of Nazareth, which leads to the return of souls and ensouled people to the eternal Father's house. It is the teaching of the Eternal, All-One, of the Free Spirit, who does not need any intercessors on Earth between Himself and His children – and this teaching is a thorn in the side of those who do not want to lose their power and influence: They are the cassock wearers of the ecclesiastical administrators of religion. They have abused the name of Jesus, the Christ, for exploitation, wars and terror in the name of God and have trampled underfoot His teaching of the Sermon on the Mount. And they also do everything today to extinguish the flame of the Spirit of the Christ of God as quickly as possible. If the sheer physical violence of torture and burning at the stake is no longer available to them for this purpose, then character assassination takes the place of murder.

Already in December 1981, through the prophetess of God, Gabriele, the law-prince before God's throne, the Cherub of divine Wisdom, revealed a part of the slander strategy of the Church, as it then actually appeared months later in church statements:

The argumentation of the unknowing ecclesiastical authorities and their followers is this: The teaching of the Lord in His Homebringing Mission are a mixture of Christian, Buddhist and Hindu knowledge. The churchmen presume to have the whole truth. They believe that people of other faiths are not accepted by Jesus Christ because they do not acknowledge Him, the Redeemer. Through their dogmatic attitude, the authorities of both churches are of the blind opinion that He, the Lord, is solely with Christianity. Only those who are wearing blinders and who listen only to the intellectual words of people to whom the true Spirit of God is silent are subject to this deception.

The assertion of an alleged "mixture of religions" (we will come back to this point) is, however, only a tiny fraction of the infamy and malice, the lies, slander, insinuations, perversions and insults that were to be spattered on the followers of Jesus of Nazareth during the following decades, first and foremost on Gabriele, the bearer of the word of the Spirit of God, who usually had to bear the burden of this persecution alone, as well.

If today, despite all attacks, the light of the messianic, sophianic age shines brighter than ever on this Earth, this is due to the heavenly luminosity and strength of the divine Wisdom: the law-prince before the throne of God and his dual in the earthly garment, God's prophetess Gabriele.

Posterity, however, shall learn what played out in all these years and what is still partly in play, for the old serpent, of which tradition speaks, is still flickering.

3. The Defamations Begin (1981-1984)

Würzburg in Germany, at the end of the 70s of the 20th century: a city with a population of 130,000, tranquilly situated on the Main River – shaped mentally and structurally since millennium one, by Catholic prince bishops with cathedral, fortress and a residence. A historical stronghold of the murder of Jews, the Counter Reformation and the burning of witches. It was here, of all places, that the Free Spirit, the Christ of God, raised His voice mightily.

From then on, a handful of people, later a few dozen, met regularly in a room open to the public, to hear the word of God through the mouth of a prophet – in the Homebringing Mission of Jesus Christ, the work of teaching and enlightenment of the Spirit of the Christ of God and the basis for the later Universal Life.

Through the prophetic word, visitors in Würzburg and several other cities received deep spiritual teachings about correlations previously unknown to humankind, for instance, about the nature of God and the make-up of the Kingdom of God, about the make-up of the soul, about life after death, about the power of prayer, but above all, about the path to within, which can be taken by every soul and every person who opens his heart to God.

At first, the Vatican Church, dominating in Würzburg, merely observed the development. Like all Catholic and Lutheran bishops in Germany, the Catholic Bishop of Würzburg, Paul-Werner Scheele, had received a letter from the Cherub of divine Wisdom in January 1981, including the message:
The word of God is in the temple of flesh and bone and not in external churches, and becomes a power of grace for those who humbly seek God in themselves ... For it is essentially written: You are the temple of the Holy Spirit, and the Spirit of God dwells in you.

"God in us" – this was and is one of the core statements of the message of all true prophets of God. Already Jesus of Nazareth, the greatest prophet of all time, taught: "The Kingdom of God is within you." But this message, which is, without exception, always directed to all souls and ensouled people, stands in sharp contrast to the behavior of the priests and theologians of the various denominations, who bind the people to external stone houses, to dogmas and rituals, who persuade the believers that they are mediators between them and God, and who therefore obstruct the direct access to God in the inner being of every ensouled human being.

In doing so, these churches invoke God, the All-Highest, and call themselves "Christian." The prophets of God have denounced this fraudulent labeling at all times: Anyone who does not do the will of the eternal Father in heaven should not invoke Him, the All-Highest. And anyone who tramples underfoot the teachings of the Nazarene, the high ethics and morals of the Sermon on the Mount, should call himself Catholic or Lutheran, but should not adorn himself with the name of Jesus, the Christ.

In December 1981, as mentioned, the letters of the Cherub of divine Wisdom were made public and addressed to all people "who want to free themselves from constricting communities of Christians."

The reaction came promptly – and it came in a devious manner. At that time, Gabriele and her family were living in a row house on the outskirts of Würzburg. An eyewitness and friend of the family remembers the following incident:

At Christmastime 1981, on the evening of December 24th, around 6 p.m., in the home of our sister

[Gabriele], there were several phone calls from the same speaker, also with the same voices in the background. The caller said that he was with a suicidal man who wanted to come to our sister's home this Christmas Eve. It was explained to him that if he would like to come to prayer at 8:00 p.m., then he is cordially invited; our sister cannot do more for him. Voices were heard in the background, then the speaker hung up – the "suicidal" person did not appear. We had the impression that it was a faked call. During the following time, there were repeated threatening phone calls to our sister's house. These calls became a matter of course. Even at 2 o'clock in the morning, imprecating and cursing threats were made. Shortly after the telephone receiver was hung up, the next call came, with which the cursing continued, then a third one which concluded it. Voices were likewise heard in the background.

Such telephone terrorizing is nerve-racking. Whoever it was that kept calling continuously, and several times in a row, to dump his message of imprecations and cursing – was acting in "good" Catholic tradition. For the cursing of "heretics" and "witches" has been part of the fixed repertoire of the Vatican Church for centuries. The reference book collections of Catholic dogmas are still teeming until today with curses on all the people who dare to doubt even one of the Catholic dogmas. Anyone who does not change his mind in time – that is the message – will burn in eternal hell!

Catholic Falsehood, Packaged as "Opinion"

Meanwhile, behind the walls of the Episcopal office buildings, measures of a different kind were being devised. The ecclesiastical hunt quickly took off at full speed. The first major public attack took place on June 20, 1982. The *Würzburger Katholisches Sonntagsblatt* (newspaper) published a full-page article under the heading "No Liability for Damages!" A Catholic journalist named Jutta Falke is mentioned as the author of the article.
The article demonstrates the church procedure and is the opening of the long-standing strategy of persecution with the means of the present time. The Church does not even consider dealing with the content of the divine revelations of the Spirit of the Christ of God. Instead, the reader is presented with slick falsehoods right from the start. For example, it is claimed that in the healings through prayer and faith offered in the Homebringing Mission of Jesus Christ, healing is "promised." This is untrue.

It is further claimed that in the Homebringing Mission, the faithful are instructed to read no other literature than that of the Homebringing Mission – another falsehood.

Anyone who deals with such church attacks on "heretics" will repeatedly come across a pattern of thinking that in psychology is called "projection":
If someone wants to fight something blindly, he often imputes to his opponent wrong attitudes and behavior patterns, that are, in reality, his own. This is also the case here: An index of forbidden books, which Catholics were not allowed to read, existed in the Roman Church until the 1960s.
The article goes on to say that the faithful of the Homebringing Mission should "not think, not form their own opinion." Their critical faculties are "systematically reduced or even destroyed and reason is switched off." In the Homebringing Mission, the people are "made servile, enslaved in dependence, stultified, until they narrow-mindedly represent only what they are told." There could not have been a better description of the educational practice of the cassock wearers over the last 1500 years.

The fact is that the Christ of God teaches freedom in the prophetic word through Gabriele, because the law of God contains the absolute freedom of every being. The person should find his way to God, who is in him, deep in the bottom of his soul; he should find his way to himself and learn to think independently, to orient himself solely toward God and to make himself independent of the opinions of others.

In this article, the church institution also directly attacked the person of God's prophetess – meagerly embellished with a few condescending words that in their hypocrisy seem almost embarrassing: "A dear, good, harmless person, a housewife … like you and me, founds a 'church'…" (After all, not even men are allowed to do that in the Catholic Church! But nothing is further from Gabriele's mind than wanting to found a church). It said that she spread "lies" (which ones, however, it doesn't say) and sowed "hatred." This probably refers to the fact that a few months earlier, some followers of Jesus of Nazareth had begun to give informative lectures about the facts from church history.

It goes on to say that the prophetess of God is *degraded to a puppet without will, who is directed by a "spirit" invisible to the general public, who pretends to be a "Cherub of Wisdom before the throne of God," but cannot have seen God from afar – how else could he spread lies that are verifiable as such in comparison with the Bible.*

Anyone who knows the history of biblical falsehoods knows who is exposing himself as a liar in this comparison, namely, the father from below. But the mockery of the Cherub of divine Wisdom goes even further. It says:
Otherwise, how else could he sow hatred by bringing up and publishing an abominable church history ...

The cassock wearers themselves thus admit that their own church history is abominable. Here, again, the projection and the perfidious distortion of facts become apparent: It is not the one who has committed the most heinous crimes who sows hatred – but the one who brings to light the Church's responsibility for them! The strategy of the Church: Whoever dares to tell the truth about the cassock wearers and bring it to the public is defamed by them.

Enclosed in a box in the middle of the article, one can read who is actually behind this accumulation of untruths, false quotations and vituperations: "The Great Sign – the Lady of All Nations" – and the Würzburg branch of this spiritualistically inspired Catholic Marian group was headed by the journalist Franz Count von Magnis (1926-2004). Bishop Scheele of Würzburg had commissioned him or his organization to watch "sects" in the diocese of Würzburg.

The "Lady of All Nations"

The name of the organization is derived from the Book of Revelations of John in the New Testament, where there is mention of a "Lady of All Nations" – which the Church usually equates with Mary.
"The Great Sign – the Lady of All Nations" is a sectarian group within the Catholic Church, which refers to an apparition of Mary in the 20th century in Holland and has taken this name. In connection with this alleged Marian apparition, spiritualistic phenomena such as strong odors, noise and gunfire occurred. But the Catholic Magnis apparently had no fear of contact with such astral-occult parapsychological phenomena. A few years later, he had circular letters sent under a pseudonym to the addresses of Original Christians, in which an "observer of the degree of faith" from Flensburg – in reality, a somewhat confused pensioner – claimed to have determined the "vibration frequency" of known Original Christians by means of a "radio-aesthetic pendulum."

And such a group now wants to "enlighten" the Catholics about the prophetic inner word of God …

The German branch of this association was founded by Count Magnis in 1968 in Würzburg. What kind of person was Magnis?
Among other things, he had been active for many years as a big game hunter on various continents and had also written a book about it, in which he informs the reader, among other things, about the best methods for hunting and slaughtering exotic animals. "The daily chase had become a source of strength for me," writes the passionate hunter – obviously so much so that he later sought and found this macabre "source of strength" by hunting people of other faiths.

In the Würzburg City Library his hunting book was found among the "Children's and Young People's Books."
So the count had nothing against passing on this kind of Catholic "values" to the youth. "Youth endangering," on the other hand, was to him, for example, a book by the Jesuit Count Spee, who had stood up against the burning of witches during the 17th century. In October 1986 Magnis put this book on a list of books that he wanted to have removed from precisely this city library.

So much for the person of the journalist Franz Count von Magnis, the chairman of the Würzburg group "Lady of All Nations." For his merits in the persecution of religious minorities, Magnis was awarded the Papal Silvester Order by Pope John Paul II in 1987.

And Gabriele, the prophetess of God, wrote a short reader's letter to this organization "Lady of All Nations" on July 1, 1982, that is, a few days after the inflammatory article appeared in the *Catholic Sonntagsblatt*:

Greetings in God!
Would the Lady of All Nations have spoken so cynically and polemically?
I cannot be insulted. Through the power of the Spirit of God, I stand above these provocations and rest in God, my Lord. Through the mystical path, which I am allowed to walk thanks to the grace of our Lord, I recognize the state of consciousness of my fellow people, including those who disparage the work of the Lord and me. Since I have knowledge about the law of cause and effect and am going through a corresponding spiritual training, it is possible for me to meet my fellow human beings in pure neighborly love.
Dear Mrs. Falke, dear gentlemen, you, who are my brothers and sisters before God, the more you make

me despicable, the more pure neighborly love I will show you. I walk the path undeterred, despite polemics, distortions and perversions of the eternal truth. Divine love will prevail. The time will come when we will meet on another level, then the blindfold will also be removed from your spiritual eyes. We will then see who had the truth.
In love for God and for my neighbor, I remain linked with all people.

... PS: If you are not afraid of your readers, then publish this letter in its entirety.

The letter was not published, neither unabridged nor abridged. Despite the character assassination, despite the public discrediting and the attacks against the word of the Spirit of the Christ of God and against her person, Gabriele remained faithful to the Spirit of God, the love. But how did she fare as a person in this situation? Even though Gabriele lives in God and is thus linked in her inner being with the Eternal, with Christ and with the Cherub of divine Wisdom, as a human being, she still had to withstand this malice of her fellow human beings. For many years, she has made every sacrifice in order to bring the highest spiritual good into the world, and to bring the people the path of Christ that leads to the love for God and neighbor, to a life in freedom, unity and peace – and in return, she reaps scorn, mockery and persecution. And this is done by the priestmen of an organization that for centuries has trampled underfoot the teachings of Jesus of Nazareth, that subjugates its fellow people with its dogmas and the threat of eternal damnation and is responsible for the cruel death of countless men, women and children.

The spiritual world stood by Gabriele. But who could support her as a human being in this situation? Who was capable of empathizing with her? There was merely a small circle of active people around her, all of whom had a job and were often occupied with their own problems.

"Does the Church Live According to the Bible?"

The balance of power in comparison with the churches was extremely unequal: Here, two powerful religious conglomerates with thousands of well-paid officials, with immense financial and media power – church newspapers, publishing interests, seats on the broadcasting councils – and with great influence on church-educated and enlisted journalists and politicians. There, a small movement, kept going by a few dozen people, who could commit themselves to the word of the Christ of God only in their free time; with limited financial means and without any influence on mass media or politics.

What possibility of countering such a defamatory article remains for a minority that has neither a high-circulation press organ of its own nor a press agency with appropriate contacts to the daily press? In the end, merely a paid advertisement.

On July 7, 1982, a large-format advertisement appeared in the local newspaper with the headline: "Have We Been Forsaken by God?" In this advertisement, the followers of Jesus of Nazareth indicated with scholarly accuracy contradictions in the Bible, and pointed out the horrors of a bloody church history. The inflammatory article in the *Sonntagsblatt* was therefore not answered with a speech of justification or defense, but with verifiable facts about the churches – and with counter questions.

Here are just a few examples.

So the question was asked: *Does the Church live according to the Bible? – such as Jesus' commandment, "Love your enemies"?*

The Catholic theologian Bruno Bauer was quoted among others: *No other religion has demanded* so many human sacrifices and slaughtered them in such a shameful way as the one that boasts of having abolished them forever.

Or does the Church obey the commandment: *Do not heap up for yourselves treasures on earth where moths and worms destroy them?*

Here follows a quote by Karlheinz Deschner, among others: *The total stocks and capital holdings of the Vatican were estimated at about 50 billion German Marks in 1958.*

Jesus said: *For I was hungry and you gave me nothing to eat.* – But: *Thousands of people starve to death on this Earth every day, yet the Vatican parts neither from its art treasures nor from its stocks and real estate holdings.*

At the end, follows a reference to the Homebringing Mission of Jesus Christ: Christ: *"I will send you prophets" … can you bear it now? … In the work of the Lord, there is no orientation to any person. We hear His almighty word through His instrument, His prophetess. One believes and lives by it, the other rejects it – we have no influence on either. … Though the Homebringing Mission of Jesus Christ and all those who follow the Lord are mocked and scorned by the Church, and though all evil is attributed to the work, and though the word of God is twisted and disdained: We steadfastly walk the Inner Path, which sets us free. For Jesus said and continues to say: Follow Me! The Kingdom of God is within you.*

A Lutheran Pastor Speaks Up

The Church had probably not expected this courageous reaction, which was based on a suggestion of Gabriele. The press office of the Episcopal ordinariate was obviously not able to answer the specific questions, nor did it deal with the facts about the churches that were presented. Instead, in a reader's letter to the *Main-Post* newspaper (July 10, 1982), the Church accused the Original Christians of "evil anti-Christian, especially anti-Catholic propaganda." It is a "murky water, from which is drawn here."

The history of the Church is indeed very murky water, from which all kinds of deplorable things can be brought to light. Among these murky waters of history is also the centuries-long persecution of early Christian movements by the Church Inquisition. And this has long been the case in the Lutheran Church, as well. Martin Luther also called upon the authorities of that time to "resist the heresies and physically punish the adherents."

Luther, literally: *With heretics one can give them short shrift, one can damn them unheard. And while they perish at the stake, the believer should wipe out the evil at its root.*

Luther also urged the believers to denounce others, saying that if something is learned about a dissident, he should immediately tell the Lutheran pastor.

> Yesterday – Inquisitor: Persecution all the way to murder
>
> Today – Sect Commissioner/Sect Expert: Persecution up to character assassination

When it comes to the fight against "heretics," apparently the Bishop's Ordinariate of Würzburg also makes use of the "help" of the other denomination – even though it has also publicly demonized it as "heretical" for a long time and still does so in its books of dogma. A few days later, the Lutheran pastor Friedrich-Wilhelm Haack from Munich spoke out for the first time. In 1969, Haack had already been appointed by the Bavarian state Church as a full-time "commissioner for questions of sects and ideologies." He described himself as an "expert on sects" – and he was indeed an expert on demagogy, reminiscent of the dark times of the Inquisition.

On July 12, 1982, the *Lohr Zeitung* (newspaper) stated that the afore-mentioned advertisement of the Homebringing Mission had prompted him, Pastor Haack, "to warn Christians against this sect."

> **Mendacious Opinions:**
> An untruth = Lies that are so formulated by "experts" that they are legally classified and permitted by the courts as "opinions" because their truthfulness is not checked. The credulous citizen does not know the difference between a permitted lie in the guise of opinion and fact. He therefore considers the lie to be a fact that the court has verified.

That it is "a new spiritistic sect," which "mixes Hindu and Christian ideology."

Here it is, the mendacious opinion that the Cherub of divine Wisdom had predicted already at the end of 1981. But it is again a projection – because hardly any other world religion has absorbed so much foreign thought, so many thought patterns, rituals and ceremonies from ancient pagan cults as the Roman Catholic State Church, from which the Lutheran Church later split off.

And it was a Lutheran pastor, of all people, who was the first to use the term "sect" in connection with the Homecoming Mission of Jesus Christ. For centuries, it was precisely the Lutheran Church that the Vatican Church has disparaged with this insult, just as it branded the so-called heretics with it during the Middle Ages. In early modern times, both denominations then persecuted the "witch sect" together. But the term is much older: Already the followers of Jesus of Nazareth were discriminated against by the scribes of the time as the "sect of the Nazarene," as can even be read in the Bibles of the churches (Acts 24:5).

Pastor Haack further "warned" against the "claim to absoluteness of such pseudo-prophetic and pseudo-revelational movements" and against a doctrine which in his opinion "often monopolizes all spheres of life."

Here, the pastor quite obviously ignored the fact that the Ten Commandments of God through Moses and the teachings of the Sermon on the Mount of Jesus of Nazareth also apply to all spheres of life – respecting, however, the freedom of the individual. This also results from the wording of the Ten Commandments of God, in which it says: "You shall ..." and not "You must ...", and from the teachings of the Sermon on the Mount. At the end of His speech, Jesus of Nazareth said: *Everyone then who hears these words of Mine and acts on them will be like a wise man who built his house on rock. ... And everyone who hears these words of Mine and does not act on them will be like a foolish man who built his house on sand.*

So, this accusation is also a pure projection: After all, it is the church institutions that disregard the free will of people, and, from cradle to grave – that is, from the baptism of the infant to confirmation, the wedding, the so-called sacraments up to their funeral – prescribe to the people to obey their church laws, under threat of eternal damnation for all those who do not submit to it.

And in the churches' own Bibles there are also numerous references to the gift of the prophetic word. Jesus of Nazareth announced the Comforter, the Spirit of truth, whom He would send to lead the people into all the truth.

*God, the Free Spirit,
Cannot Be Appropriated*

Despite the church attacks on the Homebringing Mission of Jesus Christ, the number of people who gathered around the prophetic word through Gabriele increased.

After it became obvious that the spiritual good that is given through Gabriele contains an immeasurable wealth of true spirituality, of divine wisdom – which the churches lack – and that the word of the Christ of God through His prophetess could not be silenced, Count Magnis declared quite openly on the telephone to a supporter of the Homebringing Mission that he would wish to see this movement within the Church.

This was not the only attempt to integrate Gabriele, the prophetess of God, into the Catholic Church.

Another caller pretended to be the contact person for the Bishop of Augsburg and also offered to integrate the Homebringing Mission of Jesus Christ into the Catholic Church. The book "The Rehabilitation of the Christ of God" describes how it continued:

Humbly and modestly, God's prophetess then asked the Spirit of the Christ of God what His will is. The answer was clear and unequivocal:

"His prophetic word, the word of the Spirit of the Christ of God, remains outside of the institutional churches."

Thus, the all-wise Free Spirit, whom we in the western world call God, the Creator of all life, does not give revelations within the institutional churches, nor does the Christ of God. The Spirit of God blows where It will. The written answer to the Church's caller was then limited to the statement: "I think it would be better if we march separately" ... (p. 85f)

When this answer was also conveyed to Count Magnis in its sense, as a modern day inquisitor, he unabatedly continued his smear campaign.

Catholic "Sunday Newspaper" Warns of "Risk of Infection"

In September 1982, Count Magnis published a special writing under the name "Lady of All Nations," which bears the title: "Critical Comments on the Alleged Homebringing Mission of Jesus Christ or the Inner Spirit-Jesus-Church." Already in the title a sloppy and condescending handling of the truth can be seen: He cannot even correctly copy down the term "Inner Spirit=Christ Church."

What the count writes about Gabriele in this diatribe literally drips with scorn, falsehood and condescension: She is a "pitiable woman entrusted to our prayer," and therefore "a public confrontation with her seems cruel and merciless to us. ..."
This is how the count writes about the woman whose movement he wanted to see "within the Church" shortly before! Anyone who does not want to submit to the power of the Church and can even become dangerous to it is fought against mercilessly.

His compassion is feigned, and with his assertion that a "public confrontation" seems to him to be "cruel and merciless," he proves himself a liar, for in the same writing, he fires a veritable arsenal of brazen untruths and distortions at Gabriele and the Homebringing Mission.

Thus, it is falsely insinuated about Gabriele that she describes herself as a "spiritistic medium of Jesus." Or it is indirectly asserted that in the teachings of the Homebringing Mission of Jesus Christ there is no personal God – this is also untrue. The teaching proclaimed there is said to be a "patched-up edifice of thought consisting of Eastern wisdom, Christian scriptural passages, alternative health proposals"; it is based "on hatred of the Catholic Church"; it is a "false spirit" that is speaking here and "untruthfully pretending to be the Jesus-Spirit." (How carelessly Magnis works can be seen even in the choice of words: The term "Jesus-Spirit" is unknown in the Homebringing Mission of Jesus Christ).

In his eagerness to slander, Magnis gets entangled in contradictions: On the one hand, revelations are said to be "so boring" that "listeners sink into a gentle slumber." On the other hand, the "simple, credulous people" let themselves be enchanted by the "magical atmosphere." (There is no doubt that a normal Catholic service moves between these poles). Magnis further claims: "Everything the prophetess proclaims to her followers must be accepted without criticism." Thus, "the critical

consciousness is switched off"; the followers are "loaded with the teachings like a computer."
Isn't that an apt description of church indoctrination from childhood on?

At the end of the text, Franz von Magnis makes an appeal to the readers with words from the church Bible:
Put on the whole armor of God ... For our struggle is not against flesh and blood, but against the rulers, against the authorities, against the powers of this dark world and against the spiritual forces of evil in the heavenly realms. (Eph. 6:11-12)
Isn't that the worst kind of cheap propaganda – just because people follow the Free Spirit and not the dictates of the Church! The blood trail of the churches through history clearly shows where, in truth, "the master of this dark world" is enthroned.

Meanwhile, the campaign against Gabriele and the Homebringing Mission of Jesus Christ continued for months.
Under the headline "The Fixed Idea," Jutta Falke writes on October 3, 1982 in the *Katholische Sonntagsblatt* about the "temptations" of the Homebringing Mission and warns the faithful of an "unconditional, blind obedience" (and that, of all things, in a Catholic newspaper) and of the fact

that their "idealism could be abused." She does indeed admit that the "genuine mystics" also had known about an "inner word." But says it is much too dangerous to engage in it without the "official authority of the Church."

Therefore, a person has to submit to the Church – that is the ecclesiastical credo, and there, too, "unconditional, blind obedience" is demanded! And to where has the "official authority of the Church" led countless people? That becomes more and more apparent in the state of this world.

The "demonic," the *Sonntagsblatt* continues, is lurking here for people and one could fall into a "mental illness."

How similar the statements are! Even the scribes of that time accused Jesus of Nazareth of being in league with the "head demon."

A Catholic has the right, it goes on to say, to keep away from "people with a fixed idea …" if there is a "risk of infection."

"Risk of infection" – that's what the inquisitors of the Middle Ages also warned the faithful about. At that time, as a Catholic, one had not only the "right," but also the "damned duty and obligation" ("damned" in the literal sense of the word) to stay away from "heretics" when death threatened – for after all, they could "infect" anyone.

In a certain sense this is even true: When one comes into contact with the message of God through the bearers of His word, one could very well be infected – namely, with justified doubts about the supposedly infallible dogmas and doctrines of the supposedly only saving Church, for, this is how it continues:

The greatest lie of the Homebringing Mission of Jesus Christ is the assertion that Jesus is the natural son of Joseph and Mary.

A fact that many people hold to be true is described by the Catholic Church as the "greatest lie," and Gabriele is publicly pilloried for it. It seems "more merciful," thus stated condescendingly, "to be in pastoral letter contact with the personalities of the Homebringing Mission for the time being ..."

"Pastoral Care" the Catholic Way

This "pastoral care" was such that every Friday evening Gabriele found a new Catholic writing of invective in her mailbox. The alleged mercy was expressed in the fact that these invective writings, with the vilest disparagements of Gabriele, were distributed at bus stops everywhere.

Here, the handwriting of the Inquisition is already evident, because church tradition always referred to the Inquisition also as the "care of souls." Such a tradition may exist among cassock wearers, but how would you, dear reader, feel, if you, as a blameless citizen, were attacked in such a devious manner?

> **Inquisition:** Persecution and eradication through lies, slander, discrimination, torture and murder of all those who do not submit to the prevailing religious caste.

In November 1982, the *Katholische Sonntagsblatt* claimed that in the Homebringing Mission "families are broken up," and that the followers were acting "heartlessly toward their own family, abandoning and destroying them as a result, or tyrannizing their own with their false teachings." It said that they were particularly heartless towards the Catholic Church, and that they even used statements by atheist authors in their criticism of the Church – the culmination of wickedness.

But the accusation of "destroying families" falls back on the Church itself, when one knows what the character assassination work of the Church did just to the family of God's prophetess. A part of Gabriele's family did not withstand the incessant church attacks and public damage to her reputation. Her relatives turned away from her in order not to fall under the church ban and to be exposed to ostracism and persecution by the caste of priests in their hometowns. The sect commissioners even snooped around in the church register of the birthplace of the prophetess of God to see if there was anything to be found there that could be used to discredit Gabriele. They found nothing, but the infamous accusations continued.

These are the church institutions. This is how they were, this is how they are to this day, the cassock wearers.

Occasionally, the church sect commissioners tried to attribute a marital crisis or separation to the fact that one of the spouses felt that he or she belonged to the Homebringing Mission. But here, again, the reality was quite different. In November 1987, for example, a big article appeared in the *Passauer Woche* (newspaper) in which a husband was accused of neglecting his family because he was close to Universal Life. Headline: "Cried, Argued, Pleaded."

The Passau "sect expert" claimed that Universal Life had already caused many to "lose house and home." The "sect" had "already driven many into religious delusion" by "banning alcohol, nicotine and sex."
Anyone who reads the books of Universal Life about the "Path to Within" immediately realizes

that something must be wrong here: They expressly warn against fanaticism and repression.

To get back to the specific case: In reality, the family in question was financially secure; the separation was only temporary. The couple's difficulties, however, were massively increased at the very time when Catholic clergymen began to influence the wife to prevent her from "also" succumbing to this "sect." Thus, it was not Universal Life that increased the temporary marital problems, but the opposite: the Church's intolerance of any "deviation."

> As a Reminder – Sect: A term of abuse used by the respective prevailing religious caste for all those whom their Inquisition is directed against.

We see from this example that church sect commissioners even abuse personal conflicts and hardships to publicly harm a non-church minority using freely invented, allegedly sensational stories.

Direct pressure right into the private sphere has always belonged to the instruments of power of the Vatican Church – also in the area of Würzburg. It began with the fact that newspaper clippings from the *Sonntagsblatt* were sent to various addresses of employees and sympathizers of the Homebringing

Mission. When some of those harassed in this way began to refuse to accept further letters and to send them back with the note "Return to sender," this was promptly played up in the next article as: "Conversations Are Rejected."

Healing as in Original Christianity – That Cannot Be!

The Original Christians drew the population's attention to the message of the Christ of God in the prophetic word with flyers and small advertisements. When a marketing company from Limburg approaches the Homebringing Mission of Jesus Christ in March 1983 with a proposal to publish an advertisement about Original Christian healing by faith on a poster for "cancer prevention," those involved agree. The poster is displayed in numerous medical practices.

The *Catholic News Agency* promptly responds and distributes a "warning" by the Episcopal Ordinariate of Würzburg "against miracle healers." It says that a prophetess speaks "in a trance" and gives advice on health and that "Healings as in Early Christianity" are promised. And, "If the sick person seeking help in good faith fails to be healed, he is told that his faith is not enough."

Here, too, a whole sackfull of mendacious opinions is poured out in a very small area. The Original Christians do indeed hold events where they pray for people seeking healing, just as Jesus of Nazareth and His disciples did. But no one is promised a healing. Nor is anyone accused of a "lack of faith." Instead, people are explained that it is, first of all, about the healing of the soul. Once the soul is cleansed of its burdens, the body can also experience relief or healing, if it is good for the soul of the person. This is also what Jesus of Nazareth did.

Gabriele, the prophetess of God, does not speak in a trance, either, but in full waking consciousness. This circumstance is by no means insignificant, but is, rather, an indicator of the true prophecy of God. In a state of trance, the soul leaves the body – similarly as in sleep. In contrast, the soul of the true prophet of God remains in the body during the prophetic speech, so that the prophet consciously perceives everything that God, the Eternal, communicates to the people through him.
It is not by chance that the Church reacts so allergically to the topic of "Healing as in Early Christianity." This is one of the Church's "unredeemed promissory notes," as the church historian Walter Nigg put it. Healing via prayer and faith was taken

for granted in early Christianity. But it was very soon lost. Anyone who revives it today is fought by the Church – at least, if he does so outside the institution of the Church.

Behind the scenes in Würzburg, criminal charges were even filed for an alleged violation of the law on naturopathy. However, when the Original Christians showed that according to the Bible, Jesus of Nazareth Himself gave His disciples the task of healing, this underhanded legal attack was taken off the table.

The "Delusions" of a Pastor

When the Homebringing Mission of Jesus Christ invites people to events with healing meditations in Bonn, a Lutheran pastor, "sect commissioner" of the Protestant Lutheran Church in the Rhineland, reacts. He first attacks the city of Bonn, which dared to rent rooms in the center of the old town to the Homebringing Mission of Jesus Christ. The city defends itself: It refuses to "examine the political or religious convictions of the lessee" and states that it is not possible to get out of the contract. But it doesn't want any trouble either: No more rooms will be made available for future events. The head of the city's Youth Welfare Office is more in line with the pastor's way of thinking: He has "no doubt that the city will take legal action against the Homebringing Mission of Jesus Christ if it is convinced that it is a sect that endangers young people."

The terms "youth religion" and "youth sect" had already been spread in public by the Lutheran pastor Haack from Munich during the 1970s, in order to discredit various non-church religious communities, although by no means were only young people to be found in these communities.

The cassock wearer reaches deep into the slander box, talks about "soul catchers," through whom the young people could become "dependent without questions." The prophetess suffers from "religious delusions" and the meditations are "peppered with occult elements."

The prophet is a fool, the man of the spirit is mad – this is how the prophet Hosea was already insulted by the priests and scribes of that time. (Hos. 9:7) But how does a woman who has taken on the heavy burden of serving God, the Eternal, in this day and age as His prophetess, feel when she is so publicly slandered?

The Homebringing Mission of Jesus Christ answers with a public event, during which the Original Christians take a stand regarding the defama-

tions. 300 citizens attend – but how does the press report? "Homebringing Mission Fights Against Pastor" reads the headline of the *Bonner Rundschau* (newspaper) on April 23, 1983, which states that they "zeroed in" on the youth pastor and "threatened legal steps."
Not a single sentence is written about the facts and corrections presented in detail that evening. Instead, the professional defamer is played up as a "victim."

The press plays exactly the role that the Church has assigned to it – good prerequisites for the man of the Church to further stoke the fire. Through the "Arbeitskreis gegen destruktive Kulte" (Work Group Against Destructive Cults) in Bonn, he publishes a brochure about "youth sects," in which he accuses the Homebringing Mission of Jesus Christ of caring solely about the property and assets of its followers. In his presentation of the teachings of the Homebringing Mission, one untruth follows the other, for instance: It is taught that "even in the earthly body ... one could make contact with the spirits of the deceased" – on the contrary, exactly this is warned against by the Homebringing Mission of Jesus Christ. It is claimed that "salvation is possible only through the HBM meditations" – such a claim of sole agency is not found in the

Homebringing Mission of Jesus Christ, but in the Church.

At least, in 1983, the sect commissioner still knows that the Homebringing Mission rejects "rebirth in animal or mineral form." Three years later he will turn even this last remnant of factual accuracy into a lie and claim: "Unbelievers, on the other hand, must expect to experience a much lower rebirth in their next life, for example, as a plant or as an animal. ..."

What Does a "Sect" Do with a Swimming Pool?

No matter how absurdly church representatives twist the truth – their assertions make the rounds, first, in church newspapers and parish letters, then also in the daily press.

And they are – at the beginning of the 1980s, before the later financial scandals of the Church, before the exposure of sexual crimes committed against children by priests – still simply accepted unchecked and at face value by most people. At that time, the Church still enjoyed a certain trust and back then, hardly anyone could imagine that church representatives so uninhibitedly tell the untruth.

On November 29, 1983, the director of the Catholic Caritas in Nuremberg claimed in the *Nürnberger Nachrichten* (newspaper) that a young woman had severed "all ties to friends and family." It said that the families were desperate, that every domestic discussion ended in quarrels. It is one of those cases that – as in the medieval Inquisition – are presented anonymously, so that a reply is not possible: Who is meant here? It is significant that it does not occur to the Caritas director to question his own nephew, who is active in the Homebringing Mission of Jesus Christ, on this topic before he goes public. Instead, he praises the good collaboration with Pastor Haack in Munich.

Pastor Haack, in turn, became active in March 1984 with his "parents' initiative" in Würzburg. Haack had founded this "initiative" in 1975 in Munich, in order to be able to better tug at people's heartstrings in public during his inquisition work. In reality, hardly any parents belonged to it, but all the more priests and theologians.

In Würzburg, a rumor had been started that the Homebringing Mission wanted to buy a swimming facility. The rumor-mongers did not waste a thought on the difficult question of what a community of faith would do with a swimming pool.

But it illustrates the hysteria that church representatives like Count Magnis stirred up in the Catholic city of Würzburg in just a few months. In the years that followed, similar rumors were spread again and again, when a property was up for sale somewhere in the Lower Franconia region – and the buyers and sellers dutifully declared that they had nothing, absolutely nothing, to do with the Homebringing Mission. Malicious tongues even thought they knew that such rumors were sometimes spread deliberately – in order to drive up prices or to create a "favorable" buying climate, because: The "sect" must not get it!

The Junge Union (political youth group) and Haack's parents' initiative eagerly take up such nonsense in order to "mobilize against the project" and demand, for example: "No sect center in the Swimming Club 05 swimming pool!" A Junge Union activist, an intelligent student of Haack's, sees an opportunity to make his mark here. He warns of the "dangerous psycho sect" that "shamelessly exploits especially young people's longing for meaning and security, for the financial interests and lust for power of their leadership clique." And: "Würzburg must not become Franconia's sect center." The Original Christians answer with a leaflet: "The cult madness strikes ever new capers! Will the Homebringing Mission of Jesus Christ soon buy up all of Würzburg"?

One must always be clear about who is publicly being pilloried here by the churches and their accomplices in the state:
It is the prophetess of God, who once again brings the teachings of love for God and neighbor to the people from the Kingdom of God; they are people who keep the laws of the state, yet have freed themselves from the church dogmas and the regulations of the priestmen. They strive to follow Him, according to the Ten Commandments of God and the Sermon on the Mount of Jesus of Nazareth, in all freedom, that is, without priests, ceremonies and judgments of condemnation – just as the Spirit of the Christ of God teaches through His prophetess Gabriele: The Free Spirit – God in us.

These people, who do nothing wrong, but merely want to claim their right to freedom of religion, are systematically subjected to character assassination by state and church – and this does not remain without consequences, as we will learn later on.

The Church Hardliners Prevail

The Lutheran Church also takes up the topic of "sects" and makes it the focus of the "17th Main-Franconia Conference on Faith" in Würzburg in March 1984, with Pastor Hans-Diether Reimer from the *Protestant-Lutheran Central Office for Worldview Issues* in Stuttgart as speaker. In his attacks against the Homebringing Mission of Jesus Christ, Reimer rather stays within the field of theology. He wants to see the revelations tied to the "examination by the community" (whereby he understands "community," as the church, of course), otherwise he describes the Original Christians as "a faith group like any other."

A year before, four followers of the Homebringing Mission of Jesus Christ had been given the opportunity to present their faith in short talks at a conference of the central office branch in Würzburg. This, by the way, remained the only time, ever since the foundation of the Homebringing Mission, that an official church office engaged in a normal conversation with the "heretics." However, the results, and this is also significant, they preferred to keep to themselves.

But to the Catholic Church leadership in Würzburg that is apparently not mean enough. In a country in which more and more people are leaving the Church, theological statements have long ceased to be enough to stir up the masses against a minority faith. The people have to be well and truly frightened with totally different topics, providing them with shocking stories, for example, about health, family or working conditions and the like.

Even the Pharisees and scribes did not slander Jesus of Nazareth with arguments of faith to the Roman occupying power, but flatly claimed that He wanted to take over political power. In this way, they finally achieved His cruel murder.

And so, something remarkable now takes place: On the same weekend that Reimer's lecture takes place, the cathedral school and the Episcopal Youth Office hold an "Academy Conference" in Würzburg – also on the subject of "sects"! And whom do they invite as speaker? The Lutheran pastor Haack! The *Main-Post* (newspaper) immediately calls him the "best authority on the occult and sect scene in the German-speaking world."

Within the mainstream churches, it seems that there is no complete agreement yet on how best to wage the war of slander against the "sects," and this conflict is carried, as it were, on the back of the Homebringing Mission of Jesus Christ. The process has a symbolic character: the hardliners prevail.

They invent the more memorable slanders, have the more malicious slander strategy of character assassination, and are more likely to make it into the press. Just as Pastor Haack did on March 20, 1984 in the *Main-Post*. There, Haack proclaims, as the inquisitors in former times at their first sermon in the village, the well-known "criteria" by which one can unmistakably recognize a "sect": a "holy master," a "saving principle," a hierarchy, worldly businesses. ...

That these, in reality, are all characteristics of the churches does not seem to be noticed by anyone. Then – as if by chance in-between – the decisive sentence: "Haack explicitly warned against the 'Homebringing Mission of Jesus Christ,' as well."

Vegetarians – Godless Heretics!

To keep the iron hot, right at Easter 1984, the "expert" of his own denomination, Franz von Magnis, now speaks at the spring meeting of the Catholic Diocesan Council of Würzburg. He tries to build a contradiction between the statement of the Homebringing Mission, "to get along without priests, without statutes, without ceremonies," and the life of the Original Christians. He claims that Gabriele said in a meeting that the "Homebringing

Mission's own pastor had been consecrated." Gabriele never said this; it contradicts both her use of language and the teaching given through her. – So what really happened? One of the Christ-friends had taken on the task to speak a few words in his free time at funerals (of people who had left the church, anyway).

Furthermore, Count Magnis claims that the prophetess allowed her followers to "hear voices." He says that she spreads a "totalitarian spiritualistic teaching"; he speaks of a "dangerous, deep-psychology phenomenon" and of the demand for "total submission of the followers."
This is a particularly dirty and malicious defamation against a person who has devoted her whole life exclusively to the service of God, the Free Spirit, and of His Son, Christ, the great teacher of peace and freedom. Anyone who wants to read in black and white where there is actually a demand for total submission will find it abundantly in the dogmas of the Catholic Church. Here are just two examples from "The Teaching of the Catholic Church" by Josef Neuner and Heinrich Roos:
Furthermore, we declare, state and define that it is absolutely necessary for the salvation of all men that they submit to the Roman pontiff.
(Margin Note 342)

And: *We decree that the Holy Apostolic See and the Roman Pontiff have primacy in the whole world ...* (Margin Note 349)

The modern Inquisitor Magnis created totally new accusations: He wrote: *It is known from the practice of far-eastern schools of philosophy that the abstention from animal protein can make people docile, controllable and manageable by weakening their own will. Undoubtedly, this protein deprivation also leads the followers of the HBM* [Homebringing Mission] *to a total readiness to be led, to open themselves to the teachings by way of meditative indoctrination.* The resistance of the followers is *gently reduced by means of nutritional instruction, skillful didactics, emotions and meditation.* Later he adds that this instruction is *life-endangering.*

Today, a few decades later, it is clear to anyone how absurd such claims are – just as absurd as the belief that the sun revolves around the Earth. That the abstention from meat foods is not only physiologically harmless, but even extremely advantageous healthwise – not to mention animal protection and climate protection – is known to every child today. But at the beginning of the 1980s, a vegetarian diet was still an "alternative" topic, with which one could easily arouse negative emotions among older Catholics, especially, in connection with Far Eastern esoteric "mystery mongering." The count's "exposures" are fatally reminiscent of witchcraft stories of earlier times: In those days, as well, one did not have to prove anything, but could be sure of an eagerly listening audience.

Perhaps Count Magnis secretly thought back even further, to a time when a vegetarian diet was indeed "life-threatening": In antiquity and in the Middle Ages, when "heretical movements" such as the 4th century Priscillianists or the 12th/13th century Cathars were killed by the Catholic Inquisition precisely because of this way of life! Already in ancient times, the Catholic Church condemned the meatless diet as "godless heresy" in a dogma that is still valid (!) today. (For more details see the book: "Vegetarians – Godless Heretics? What vegetarians and meat-eaters alike should know.")
The Original Christians only learned about the dubious ways in which the inquisitor had built up an abstruse „black legend" against them three years later in connection with the founding of a natural clinic – we will get back to this later. Some of that, however, can already be anticipated here, because the example of the allegedly "life-endangering nutritional teachings" shows, in an especially impressive way, how deviously the modern inquisitor

proceeded, in order to denigrate Gabriele and the Original Christian teachings.

Through Gabriele, the Spirit of God teaches respect for God's creation and thus, a vegetarian way of life. Against this, the church demagogue – as already mentioned, a passionate big game hunter – proceeded as follows: He commissioned a nutritionist to prepare an "expert opinion" on the vegetarian diet of the followers of Jesus of Nazareth. For this purpose, in support of his absurd thesis – the "danger" of a meatless diet – he deliberately provided the scientist with false information about alleged statements of the Spirit of the Christ of God through His prophetess, Gabriele. The expert witness fell for the churchman's lies and wrote the requested report as the Church wanted.

After the scientist had been informed about the true facts in the summer of 1987, he realized that the Church had hoodwinked him. He revoked his report in March 1988 and expressly forbade Count Magnis from using it any further. However, the mendacious opinion was in the world and was further spread without restraint by other sect commissioners and compliant journalists, in order to denigrate the word of God through the prophetess of God, Gabriele.

> **Mendacious Opinions:**
> An untruth = Lies that are so formulated by "experts" that they are legally classified and permitted by the courts as "opinions" because their truthfulness is not checked. The credulous citizen does not know the difference between a permitted lie in the guise of opinion and fact. He therefore considers the lie to be a fact that the court has verified.

But that was not the end of it. The ban against further use was circumvented in other ways as well:

An almost identical "expert opinion" appeared in another writing by Count Magnis in 1990. The "expert opinion" on the dietetics of Universal Life, which is literally congruent (!) over longer passages and which came to the same demonstrably false conclusions as the first one, was prepared by a certain Professor Seewald of the Mayo Clinic in Rochester, New York in the United States – or rather: copied and signed. According to an inquiry, Professor Seewald left the Mayo Clinic a little later with an unknown destination.

Thus, we see that modern Inquisition has no scruples where harming reputations is concerned. When the untruth of a character assassination attack comes to light in one place, it can nevertheless be spread further elsewhere.

Such procedures of the modern Inquisition was characterized by the then already well-known

Catholic theologian Hans Küng in the newspaper of October 4, 1985 with the words: *No one gets burned to death anymore, but mentally and professionally destroyed wherever necessary.* That is the church institutions. That is how they were, how they are, the cassock wearers, until today.

"The Truth Will Prevail!"

In April 1984, Gabriele decides to give an answer to this and other defamations – even though it is already foreseeable that again, none of this "answer to the churches and their representatives" will be printed in the press.

A few sentences are quoted from this document with the headline "The Truth Will Prevail!" Gabriele writes on the topic of nutrition:

It is noticeable how "seriously" our critics are concerned about our nutrition. It is, of course, unimaginable to people whose happiness depends on cutlets and ham to do without them.

The fact that, for example, the majority of the 500 million Hindus and hundreds of thousands of highly civilized Europeans and Americans are also vegetarians should actually be known. So are all of them "weak-willed for lack of protein" and possibly submissive to those who eat meat? Since, according to my critics, I demand and also achieve "total submission" from "my followers," this should contradict the fact that as a vegetarian, I myself must also be weak-willed.

On the topic of "hearing voices":
It is not about "hearing voices," but about hearing the voice of God. ... Paul also testifies that in the early church the Holy Spirit spoke through the mouth of human beings.
If in today's churches no one hears the voice of God or has the gift of prophecy, then this is because of the Church and not because of God. For Christ teaches us that all people should hear the voice of their Father in them; if they are not yet able to do so, then they should purify themselves by living according to God's laws ... All other voices, that are rightly warned against, among ourselves, too, are heard by people who are still very earth-bound.

At this point, Gabriele takes up a statement by Lutheran theologians from the German state of Hessen according to which the Homebringing Mission belongs to the realm of "spiritism in revelations." Gabriele explains this:
These theologians should be more careful with their classifications. They base their faith on the word of God, which they believe is revealed in the Bible. –

But how did God reveal Himself in the Bible? In 2500 passages it says: "And God said." The divine Spirit has always revealed Himself in a human being who then proclaimed His word – most powerfully, in Jesus of Nazareth. He has revealed Himself again and again during the last 2000 years, in that His Spirit spoke through people, some of whom were subsequently even canonized by the Church.

Taken at its word, therefore, the whole of Christianity is spiritistically grounded, and the churches are the largest spiritistic associations. If our critics are not able to distinguish between the revelations that Christ gives through me and what a poor soul "reveals" at a séance table in vulgar spiritism, that is their problem, not ours.

On the subject of family conflicts:
The representatives of the institution church continue to accuse the Homebringing Mission of destroying marriages without regard to economic consequences. To this it should be said: Those who live in glasshouses should not throw stones. Are all the marriages that the Church has blessed in good order? Where there is no love, the church's blessing also does not prevent separation. – Throughout the centuries, the Church has taught and practiced intolerance towards non-Catholic spouses. It does not surprise me that it also does so now toward the

followers of the Homebringing Mission. The ones who sow discord are the priests who mislead the Catholic spouse into intolerance. Does this correspond to the love that Jesus taught? ... God does not see Catholics and Protestants. He loves all His children equally and wants them to live together in harmony. ... If there were more tolerance in the families, indeed, if there were more tolerance in the Church, then the man or woman would let the awakened soul of the partner follow the path to truth, if the right kind of love is there.

Gabriele asks further: *Why do the representatives of the institution go against the prophetic word of God and against our clarifying lectures? Why do they resist, reject the word of God and suppress the holy message? Because they are afraid. Anyone who is afraid does not have the truth... If the representatives of the Church were sure that they have the sole beatifying grace and truth, they could remain calm, because the truth will prevail.*

Who or What Is Totalitarian?

Because – as to be expected – no newspaper wants to print any of these clarifying words of Gabriele, the Original Christians distribute them again from hand to hand in duplicated form. The modern inquisitors have quite different possibilities; they have an almost unlimited fund of money, personnel and influence at their disposal. And they know that the persecution zeal of their faithful will always decrease if fuel is not added to the fire. Anyone who met the Original Christians without prejudice in daily life found them trustworthy, and usually found that they could easily befriend them.

In June 1984, Pastor Haack moved the annual conference of "his" parents' initiative to Würzburg – a "coincidence" that will be repeated in the following years. His main focus: "Against the abuse of religious freedom – experts and parents warn against the psycho-cults" that "bring young people into psychological dependence" and "inveigle" children. They are looking for ways "to liberate someone from the belief of the gurus again." But much more importantly, he said, is to talk about "how to reduce the long-term effects of soul-washing that these totalitarian societies carry out with great skill."

Here the word "totalitarian" appears for the first time. With unerring instinct, the defamation specialist Haack recognized that this term makes a special impression in Germany because it evokes associations of the Hitler era. "Totalitarian" was originally the label given to a state that uses all its state power to forcefully bring its citizens into line and control them right into their private sphere. Now, this word is suddenly being applied to communities in a liberal, constitutional state, in which there are laws that protect the freedom of the individual, and in which one can leave a community if one feels restricted there. So what does this term mean, at this point? If it is supposed to refer to a total monopoly on the use of force, it is nonsense. If it is supposed to express the fact that a denomination hoards power and money in order to exert the greatest possible influence on society, then the mainstream churches are the best example of this – Catholic theologians such as Küng, Greinacher or Drewermann are not without reason in unanimously describing their own church as "totalitarian." But if it is to mean that a religion tries to give answers and guidance for all areas of human life, then Jesus of Nazareth was also "totalitarian" in His Sermon on the Mount.

But which newspaper reader would even take the trouble to question such a term? Who would even think it possible that despite the constantly decreasing importance of the churches, a priest defames and deliberately speaks the untruth?

But for the Catholic inquisitor colleague Count Magnis, this is not a question. Thus, in July 1984 in his latest pamphlet, he quotes from the local press: *The Homebringing Mission of Jesus Christ, which is based in Würzburg, is, by the way, seen by the Munich pastor Friedrich-Wilhelm Haack as a "spiritualistic sect with a pseudo-prophetess at its head, who fully co-opts the human being."*

Who is the cassock wearer talking about? Gabriele is the prophetess and emissary of God in this time. May the one who can grasp it, grasp it; may the one who wants to leave it, leave it. But whoever takes action against the prophetess of God with lies and vituperation bears witness to the fact that he is the one, who is walking in the footsteps of those to whom Jesus of Nazareth said: *You have the devil for a father. He was a liar and a murderer from the beginning.*

The Theologians Take to Stonewalling

To defend themselves against the lies of church opinions, the Original Christians again had no alternative outside of newspaper advertisements. On June 2, 1984, such an advertisement appeared in the *Süddeutsche Zeitung* (a major newspaper). Pastor Haack was called upon to prove that the Protestant-Lutheran Church possesses the truth and that Martin Luther, in particular, spoke from the divine truth in his diatribes against Jews and peasants. Anyone, who cannot prove that he himself speaks from the truth cannot deny that others have the truth, either. The Original Christians publicly offered to face the public with Pastor Haack.

This was to be repeated several times during the following years: The church agitators were repeatedly called upon to prove in public that their claims about the Homebringing Mission of Jesus Christ correspond to the truth. But the demagogues never responded to this. Why not?

Haack never complied with such a request, either – nor did any later sect commissioners, regardless of denomination. A fair, equal discussion in public would very quickly reveal to the unbiased observer the untenability of the churches' assertions. The person who damages reputations needs the ambush, the unassailable position of power that he automatically enjoys today in the media dominated by church broadcasting councils and church-controlled capital.

So what did Haack do? He fled into a further slander. On June 14, 1984, one could read in the *Süddeutsche Zeitung:*

Prophecy Competition

The sect commissioner of the Protestant-Lutheran Church in Bavaria, Pastor Friedrich-Wilhelm Haack, has been called upon by the Würzburg-based "Homebringing Mission of Jesus Christ" to engage in a competitive prophecy. As Haack explained, a leading representative of the community of faith, which he classifies as a "neo-spiritistic sect," has invited him in writing to prove his abilities in the field of prophecy in a joint event with the prophetess of the Homebringing Mission. Certain conditions, such as previous fasting by both participants and holding one's legs completely still during the prophecy, were attached to the religious comparative test. Haack, who, according to his own statement, does not possess any special abilities of this kind, declined the invitation. According to the sect commissioner, such competitions were suitable "for the circus or the zoo," but not for a serious discussion of religious issues.

What here was meant to be a humorous report, is, in truth, another mendacious opinion. The diabolic "art" of an inquisitor consists of twisting everything – including the exposure of the church, into a further invective against the "heretics."

If the *Süddeutsche Zeitung* had taken the trouble to ask the Homebringing Mission of Jesus Christ what really happened, it would have turned out that there was indeed an invitation, but back in September 1983, which went not only to Pastor Haack, but to all theologians who until then had publicly dragged the Homebringing Mission through the mud. Of course, the theologians were not supposed to "foretell" or "prophesy"; they were supposed to face the public together with the prophetess of God and talk for one and a half hours – in their own way – about a spiritual topic that was to be announced to them only shortly before. On the occasion of great revelations, the prophetess of God also learns from her inner being only shortly before, what the subject will be. Nor should the theologians "fast," but should come to this comparison under the same external conditions as Gabriele, that is, with only a light breakfast. Like Gabriele, they should stand before the audience without a concept of speech and speak to them with closed eyes and hands raised for a long time – just as Gabriele regularly did during great revelations at home and abroad. The text of a revelation of the Christ of God was also sent to the theologians, in which it said:

My word and My teaching in the present time are rejected and My prophetess, My instrument, is slandered. So I offer to all the possibility to comprehend what My prophetess, My instrument, accomplishes through the power of My love at every revelation in public. All those who express themselves in a reprehensible way can now face My word under the criteria given by Me, which My instrument has to fulfill constantly. All slanderers will then recognize where the power and the word of My instrument come from. They themselves can then experience how far their own powers reach! This shall happen in front of a great number of listeners! ... Everyone can examine for himself where the Spirit of God truly blows! ... The Lord once again extends His hand to all doubters, slanderers and all those who mock and speak evil of His work. Check for yourself! Who has the living Holy Spirit in himself? The theologians, the many slanderers of the Homecoming Mission of Jesus Christ? Or the prophetess of God for the present time?

This offer was accompanied by the addition that it was valid for an unlimited time, *until one of the theologians addressed has the strength and courage to accept this offer.*

As was to be expected, there was no reaction to this offer either, except the one quoted above from the *Süddeutsche Zeitung*, three-quarters of a year later. This occurrence is also an example of the fact that the public always learned only a fraction of what really happened with regard to the Homebringing Mission of Jesus Christ – and if so, then only in a completely distorted form through the eyeglasses of the church representatives.

Those Who Are Hit Rebel

In February 1987, Gabriele, the prophetess of God, was interviewed at length by the magazine "Der Christusstaat" (The Christ State). Among other things, she was asked why she, as the prophetess of the Lord, was repeatedly exposed to attacks from the churches. Her answer is reproduced here (slightly abbreviated), because she also deals with many other questions that are frequently raised. Note the clarity, calmness and objectivity with which Gabriele counters the vituperations and lies of the church representatives:

When I read the first defamations, I could not understand that people give voice to claims that they cannot prove. The representatives of "The Great Sign – The Lady of All Nations" poured dirt over me and I had to realize over and over again that it was only spitefulness, nothing else.
Today I know that it was out of fear. They believe, for example, that the teaching of reincarnation is unchristian, because it is not literally written down in the Bible. The teaching of reincarnation is a law, and Jesus of Nazareth taught and lived the law. The Bible does not contain the complete law. Christ teaches the law through me, and He doesn't ask whether it fits with the teaching of the Church or not.

If the representatives of the Catholic and Protestant-Lutheran Churches had the truth, they would be free, and they would not have to denigrate, slander, mock, ridicule and pervert the revelations of the Lord. The one who has found the truth knows that the truth works for the people and that the truth will bring everything to light.

When the first defamations came, I asked God in my inner being and He said to me:

"What happened in and through the church institutions, and still partly happens today, is not the will of God. God is love. God does not kill. Love is not brutal. Love does not strike. Love clarifies. And so, I have sent you to My own to clarify about the injustice partly that still vibrates in the atmosphere and is effective in the astral planes, and to give an understanding of it to those who are in the earthly garment, and who should atone for it, that is, ask for forgiveness. The rebellion of the churches is nothing more than the fact that they have been hit by Me," thus, spoke the Lord.

Jesus of Nazareth said: "Just as they persecute Me, they will one day persecute you." Aren't the churches then taking action against God with their attacks? Aren't they blaspheming God?

In a way, they are blaspheming God, because when they condemn people, when they discriminate against people because of their faith, they are violating the law of neighborly love. The Catholic and Protestant-Lutheran Churches cannot prove their belief. Consequently, the representatives of the Catholic and Protestant churches cannot reproach those of other faiths, nor accuse them of a wrong belief and enticement.

It has been this way at all times and it is also this way today. Anyone who raises a word against the church institutions is pilloried; he is defamed, mocked and ridiculed. He is accused of the satanic, even though the one accused has not caused anything. On the other hand, we know what a bloodbath the church institutions, particularly the Roman-Catholic one, have caused in this world. Jesus said: "Love your enemies, do good to those who hate you."
If we include the words of Jesus in our lives, then we can forgive, and if we live the words of Jesus as truth and accept them as a source of strength, then it is also possible for us to turn both cheeks. So I have always turned both cheeks in response to the slander and I will continue to do so, because I know that I have found the truth and the truth has set me free. I know that the just God who speaks through me will bring everything to light.

We know that the mills of God grind slowly. This also applies to the church institutions and to "The Great Sign, the Lady of All Nations." I know that God's justice will open the eyes of many. When – we leave that to God. And I know: I will meet my detractors again, whether on this Earth or in other worlds – we leave that to God. I know that my detractors cannot stop me on the way to the heart of God. I do not need to forgive them at all, because I have not accepted their slander. ...

Why are the prophets and many people who believe in God slandered? Because those who slander do not have the truth, since the one who slanders has no truth. He thinks only of himself and wants to justify himself and wants to put himself in the right light. ...

When Jesus stood before Annas and the servant of the high priest hit Him, Jesus asked: "Have I spoken wrongly? Why do you strike me?"
I would like to ask the same question of the representatives of the church institutions: "Have I spoken wrongly, then prove it to me; but if I have spoken rightly, why do you slander me? What have I done to you? If you have the truth, then prove the truth." That would be close to the Christian way. But until now, the "Christian" institutions have not proven their truth. Because if they were from the truth, the world would be in a better state.

4. The First Enterprises of the Original Christians Are Fought Against or Hindered (1984)

Despite all hostility, the Homebringing Mission of Jesus Christ grew to considerable size within a few years. In well over a hundred meeting places, the Inner Spirit=Christ Churches at home and abroad, Christ-friends gathered, books were translated into the major European languages, thousands of people attended the courses of the Inner Path or did the schooling at home with the help of cassettes or books.

Once the Spirit of truth, the Spirit of the Christ of God, had taught many of the lawful principles of the heavens in word and writing, and had given the Inner Path to God, around the year 1983, in several revelations the Eternal called upon craftsmen, merchants, farmers, doctors, people of nearly all occupations through His prophetess Gabriele – to consider whether they would like to apply the divine laws in community.

Thus, it was now increasingly more about doing the Sermon on the Mount, about implementing the divine teachings in daily life, according to the words of Jesus of Nazareth:

Everyone then who hears these words of mine and acts on them will be like a wise man who built his house on rock. The rain fell, the floods came, and the winds blew and beat on that house, but it did not fall, because it had been founded on rock.

And everyone who hears these words of mine and does not act on them will be like a foolish man who built his house on sand; and the rain fell, and the floods came, and the winds blew and beat against that house, and it fell – and great was its fall!

In 1984, Christ now created the work of the deed, Universal Life, from the root of the work of teaching and enlightenment, the Homebringing Mission of Jesus Christ.

Universal Life is thus the step from the inner to the outer: What has grown internally should also become visible externally. This means that people who want to help in this also join together in the external world, that they live together in the Spirit of God and found businesses and social services, that they put the Ten Commandments of God and the teachings of the Sermon on the Mount into practice in their daily life and work, step by step.

It took a few months until ecclesiastical twisters of truth got wind of this. Then, they also learned that the Original Christian farmers of a newly acquired farm also sold their vegetables from peaceable cultivation at the weekly market in the city Würzburg.

People who live and work together and are oriented toward the Original Christian goals? Combining spiritual, ethical-moral and economic activity? In the view of the church leaders, monasteries and cloisters may combine religion and economic activity. But what about people who organize themselves economically outside the churches, thereby making themselves independent? You can no longer exert existential pressure on them from the side of the Church, for example, by denouncing them to their employers. For the churches it was therefore quite clear: This must not be allowed and will be fought against with all conceivable means – especially because the churches also see their power endangered as soon as people prove with their life and thinking in everyday life, that the Sermon on the Mount can be lived and that for this, no external priestly religion is needed.

The Würzburg Episcopal Ordinariate held a press conference on July 16, 1984 – in a big way. Not only Count Magnis appeared, but also a cathedral canon and a media consultant.
And the count also brought along a "piece of evidence": a radish, purchased a few days earlier at

the market stand of the farm run by followers of Jesus of Nazareth. After a few days, of course, the radish didn't look quite so fresh anymore – which prompted the reporter from the *German Press Agency* to describe it as "downright pathetic." Which, in turn, leads to a sneering headline in the *Ingolstädt Donau-Kurier* (July 17, 1984): "A Pathetic Radish as Proof of Business in the Name of Jesus."

For the first time, the Church "sect commissioners" spread their mendacious opinions throughout Bavaria – thanks to the *German Press Agency*, which is glad to be of service to them. And the regional press willingly follows suit without checking anything. "The Sect God Is Called Mammon" is the headline in the *Nürnberger Zeitung*.

With the air of sanctimony, according to Count Magnis, there has been an "expansion of economic activities" *(Main-Post)*, a "questionable combination of religion and 'Ltd. & Co'." *(Burghauser Anzeiger)* – as if especially for the Church a "combination" of religion and business is something fundamentally foreign. But it belongs to the usual behavioral repertoire of an inquisitor to present even quite serious events as something deeply reprehensible and abhorrent: for instance, that people earn their living together with honest work and keep to the Sermon on the Mount of Jesus – whereby until today, this is dismissed by both church institutions as a kind of utopia.

The Catholic *Fränkische Volksblatt* noted with satisfaction that the Church has "fired a strong broadside" here. As the only one of the reporting newspapers, the *Main-Post* considered it appropriate (even this remnant of liberality, however, was lost in later years) to quote at least in one sentence something from a statement of the Homebringing Mission of Jesus Christ. If all journalists present had fulfilled their obligation to exercise diligence, they could easily have determined what the Church "broadside" consisted of: hateful polemics, unscrupulous distortions and outright untruths.

For example, it is claimed that the Homebringing Mission of Jesus Christ acquired a "villa," a farm and two bakeries. Magnis speaks of "millions." In reality, it is a normal residential house, which, like the farm and the bakeries, was purchased by private individuals.
In contrast, the Vatican Church itself actually owns innumerable properties in Würzburg, some of which are in prime shopping locations in the city

center. This is where the "millions" sit, and not only here:

The mainstream churches in Germany, in particular, have assets of an estimated 500 billion Euros, including shares and funds on a large scale. They are the largest private landowners. Here, the "sect god" is actually called Mammon! And their social service institutions Caritas and Diaconate generate more revenue than Lufthansa Airline or the German Federal Railway – and on top of that, they are subsidized to nearly 100 percent by the general public. (For further details: see the following books in German by Carsten Frerk, "Finanzen und Vermögen der Kirchen," "Caritas und Diakonie in Deutschland," "Violettbuch Kirchenfinanzen.")

And then, a few medium-sized businesses – as we will see later – are repeatedly called "economic conglomerates," of all things, by these churches, which are worth billions, simply because they are not run by Catholics or Lutherans, but by simple followers of Jesus of Nazareth.

Count Magnis makes use of the chance to set a few more untruths into the world. Thus, he claims that during the prayer healing of the Original Christians, those seeking healing are "stroked with the hands." In reality, they are not touched at all. Magnis continues: The path within is about "self-redemption" (there can be no talk of this) and about an "adoption of far-eastern practices." *(Fränkische Nachrichten).*

The church representatives – this, too, is significant – can apparently imagine a higher wisdom and spirituality solely in the east. If someone really wanted to visit such an "adoption," then at that time he would only have to attend the Zen courses of the Benedictines of Münster-Blackzach in the "House of Benedict" in the middle of Würzburg. Thus, one imputes to others exactly what one does oneself.

The Enemies of Divine Prophecy in Action

But above all, the Catholic inquisitor Magnis is concerned with purposefully arousing fears – for instance, that young people r*un the risk of being financially abused and exploited by their own "youth church" of the "Homebringing Mission."* *(Neue Presse Coburg)*
This filth, too, falls back on the Church a thousandfold – in the meantime, it has been revealed that thousands of children and young people in ecclesiastical children's homes suffered from maltreatment and exploitation, and thousands of children were often sexually abused by so-called cler-

gymen over many years. And these are facts about actual crimes!

The mainstream churches are particularly concerned with making a mockery of the prophetic word of God. Magnis tries to do this, among other things, by bringing into play *"one of the prophetess's closest associates,"* who is *"a professor of economics at the Fachhochschule (university), an expert in marketing issues." (Kitzinger Zeitung)* Already in his writing of 1982, he called this professor – it is Professor Doctor Walter Hofmann – Gabriele's "mentor" and mentioned that he had traveled to India several times. With this, Magnis obviously wants to connote: The revelations are merely feigned; in truth, everything comes from a worldly source: modern marketing mixed with a pinch of far-eastern wisdom.

A little later, the Lutheran dean of Würzburg, Professor Martin Elze, also takes this legend of the count and develops it further: Walter Hofmann, for example, introduced reincarnation and the law of karma into the teachings of the Homebringing Mission. This, too, is an untruth – it can easily be proven that these (and other) teaching contents already appeared in the revelations of the Spirit of the Christ of God, when Professor Hofmann did not even yet know the prophetess of God.

The press conference described here is an example of how modern Inquisition works today and how easy it was for the Church to reawaken the ancient reflexes of fear and condemnation of "sects." As intended, the journalists immediately jumped at the presented ecclesiastical mendacious opinions and obediently used all the clichés in their headlines: "Catholic Church Warns of Homebringing Prophetess," titles, for instance, the *Fränkischen Nachrichten*, and in the subtitle it says: "Study: Followers Are Indoctrinated for Selfish Purposes, Young People Exploited." "Study" – this sounds scientific, but in reality, it is just one of the pamphlets from Count Magnis.

Incitement – modern inquisitors are perfect at this. But how little the church representatives could inwardly oppose the truth of the prophetic word of God, how little they had understood, or wanted to understand, the concerns of a spiritual movement, is substantiated by a marginal note: At the end of the meeting, Canon Heinz urged "therefore the formation of groups that talk about the gospel should be promoted" in the parishes. (*Volksblatt*) But the world does not get better by talk alone. However, if people set out to follow Jesus, the Christ, by practicing the gospel in daily life, then they are mercilessly fought against by the church institutions!

"We Have Risen Again!"

The Original Christians again react to the churches' mendacious opinions with a large-format advertisement, but hardly respond to the individual absurd accusations. However, on July 28, 1984, in the *Main-Post*, under the headline "We Have Risen Again!" they make it clear that the Homebringing Mission of Jesus Christ has no possessions and that "opportunities for selfish and dubious business ... are out of the question." Furthermore, they point to the long tradition of early Christian movements in history and to the emerging Kingdom of Peace, on which people of different occupations work together.

If one wants to incite people – the church representatives know this – one must appeal to the lower instincts – for example, fear of competition and envy. In the autumn of 1984, they therefore try to drive a wedge into the Würzburg health food scene. On October 26, 1984, Count Magnis launches an article in the *Frankische Volksblatt* with the headline: "Health Food Shops Speak of a Threat to Their Existence – Market Economy Under 'Religious Influences' – new market stands do not work according to the laws of the market economy." Allegedly, there are "dumping prices" at the market stands operated by Original Christians, because, as Count Magnis claims, followers of the Homebringing Mission of Jesus Christ work on the farm "for the wages of God." Again, a downright lie: In reality, all employees on the farm – in contrast to church nuns and monks – receive regular salaries and are correctly insured.

After that, the attacks, which are tantamount to barely veiled calls for boycott, on the market stalls of the followers of Jesus of Nazareth and the farms behind them do not stop for years. Some examples can be found in chapter 12.2, which deals, among other things, with the attacks on businesses operated by Original Christians.

The Prevented Christ Clinic in Dettelbach

Church and state "sect experts" then tried to track down and prevent in advance planned business projects of the Original Christians. And what if they are already under wraps? Then one nevertheless pulls out all stops, even if millions of tax monies are wasted in the process. This is shown by the example of the Christ Clinic planned in Dettelbach, Lower Franconia.
In Dettelbach, a Catholic pilgrimage site, a former regional hospital had been empty for a long time.

Both the district of Kitzingen (the owner of the building) and the town of Dettelbach were desperately looking for a buyer and therefore welcomed the fact that a German-Swiss group of doctors agreed to establish a clinic there for the follow-up care of cancer patients. They agreed to a purchase in mid-June of 1984, which was then settled immediately.

District Administrator Siegfried Naser (CSU - Christian Social Union) was happy that the search for a new purpose for the hospital had taken a fortunate turn. At the latest in early 1985, the 50-bed facility would be opened. Also the purchase price of 1.2 million marks "is absolutely in line with our expectations."

But a few weeks later, suddenly everything was different. It had turned out that the doctors and alternative practitioners had the "wrong" prayer book – they were close to Universal Life.

Now the mayor of Dettelbach suddenly said in a city council meeting that one must prevent "the city from becoming the center of a sect." And that "due to the experience with youth sects one has to be especially concerned ... about the adolescents." The tranquil wine village in the district of Kitzingen is close to the Episcopal city of Würzburg, so that the mayor obviously very quickly adopted the view of the Episcopal Ordinariate there. A few days later, at a higher political level, in the Kitzingen district committee, the mayor "expressed reservations from Dettelbach's point of view about the possible Christ Clinic, especially since the small town is a well-known pilgrimage site." (*Main-Post*, September 28, 1984) A city councilor had already mentioned this in the city council meeting: "We cannot inflict such things on ourselves in Dettelbach."

"Churches Pressure the District Administrator"

The politicians now had to reverse course – because the Church wanted it that way. In the *Main-Post* (Sept. 28, 1984) under the headline "Churches Pressure the District Administrator" the following appeared: "District Administrator Dr. Siegfried Naser, as stated by a well-informed source, made it clear in the meeting behind closed doors that the two mainstream churches were pressuring him, after which he had to reverse the sale of the building." A few days earlier, the District Administrator had kept all doors open for himself. He had told the *Main-Post* (Sept. 22, 1984) "in no uncertain terms" that the doctors would have his "full support" if they "worked according to the ideas mentioned in the contract and ran a proper hospital." But if "a center of the Homebringing Mission" is to be established in the clinic "through the back door," he would "exhaust all legal possibilities to get the Dettelbach hospital back."

Here, the attitude of many politicians becomes apparent: At first, they are quite pragmatically interested in new enterprises and new jobs – but when the wind of the church blows in their faces, most of them retreat quickly and obediently reverse their own decisions.

A titled councilor and hospital adviser to the district council, scion of an influential Protestant aristocratic family, for whom there was "no doubt" "that the clinic will develop into a center of the Homebringing Mission that does not fit into this landscape" also blew the horn to retreat. (*Saale-Zeitung* Oct. 11, 1984)

> **As a Reminder – Sect:**
> A term of abuse used by the respective prevailing religious caste for all those whom their Inquisition is directed against.

How absurd it is to fantasize about the establishment of a "center of the sect" becomes clear with the following comparison: If the building had been sold to a Catholic or Lutheran hospital operator, would there have been a warning that a Catholic or Protestant "major sect center" would presumably be established here?

Moreover, the doctors had specifically pointed out at a press conference that no one was to be indoctrinated in the clinic, but that the medical services would be offered without regard to ideology and religious affiliation and without any attempt to proselytize.

Retreat with Formal Tricks

But the politicians are now interested in only one thing: How do they get out of the purchase contract? With a formal trick: The purchase contract – normally a mere formality – still has to be confirmed by the supervisory authority at the next higher political level, the government of the Lower Franconia District with headquarters in Würzburg. The latter now refuses to give its approval because the sale was made "far below the estimated price" of 3 million marks – an excuse easy to see through, in view of the satisfaction of all parties involved just a few weeks previously. And an "arbitrary measure" by the state, as lawyer Gottfried Niemietz later stated in an expert opinion. But the authorities apparently felt less committed to the German Constitution than to the laws of the medieval Inquisition, according to which legal transactions and legal acts of excommunicated persons are fundamentally invalid.

The action of the government authority becomes totally incredible when one knows that shortly before, the district of Kitzingen had sold a second former district hospital, namely the one in Marktbreit, for only 800,000 marks to the Workers' Welfare Association. Here, too, the estimated price was considerably higher – but the government of Lower Franconia allowed the contract to go through without objection. ...

The fact that things turned out differently this time was something the Dettelbach church congregations of both denominations had campaigned for just a week before this strange decision – in a letter in which they appealed to the "responsible politicians" to "do everything in their power to reverse the sale" because the religious community of the medical team is an "artificial religion based on far-eastern and Christian thought" – and because "in the long run, it cannot be asked of children and young people" to "be constantly exposed to a possible pseudo-religious-ideological infiltration." How ludicrous such words sound in a Catholic pilgrimage site of all places, which is exposed to a constant "infiltration" of a quite different kind, was obviously not even noticed by the pious writers. In any case, only four days later, the district council asked the administration to negotiate with the doctors about the cancellation of the purchase contract, which the Lower Franconia government, in turn, made superfluous two days later with its vote.

However, the doctors insist on the contract being complied with, while at the same time, expressing their willingness to negotiate a higher price. They turn to the public with a "proclamation" in which, among other things, it says:

We want to make it easier for people with cancer who have been given up on by doctors to go home to the worlds beyond. ... After we purchased the clinic, the Church began to fight over a pile of stones for which it had previously shown no interest. So the point is to drive away the doctors who are unpopular with the Church. The purchase price is now being driven up. This is not about helping the sick. ...

Can a people that calls itself Christian afford once again to make differences of belief the reason for their actions, as in the Middle Ages? ... In what era are we living, anyway? ... Must Christ again bow before the finances of the Church and its influence on the governmental organs?"

Ill-gotten Goods Do Not Prosper

But it was long since decided that the offer of the Original Christian doctors should no longer be taken into consideration. And now, there is a buyer to be found, who will voluntarily pay even more. How unrealistic the excuse of the state authorities is with regard to the actual market conditions can be seen in the bizarre provincial farce that has now begun and will drag on for years.

The district council first brings the Catholic St. Joseph Foundation into the discussion, to which they want to make an offer of 1.36 million. But nothing comes of it. They now go back to private operators of old people's homes in the district of Würzburg, which they originally did not even want to have because they already had enough places in old people's homes.

Now, they sell the clinic for 1.5 million marks to a businesswoman from Güntersleben, who wants to set up a "Haus Sorgenruh" (House of Rest from Worries) there. In order to deny further access to the team of doctors, who, until a new buyer is entered in the Registry of Deeds, are still the legal owners of the building, the locks are changed in the dead of night.

But Dettelbach does not calm down. This sale also fails. The promised sum is not paid.

The building remains empty – at the expense of the taxpayers – even though the Original Christians had intermittently announced their willingness to purchase several times. In the summer of 1988, it was rented to the Protestant-Lutheran Diaconate.

However, after a few weeks, just as the renovation work for an alternative accommodation for senior citizens began, the lease is terminated again: A buyer has now been found. It is a real estate agent from the Rhineland, who buys the property for the ridiculous price of about 240,000 marks and immediately resells it – for 12 million marks to a Swedish stock company, which resides at the same address as the real estate agent himself. The intention is to build an "upscale senior citizens' residence" there. Now the reader will ask himself: How can that be? The selling price of 240,000 marks is one million marks below what the Original Christian doctors paid. Did the government of Lower Franconia approve this? It did not – because the clever district administrator arranged a deal aimed at evading the law: He first sells the building to the city of Dettelbach, which then sells it to the real estate agent, who, almost like an "Aryanization profiteer" of deplorable times, can reap the fruits of religious discrimination.

As far as the city is concerned, however, the district itself is now the examining authority. ...

The bottom line is that the district lost about one million marks (in public funds!) compared to the original offer of the medical group. And the 200,000 marks may just have been enough to pay off the affronted Deaconate.

As the saying goes, "Ill-gotten goods do not prosper." Since the Original Christians were thrown out at the instigation of the Church (and at the expense of the state), the further fate of the property was as if "bewitched." To make matters worse, the district had a clause inserted in the purchase contract that the buyer assured that he would not "sell to Universal Life or similar institutions" – another violation of the German Constitution, which expressly forbids state authorities to discriminate on grounds of faith.

5. The Smear Campaign of the Churches Against a Commercial Project in Würzburg (1985)

Thus, the Original Christians were driven out of Dettelbach – ultimately, at the behest of the churches. But they had not given up, because they wanted to put into practice what Jesus, the Christ, desires: the implementation of His teachings of the Sermon on the Mount in all spheres of life.

A 48-year-old entrepreneur offered his help with this. A few days before Christmas 1984, he went public: He said he was close to Universal Life and planned to use his private fortune to build a settlement with apartments and medium-sized artisan businesses, a community "which should live according to the laws of the Sermon on the Mount." 300 to 500 people were to produce in an environmentally friendly way, goods and services that cover the basic needs of life: food, clothing, shelter. "But also spiritual and emotional needs that have been neglected for so long are taken into account: the need for peace and harmony and spiritual development." There was also talk of "schools, kindergartens and clinics in which the Sermon on the Mount is actualized." The entrepreneur: "I want to offer jobs to people of good will."

The entrepreneur presented the head mayor of Würzburg and a mayor of the neighboring community of Höchberg with identical letters in which he asked for the sale of a suitable site in order to initiate these plans. The head mayor of Würzburg, Klaus Zeitler (SPD – Social Democratic Party), then met with him for a first meeting and, with him, viewed a possible site in the Heuchelhof district on the outskirts of Würzburg with satellite settlements and (at that time) a lot of vacant industrial land.

Zeitler, whose party is a minority on the Würzburg city council, briefly presented the project to the city council's advisory committee. On the very same day that the *Main-Post* reports the news, the Catholic chairman of the CSU (Christian Social Union) faction and a mayor on Würzburg's city council, introduces a "question," which, in truth, is a single collection of defamations: Whether the city administration is aware that this "community similar to a religion ... had caused a lot of suffering and tragedies," that people there were being "physically, psychologically and materially ruined" with "questionable healing methods"? The Homebringing Mission represents a "spiritual-emotional pollution of the environment." These outrageous claims are pure speculation and polemics – he provided no proof. Had the Christ-friends been better legally advised back then, the man would probably have been charged with incitement of the people.

At least, the mayor puts a stop to this, stating that it is one of his "principles" to "first stand up for any citizen who is associated with any kind of sect," that is, to whom his affiliation of faith is reproached. Ironically, he adds: "If a center of the Spirit emerges there," one can hardly have anything against it. ... In a pluralistic society every citizen must have the right "to at least be heard, to be taken seriously, and furthermore, to be treated properly." The "standards of Dettelbach," says Dr. Zeitler, "are not binding for me as head mayor of Würzburg." The property request, he adds a few days later, is being treated like any other: "We don't ask anyone how they do their evening prayer."
With this, to this day, Dr. Zeitler is one of the very few city leaders who dared to publicly defy the claim to power of the church representatives and their attacks against the Original Christians and to demand at least a minimum of democratic fairness toward a minority.

But the unrestrained propaganda of the Catholic city council was merely the prelude to a concerted witch hunt of the mainstream churches against a project that went against their grain – since it could have proved that the Sermon on the Mount, which they usually downplay as "utopia," can actually be put into practice.

Christ, the Son of God and Co-Regent of the Kingdom of God Gives a Revelation

Just when the storm of church defamations broke out, which is described in the further course of this chapter, Christ, the Co-Regent of the heavens, revealed Himself through Gabriele, the bearer of His word and His emissary.
On February 8, 1985, in a public revelation, He, the spiritual revolutionary, addressed the Church and secular authorities, but also all seeking people, and He prepared the Christ-friends for what was to come.

The following are some excerpts given from this mighty Christ-revelation:
I*n word and in deed, I have come once more to bring My living word to all willing and seeking souls and human beings, so that souls and human beings may again reflect on the primordial principle, on My teaching, the eternal laws, which I taught and actualized as Jesus of Nazareth, the Sermon on the Mount.*

Who acts against the Sermon on the Mount and who is against it? Only those who strive for power and prestige. It is the church and worldly authorities who, tolerate at their side nothing but their own principles, their own teachings. ...

In this epoch of time, things are not much different than at all times. Righteous men and women are persecuted, ridiculed, mocked and slandered. Evil is said about them; My teaching is rejected, called un-Christian, anti-Christian and much more. As at all times, these assertions and defamations resound from the ranks of the ecclesiastical and secular representatives and their faithful.

First, prove to those whom you slander and of whom you claim to be un-Christian that you, the ecclesiastical and secular authorities, are true Christians! First, prove that your doctrine of dogma and form is My teaching, the teaching of the true Christian life. Whatever you do to the least of My brothers, you have done to Me!

As long as you cannot prove that your doctrine corresponds to the eternal truth, you do not have the right to call your neighbor un-Christian! If you cannot prove that your teaching corresponds to My eternal truth, then keep silent! I, the Spirit of truth, say to you: The teachings you represent are truly not My word. You do speak of the Bible, teach from this book, but you do not actualize the foundation of the Bible, the Sermon on the Mount!

Without mercy and understanding for the neighbor, the brood of adders and vipers is active even today. It believes, in turn, that it can persecute the prophets and all righteous men and women in order to thus silence the Spirit. ...

I cannot be silenced. ... Verily, I say to you: I ignite the fire of spiritual revolution in those who are truly of good heart.

Why are you afraid, you who are called the ecclesiastical and secular representatives?

Why do you go against all those who are of peaceful heart, who want to live according to the Sermon on the Mount? Are those who gradually actualize the Sermon on the Mount becoming a danger to you?

Do you feel the omnipotence of My Spirit that will be victorious? – For I Am the Light of the world.

You have declared war on all those who, on the basis of facts, have held before your eyes the mirror of church history, your deeds. Your vociferous arguments say that, "this belongs to the past." But you yourselves have proven, and prove it anew every day, that the Middle Ages are far from over, that they resurge again! In the present time, as in the Middle Ages, only with other methods, the prophets and all people of good disposition are also being slandered and mocked by you.

Why are you, who are called the ecclesiastical and secular authorities, afraid of a handful of people, of a small number who want to actualize the Sermon on the Mount? Why, indeed? Because you do feel in your hearts that it is the Spirit of truth that calls you to action again, that admonishes you to actualize the Sermon on the Mount, which I taught and lived as the Nazarene and promised the people of the future a Kingdom of Peace, a Kingdom of Love.
Verily, verily, I say to you, whoever does not live the Sermon on the Mount, indeed, who is against the Sermon on the Mount, is the Antichrist.

And anyone who persecutes those who want to live a pure life follows in the footsteps of the fascists. ... The time of the Spirit has come.
Even though you continue to slander and persecute righteous men and women through your mass media and with your words, your power is broken.
All your thoughts and aspirations, your dogmatic teachings, your palaces, your rich churches are built on sand. What is built on sand will fade away.

So you are the same ones, again and again, then and now, who persecuted, maltreated and killed the

prophets. The blood still sticks today to those who maltreated, tortured and killed people in My name, also to those who gave the commands.
Recognize yourselves and ask for forgiveness. Reconcile with all people and souls who are waiting for your request for forgiveness. Smash your crosiers and bow your heads, lay them in the dust and ask for atonement.
These words are the words of the prophetic Spirit, the Spirit of Christ.
May the one who can grasp it, grasp it.

Diabolical Suggestions

Over the Christmas holidays, the church representatives and their henchmen had remained largely quiet. After all, one must keep the "sham peace." But in the meantime, Count Magnis had hurried to prepare new "ammunition" for the campaign. At the beginning of February 1985, he published a new paper with the suggestive title: "Is the So-called Homebringing Mission of Jesus Christ a Homebringing Mission of Satana Lucifer?" Already in the headline, however, he not only suggested that the entire Homebringing Mission is "satanic," but also literally described the teachings spread there as *"demonic." "A Dangerous Sect"* – *"A De-*

monic Teaching" – "Life-Endangering Dietetics" – such and similar were the headlines with their diabolic suggestions. Here, we can literally hear the hateful cry of the "father from below," who had already slandered Jesus, the Christ, as a demon.

Here again: untruths and defamations, meant to prevent people from listening and reading for themselves the word of the Christ of God through His prophetess, and freely deciding for themselves whether they want to accept it or not. The church believers were not supposed to learn the truth:

God, the Eternal, is the Free Spirit – God in us – who needs neither stone houses nor denominations nor religions, dogmas or priests, for He is in us, deep in the very basis of our soul. He is the love, the Father of us all, who loves all His children equally and would not send one single one into eternal damnation. Through the Redeemer-deed of Jesus, the Christ, it is guaranteed that no soul will be lost – Christ will one day lead every soul home, back to God.

Briefly stated, that is the message from the Kingdom of God, which Count Magnis called "demonic"!

Through His prophetess, the Christ of God teaches the love for God and neighbor and the path to the Father's house; the churches teach, as before, eternal damnation – but, they call the teaching of the Christ of God demonic!

As stated, the human being, the prophet, who speaks the truth from the Kingdom of God, has to cope with such inflammatory slogans and distortions! How would you, dear reader, fare, if you were constantly pelted in public with filth in this way, just because you speak the truth?

It is not by chance that Count Magnis, for the first time in this pamphlet, also attacks the path within, which is taught in every detail in Universal Life. This is what the adversaries of God want to prevent at all costs. In his writing, among other things, Magnis spreads the untruth that "by means of intense suggestive indoctrination by meditation" people are made "totally servile" … to these "abstruse teachings." He says that there are "instructions" to meditate "several times a day for hours."

What is it really like? The meditations that prepare for the Inner Path last between 20 to 40 minutes and are heard once a day – only by those who want to go this path to within in all freedom. It is to be expected of the externalized church, ossified in dogma and ritual, that it does not understand the nature of meditations at all: They are a profound devotion to Christ and an affirmation of the divine power in the soul and in the physical body – for as Jesus of Nazareth taught: "You are the temple of the Holy Spirit, and the Spirit of God dwells in you."

But the churchmen are not interested in the truth. Almost ten years later, the *Zürcher Tagesspiegel* journalist Hugo Stamm will repeat the count's insults almost word for word: "For the expert Franz Graf von Magnis, Universal Life is a dangerous sect, because seeking people are made dependent on the abstruse teachings of a 'prophetess' through intense, suggestive, indoctrination by meditation."

> **Mendacious Opinions:**
> An untruth = Lies that are so formulated by "experts" that they are legally classified and permitted by the courts as "opinions" because their truthfulness is not checked. The credulous citizen does not know the difference between a permitted lie in the guise of opinion and fact. He therefore considers the lie to be a fact that the court has verified.

This example shows how long-lasting such mendacious opinions can be, if they are spread with the Church's almost unlimited means of influence.

Incidentally, anyone can compare the eternal word of the Christ of God through His prophetess with the ecclesiastical dogmas – for instance, in the book "The Teaching of the Catholic Church as Contained in Her Documents" by Josef Neuner and Heinrich Roos – and judge for himself what "abstruse teachings" are.

As stated: The facts are not decisive for a modern inquisitor, anyway. Just as with the allegedly "life-endangering dietetics," he also refers to a pseudo-expert report on the path to within, as will be shown later. With this, he again wants to give the appearance of scientific objectivity to a poorly concealed defamation. Since this is further proof of his approach, this procedure will be briefly described here.

The Spall – "Expert Report"

On the heels of the dubious expert report on dietetics, Magnis commissioned another one in 1985. He commissioned the Würzburg graduate psychologist Alfred Spall to prepare a report on the effects of the meditation texts of Universal Life. Spall was a full-time employee of the Catholic Caritas in Würzburg, so he was anything but an objective expert. He did not, for example, scientifically investigate how the meditation texts affected actual meditation participants. Instead, he only made adventurous speculations about how these texts might have an effect – exclusively negative, of course – and even described their language as "pompous, emotional, inflammatory, hypertrophic, and thus, difficult to understand." He insinuated that through the meditations, Universal Life did not want "the independently thinking, and thus, adult person, but a person who submits himself to the ideology without criticism."

A professional Catholic can evidently draw conclusions about others only from the perspective of his religion ... and the Catholic doctrines speak for themselves: *Whoever wishes to be saved must, before all else, hold the Catholic faith: for unless each one maintains it whole and inviolate, he will certainly perish in eternity.* ("Compendium of Creeds, Definitions, and Declarations on Matters of Faith and Morals" by Heinrich Denzinger and Peter Hünermann, No. 75)

When, for example, Pope Pius X died on August 20, 1914, the Vatican correspondent of the *Berliner Tageblatt* (newspaper) wrote an obituary on the same day:
He laments the freedom of dissenters and wants *it limited to the Church and its doctrines. (...) Freedom of faith and conscience was an abomination to Pius X.* In 1954, Pius X was "canonized."
Through the meditations, Spall continues, feelings of guilt and fear are awakened; people are "indoctrinated" in an authoritarian way. Spall reaches the conclusion: *One must assume that at least some*

of the participants are "considerably harmed mentally" by such an approach. He then claims, freely invented: *In a considerable number of individual cases, psychotic or psychosis-like conditions were observed in young people, who had undergone a series of corresponding sessions.*

This, too, is obviously untrue. In his expert report, Spall does not cite a single empirical case for these brazen assertions! At the beginning of 1988, it then turns out by chance that, through the arrangement of Count Magnis, he only had one single "counseling interview" with a mentally unstable young man, who had participated about two or three times in events of young Original Christians (for instance, a movie about Francis of Assisi), but had not attended any meditation events there. His mother spoke up at a lecture by Pastor Haack in Hettstadt and tried to blame Universal Life for the psychological difficulties of her son (which had already existed before his sporadic contact with the Original Christians!) By the way, the stepfather of the young man is a theologian.

This "expert report" already is, by its very approach, but also in its concrete formulation, completely unscientific, a pure propaganda writing of the Church aiming to discriminate against those who think differently. Nevertheless, in the following years it was repeatedly quoted as alleged "proof" of the "harmfulness" of the Inner Path in Universal Life. The Original Christians therefore took the trouble to have a total of four counter-evaluations prepared, which all proved the academic untenability of Spall's commissioned work. For example, the scholar of comparative religion, Professor Doctor Hubertus Mynarek attested about Spall, among other things, that Spall, had "no idea" what was actually to be understood under the term "meditation." Apparently, Spall had related this term only to "non-representational," silent meditation in the far-eastern sense, and therefore, from the outset, disparaged meditations, that is, contemplations, on a text, as offered in Universal Life, as "intrusive." Yet, even within the Church, meditations with words or images are nothing unusual. But everything, really everything, no matter how good, is fought against by the Church, if it is not under its hegemony of power.

Professor Mynarek also subjected the individual meditation texts to a detailed examination and came to the conclusion, quite differently from Spall, that here, the positive in the person is addressed and affirmed, whereas in the church doctrine, the emphasis is mostly on the negative, the "sinful," the denigration of the possibilities of the individual being in the foreground. Feelings of guilt and fear are conveyed precisely through meditations that are shaped by *Catholicism*, like the spiritual exercises of Ignatius of Loyola or texts of Opus Dei; likewise authoritarian or indoctrinating "exercises" are a domain of the Catholic Church. With his polemical attacks, Spall thus directed them to the wrong people.

Nevertheless, the pseudo-"expert report" of Alfred Spall, which could hardly be surpassed in its lack of academic scholarship and tactical transparency, was repeatedly brought up by church representatives and compliant journalists for years.

The Constitution Is Trampled Underfoot

Back in the city of Würzburg of 1985: Church representatives and politicians servile to the Church from the "C" party now feed each other lines. The Junge Union of Würzburg finds the idea "unbearable" that the city could sell land to an organization "that in its self-image has the destruction of the family as its goal" and is a "dangerous youth sect." The city may not sell "even one square meter of land," according to the local Junge Union (JU) chairman and its regional manager (who is in close contact with pastor Haack). The Frauen Union (women's political union of CDU and CSU) criticizes the official church representatives because they were "so reserved."

The Original Christians then call upon both the Junge Union and the Frauen Union to prove that their request that land be sold only to those who are approved by their religious superiors corresponds to the Constitution. In it, is written that no one may be favored or disadvantaged by the state because of his or her religion. As far as the alleged destruction of families is concerned, the public should examine how many marriages among the members of the Junge Union and their mother party are troubled and, in comparison, how many among the Original Christians. The Junge Union should "show us the young people who are under 18 years of age who walk the Inner Path with us" – because the preparatory meditation courses for this path are not even accessible to young people under 18 years of age. The political organizations should furthermore prove "that their politics, their faith and, above all, their actions, correspond to the teachings of Christ."

A "Clarifying Word," that Isn't One

The Original Christians receive no answer. Instead, in mid-February, a so-called "Clarifying Word" is published by the Würzburg deans Helmut Bauer (Catholic) and Martin Elze (Lutheran) against the Original Christians. In it, they accuse the Homebringing Mission of Jesus Christ of "massive economic interests." The Homebringing Mission is "not Christian." According to the "belief of Christianity," the "revelation of God has found its unparalleled culmination and conclusion in Jesus Christ." **In plain language, this means that the mainstream churches impose a ban on God speaking. According to the churches, He has nothing more to say. Then whose side are they on? Who is the one who is against God? Who is the one who does not want Him to speak?**

The concept of God in Universal Life, the "clarifying word" continues, is limited to a "personal primal force"; "a positive attitude toward creation is not possible according to the teaching of Homebringing Mission." Exactly the opposite corresponds to the truth: Through Gabriele, God, the Eternal, teaches the unity of all life – everything and everyone belongs to the great family of God. Original Christians, therefore, practice peaceable farming in harmony with nature; they advocate for nature and animals and, out of love for their fellow creatures, the animals, they abstain from eating meat. The churches, on the other hand, deny the immortal soul of the animals; they approve of their being used and consumed for the benefit of human beings, with the result that animals are tormented and cruelly murdered millionfold.

What the churches really think of the Kingdom of God, which Jesus once proclaimed, is what the two deans themselves write in black and white in their allegedly "clarifying word": "The Kingdom of God is not feasible."
Then, which kingdom of which God did they build over the centuries? And: Why, then, do they pray "Your kingdom come, Your will be done" in the Lord's Prayer if they do not believe in it? That's all then just for show...
In short, the deans do not provide "clarification," but insinuations, distortions, false citations.
Through the use of quotation marks, for example, they give the impression that the Original Christians, with reference to their teachings, themselves speak of "self-redemption" – in truth, according to the conviction of the Original Christians, redemption is possible only with the help of the Christ of God. When the deans are made aware of the

obviously wrong quotations, they do not change the wrong content, but simply leave out the quotation marks in a new edition. ...

To go against those of other faiths using false quotations and distortions, is an ancient practice of the Church. Jan Hus, for example, was condemned as a "heretic" by the Council of Constance and burned at the stake, because he allegedly represented certain quotations from the teachings of John Wycliff, which, however, Hus denied. ...

The Original Christians again react with a newspaper advertisement – headline: "'Christians' Expose Themselves." It states:

We want to prove to the world that life according to the Sermon on the Mount is indeed possible. ... But before the seed of the good can begin to sprout, representatives of the institution church stand up to trample on the seedling. ... What do they fear? ... Their fear ultimately indicates that in the depths of their soul, they sense that it is indeed Christ who is now revealing Himself again through the mouth of a prophet.

If, the Original Christians continue, *the revelation of God had actually found its "conclusion" in Jesus of Nazareth, then parts of the Bible, such as the secret revelation of John or the letters of Paul, could never be a revelation of God. Then Jesus also could not* have said: "Therefore I send you prophets, ... whom you will kill and crucify, and some you will flog in your synagogues and pursue from town to town. ..." (Mt. 23) – for then, there should have been no more prophecy after Jesus of Nazareth.

And to the insinuations of the deans:
Finally, we want the evidence for these constant accusations! What is wrong with our Christian businesses being founded and run on the basis of the Sermon on the Mount? ... We are a part of the people and call upon the populace to take a position on the question of whether they agree with the defamation of those who want to follow Christ. We call out loudly into the public: Where is the evidence for the false accusations of the church representatives?

The Barrage Sets In

It was not by chance that the Original Christians appealed to the public. For it was there that the next, the decisive phase of the large-scale attack by the Church to drive out "heresy" took place. Until then, the regional press had still reported relatively objectively about the astonishing occurrence that the purchase of property suddenly became the object of a religious conflict. But now, the churches – which to this day have considerable influence on the media – pulled out all stops, nationwide and for months via magazines and newspapers: "For a Housewife a Company Head Becomes a Sect Disciple" (*Das Goldene Blatt*, January 30, 1985); "The Sect Leader, for whom a Millionaire Gave Up Everything" (*Bild der Frau*, March 18, 1985); "The False Prophetess" (*Quick*, January 2, 1986); "Grotesque News from Würzburg" (*Deutsche Tagespost*, March 5, 1985). The headlines alone expose the level of professional journalism.

On March 8, 1985, the Catholic daily newspaper *Deutsche Tagespost*, with headquarters in Würzburg, published a whole page about the Original Christians in Universal Life, with the headline: "The Sect Has Turned Them into Glorified Masks." For chief editor Harald Vocke, the revelations of the Spirit of God are nothing but "demonic inspirations." Medieval hatred of everything non-Catholic speaks from every line.

How does a person feel who – called to do so by God, the Eternal – has set out to prepare the way for the Christ of God and to prepare His coming, which, after all, is what all Christians around the world pray for – and is now being pelted with filth and the most primitive malice by those in church and politics who abuse the name of Jesus, the Christ, and who for centuries have trampled underfoot His teaching of love for God and neighbor, and that, to this day?

And how do people feel who, only a short time before, were regarded in their occupations as capable and honorable citizens; who are now energetically and peacefully preparing to put a high ideal, the ideal of the Sermon on the Mount, into practice – and are now suddenly denounced as "seduced," as "lunatics," as a kind of eczema of society, as outcasts, from whom one turns away in horror and from whom one has to warn one's children?

As for Gabriele: With the power of the Most High, she endured this and more, because she knew: The word comes from heaven. It is God-Father, the Eternal, who speaks here through her; it is His Son, Christ, and it is the Cherub of divine Wisdom.

But the raving madness of the church authorities had only just begun. The *Bunte Illustrierte* (April 18, 1985 – magazine) published a report with the headline: "Sects – with Contacts to the Hereafter – a Fortune on Earth – the Flourishing Business of a Sect and Why More and More Fall for It." About the teachings of Universal Life it merely says: "And who believes this nonsense?" *Bavarian Television* (April 4, 1985) broadcasts a report in which Count Magnis, Dean Elze and Dean Bauer have their say in detail, but representatives of the Homebringing Mission only marginally.

Der Spiegel (May 6, 1985 – news magazine) publishes a malicious article, of all times, during the hot phase of the city council decision: "Divine Power at the Tailbone." The assertions of the Würzburg Ordinariate about "meditative indoctrination," "increased Messianism" as well as "the most modern advertising and marketing strategies," with which one pushes into an "emotional market gap," are simply quoted literally without questioning them. Pages long, the journalist ridicules a faith movement in arrogant *Spiegel* style, but in no way addresses how this movement is discriminated against by the powerful mainstream Church and by state authorities. Nevertheless, it was precisely this arrogant article that first brought Universal Life to the attention of numerous people who wanted to know about it in more detail: If *Spiegel* sneers at something in such a malicious way, then there must be something positive to it!

Shortly before the *Spiegel* article, the two pastors of the Heuchelhof district of Würzburg, Ulf Claussen (Lutheran) and Erwin Kuhn (Catholic) had invited their colleague Pastor Haack from Munich to an event in the gymnasium of the Heuchelhof School. Already the headline of the Catholic *Volksblatt* (April 26, 1985) sets the direction: "Concern: Influence on Children through HBM." Haack takes off: "Religion is like a knife: You can work with it for good or for evil. Khomeini is only one example of this!"

This is another diabolical slanderous trick: From the outset, an initially open topic – in this case the religious convictions of the Original Christians in Universal Life – is put into an extremely negative "emotional framework," in this case, the assumption of power by the Muslim fundamentalists in Iran in 1979, that is, a few years earlier.

Such communities (like Universal Life), Haack continued, are for him "emergency associations of evaders of responsibility." He fears "above all the danger of indoctrination of children in the planned kindergartens and schools." (As if there were not innumerable church schools and kindergartens. And what thousands of children had to suffer under Catholic and Protestant care is meanwhile known). The children, Haack continues, could be "spiritually trained" there. And: Anyone who claims to be able to live according to the Sermon on the Mount is "overdrawing his account." (With which the pastor pretty much described exactly the derogatory position of the churches regarding the Sermon on the Mount of Jesus of Nazareth.)

The ostensibly liberal *Main-Post* writes in a commentary that in Heuchelhof one is concerned "whether the district's integration capacity is not overstretched when a community of several hundred people – subject to its own rules of life – creates completely new social, socio-political and economic structures."
Such "thoughts" would probably also have been formulated if an asylum-seekers' home had been built in Heuchelhof. But the difference is: Then one would at least have regretted this attitude and, asked, "in consternation," where this xenophobia came from – because the "*ability* to integrate" is in reality the *willingness* of the majority for integration in regard to the minority. But with "sectarians," one does not even need to make such efforts – programmed through centuries, one obviously

feels no pangs of conscience at all when one ostracizes people of different faith, who have turned their backs on the church conglomerates.

Signature Lists in the Cathedral

To keep the leading role of the churches in this ostracism from becoming too obvious, a "Citizens' Initiative to Prevent the Settlement of the So-called Homebringing Mission in Heuchelhof" is founded. The word "so-called" is adopted from the writings of Count Magnis against the Homebringing Mission of Jesus Christ, and otherwise, the so-called citizens' initiative cannot completely do without the help of its mastermind: The signature lists of the "objectors" are placed in the Cathedral of Würzburg, among other places; on the order of worship, the visitors to the services are again separately urged to submit their signatures in the parish office (!).

But when the Original Christians invite Bishop Paul-Werner Scheele to a panel discussion, he has it canceled. On the other hand, the Lutheran regional bishop Johannes Hanselmann from Munich deems it necessary to call upon his faithful at Pentecost in the *Evangelische Sonntagsblatt* (May

26, 1985) under the heading "Do Not Let Yourselves Be Inveigled": *But as for you, continue in what you have learned and have firmly believed, knowing from whom you learned it.* (2 Tim. 3:14)
For centuries, the priestmen of both denominations have long since misled the faithful into turning the Sermon on the Mount of Jesus, the Christ, into its exact opposite in many respects – and generations of pupils have had to learn this lesson in religion classes.

Meanwhile, the Catholic side also ropes in a former head mayor of Würzburg from the post-war period, Michael Meissner, who, in a letter to the city council, blatantly reminds it of "the tradition of Würzburg as a bishop's city," for which "the allocation of such a large area of land to a sect ... would present a false and inappropriate impression."

Indeed: In the "tradition of Würzburg as a bishop's city," as Meissner correctly recognized, freedom of religion and tolerance are not provided: In the 14th century, for example, all Jews in the city were expelled or murdered; in the 16th century, Prince-Bishop Julius Echter expelled all Lutherans from the entire diocese; and in the 17th century, two of his nephews (!), as Prince-Bishops of Würzburg and Bamberg, burned more alleged members of what was then called the "witch sect" than in any other German region.

Few of these politicians talk about the German Constitution, according to which no one may be discriminated against because of their faith.

The churches' smear campaign has an effect. At a panel discussion of the citizens' association in Heuchelhof, participants expressed that the plans were a "crazy fantasy," a "threat to jobs" (on the contrary, jobs would be created!). One mother is concerned that young people will be "exposed to massive influence." So it does not help that Mayor Zeitler points out that "we live in a pluralistic society in which everyone, including minorities, has the right to express their personal way of life."

But suddenly, even Dr. Zeitler, who does not have a majority in the city council with his party, has "growing reservations about HBM plans." The realistic politician has certainly not failed to notice that more and more political forces are meanwhile speaking out in favor of preventing the settlement. The local CSU association of Heuchelhof fears "for the good reputation" of the district, the local SPD association also has "reservations, given the current state of planning ... to advocate the allocation of property."

On June 1, 1985, the Bavarian party (CSU) conducts a "public opinion poll" in the streets of Würzburg ("ostracism" is what the Athenians called it); the Heuchelhof citizens' association fears a "ghetto formation" – without thinking about who introduced ghettos for the Jews during the Middle Ages: It was certainly not the Jewish fellow citizens!

The Middle Ages Are Alive

The politicians are probably not aware of this, but quite obviously many of them – not only in Würzburg – still have the Middle Ages in their "bones," that is, in their subconscious or even – if one assumes the possibility of reincarnation – in their soul garments. The obedience to the Church out of fear is apparently deep-seated.

At the 4th Lateran Council in Rome in 1215 under Pope Innocent III, it was decided that the worldly rulers should be "admonished, induced and if necessary ... compelled" to "exterminate the heretics from their territories." If a temporal ruler neglects to "cleanse his territory of this heretical foulness, let him be excommunicated." "If he refuses to make satisfaction within one year," the supreme pontiff should be informed "that he may declare the ruler's vassals absolved from their allegiance and may offer the territory to be ruled by lay Catholics. ..."

(For more information, refer to the Medieval Source Book of Fordham University in the Internet.)

However, the excommunication – and thus the condemnation as "heretics" – was also threatened in 1215 to all "benefactors, defenders and protectors" of heretics. And this was not an empty threat. During the Crusade initiated by Innocent, for example, against the early Christian movement of the Cathars in southern France (1209-1229), the Counts of Toulouse lost their entire lands to the King of France – simply because they had not fought "heresy" energetically enough.

In 1985, the Original Christians even asked the Bavarian Minister-President Franz-Josef Strauss to help them "to protect our constitutional rights." They speak of a "broad-based campaign," aiming to have people "discriminated against because of their faith." But the CSU politician does not respond.

Meanwhile, the churches continue this very campaign unabated. Pastor Erwin Kuhn writes in his parish letter that he finds it "appalling" that many inhabitants of Heuchelhof have not yet heard of the "new sect" (a medieval inquisitor could not have put it better) and stirs things up with the Bible quote: *Beware of false prophets, ... they come to you in sheep's clothing but inwardly are ravenous wolves.*

Professor Elze and Count Magnis even hold lectures against the Original Christians in the villages around Würzburg. Count Magnis, who was born in Silesia (now Poland), plays the role of defender of Franconia in a discussion organized by the Original Christians and shouts: "In our beloved Franconia, we do not like troublemakers." (A Würzburg city councilor who was present thereupon says when leaving: "If that was the official representative of the Catholic Church, then I am sorry for every penny that I have paid.")

"If You Are Thinking Inquisition with Me, You Are Right, of Course."

In mid-June 1985, a few days before the decisive session of the city council, Pastor Haack held – as in the year before – the annual conference of his "Parents' Initiative Against Spiritual Dependence and Religious Extremism" in Würzburg. According to Haack, he is "concerned" that Würzburg is threatening to become a 'Sect's Rome.'" (Here the Catholic *Volksblatt* misquotes him for obvious reasons and writes: "Sect's Home"). Universal Life is a "prophet's dictatorship"; freedom of religion does not mean "that a sect can do what it wants."

It is a monstrosity and a malicious lie to speak of "prophet's dictatorship" – on the one hand, because the prophetess of God teaches the law of freedom and lives according to it, that is, she respects the freedom of every human being; on the other hand, because with this mendacious opinion one strives to prevent seeking people from checking out for themselves and accepting or leaving the word of the Christ of God and the path of love for God and neighbor, in all freedom.

What "Pastor" Haack – as official representative of his church! – thought about freedom of religion, he had already in 1970 clearly put down on paper in an activity report to the Bavarian Regional

Church: *If we understand our faith correctly, then we have no right to "leave the other" to "his faith."* And in an interview given to the "Bavarian State Center for Political Education Work" he stated how little he thought of tolerance: *I believe that in the long run we cannot follow this western enlightenment structure, which can also be found in "Nathan the Wise," by (Gotthold) Lessing.* Or, as he later expressed it in a book: The "old, bourgeois Nathan-the-Wise naiveté" and the "Be-nice-to-each-other world championships" should be over.

What kind of person Haack is, is also made clear by a letter he himself once wrote to a representative of a religious minority persecuted by him: *If you are thinking Inquisition with me, you are right, of course.*
And to one of the Original Christians in Universal Life, he once said: *In the Middle Ages, we would have dealt with you completely differently.*

The CSU mayor, who was the first to set off the avalanche of slander by the Church, spoke triumphantly before Pastor Haack's "Parents' Initiative" of a "happy development in Würzburg": "After initial sympathies, an orderly retreat was initiated." In the beginning things had been judged "quite superficially" – that is to say: not yet through the eyeglasses of the clerical Inquisition. But in the meantime, a "great process of enlightenment has taken place."

That is the height of hypocrisy: A political stooge of modern Inquisition, who was prevented from igniting pyres, even today, only by the courageous work of the age of enlightenment, hypocritically speaks of "enlightenment."

The CSU mayor thanks Haack profusely for the "documents" (that is, defamations and untruths), without which he would not have been able to "sensitize" (a favorite word of all those who damage reputations) the mayor and the city council.

How right the philosopher Karl Jaspers was, when he wrote in his book "Der Philosophische Glaube": *The biblically founded claim to absoluteness of the churches is always on the verge of igniting the pyres for heretics.* (9th Edition, 1988, p. 73)

The City Council Declines

A few days later, first the main committee, then the plenum of the Würzburg City Council, in a closed session, declines to sell the property to the Original Christians. By all accounts, it had come down to a crucial vote, in which the purportedly "Christian" side had prevailed. Mayor Zeitler was given the task of explaining the city council's refusal to the press – with the seemingly objective arguments of the city council majority: that the plans had been too vague, that some of the people wanted to build residences instead of businesses (the responsible project manager had long since withdrawn this); for, after all, the city was interested in a "commercial settlement," and "not at all in a religious undertaking."

The question remains whether such prevarications would have also been expressed in the end, if the people willing to settle had not been deliberately declared lepers, people who allegedly represent a danger for children and young people, through a month-long witch hunt by church representatives, by journalists and politicians servile to the Church.

On the other hand, there is no question in terms of whether the adverse decision would have been made if the same plans had been submitted by people with the "right prayer book": create new jobs – yes, please!

In a newspaper advertisement, the Original Christians explained how they saw the result:
The eternal Spirit doesn't just own a small plot of land like Heuchelhof. The universe is His ... When Christians reject Christians, when they close their doors to their neighbor, then the latter will shake the dust from their feet. We Christians in the following of the Nazarene let ourselves be guided by Christ to far greater deeds. True Christians open the way to us: ...
They told the press that Original Christian businesses and facilities would develop – though not in one place.
Gabriele, the prophetess and emissary of God, would have much rather done other things than deal with church commissioners who stirred up the people and their journalist adherents. Now, through her unshakable trust in God, she made sure that the small flock of fellow comrades did not despair in the face of external superior power. Anyone who wants to build something new needs to have a lot of staying power. Gabriele already expressed this in an interview in August 1985, shortly after the "finale" on Heuchelhof:

What we are doing for the Lord in His work is to build a bridge to the next era, in which other people, but perhaps the same souls in the earthly garment, will continue to build. Many of us are building the bridge today. Tomorrow, that is, in the next era, they will continue to build where they left off today in a different garment. That is the work of the Lord.

Würzburg Afterthought

From a purely external point of view, even though the project in Würzburg, Heuchelhof was unsuccessful – its mere announcement also made the Original Christians known nationwide. On the other hand, the mainstream churches had "zeroed in" on Universal Life. Although the distortions and false quotations of the "Clarifying Word" were repeatedly corrected, for years, the misrepresentations were continuously spread and printed in church parish letters. As late as February 11, 1993, a Lutheran military chaplain distributed them at an anti-"sect" lecture in Güntersleben near Würzburg. In April 1988 the two deans had added a second "clarifying word," which again contained new distortions. Again, it was claimed that Universal Life taught that one could "redeem oneself"; it was ascribed to the Original Christians that according to their teachings, "the laws of this world, thus, also those of the state, ... should not be developed further, but changed from the bottom up" – although Original Christians emphasize again and again that they consider the Basic Law to be a very good Constitution and that one should give to Caesar what is Caesar's. From their distortions of the Original Christian teachings, the deans then again draw the conclusion that Universal Life shows itself "as a dangerous movement," and that when it "is watched by Catholics and Protestants with concern and growing displeasure," "it has to attribute this to itself." (The "justified public anger" of the incited masses was at all times happily blamed on the victims by the slanderers.)

Subsequently, the Lutheran dean Professor Martin Elze especially proved to be a master of splitting hairs in distorting the truth. Thus, in numerous lectures until well into the 1990s, he claimed in various places of the Federal Republic of Germany that the word "Christ" had disappeared from Universal Life – although the Christ Key with the caption "Christ, the Key to the Door of Life" is widely and still to this day the symbol of recognition of the Original Christians. As mentioned, he also made the claim that certain elements of the teaching were always brought into Universal Life only by certain people or "fashion trends" – for example, the teaching of reincarnation by Professor Walter Hofmann, the Sermon on the Mount through the books of Franz Alt, the Father-Mother-God through feminist theology, the vegetarian diet, only once the Original Christians owned farms, etc. Some Original Christians made the effort to prove to Elze in detail that all these things were included in the teaching of the Homebringing Mission from the very beginning (1978-1980). Thereupon, the churchman omitted some of these assertions – but only when he knew that Original Christians were present in the hall. If none were present, he brought up the old lies again.

This is the unscrupulousness of not only the "modern" inquisitors: They trample underfoot as often as they can the eighth commandment of God through Moses – *You shall not bear false witness against your neighbor.* But these insidious attacks, in turn, were ultimately directed against Gabriele, the prophetess and bearer of the divine Wisdom, who brought the entire teaching of the heavens to Earth under unspeakable sacrifices – and had to bear and endure all of this.

When Dean Elze retired in 1992, his Catholic colleague Helmut Bauer was promoted to auxiliary Bishop of Würzburg. The entrepreneur, in turn, who had wanted to build the settlement with apartments and artisan's enterprises, left the Original Christians a few years later, taking his millions with him. That millionaires came and went, happened several more times over the course of the years, for with the Original Christians, the principle applies: "Spirit before money." Anyone who wants to work as an equal among equals and also wants to participate in decisions is welcome. However, anyone who tries to derive prerogatives with his means, will push himself away. Or, as Jesus of Nazareth put it: *It is easier for a camel to go through the eye of a needle than for a rich man to enter the Kingdom of God.*

6. The Expulsion of the Friends of Christ from Hettstadt (1985-1996)

What happens when water is held back, for example, by a boulder falling into a streambed? It flows around the outside and seeks another way. Already in July 1985, a few days after the prevention of the settlement of Christ-friends in Würzburg, a contact was established between an architect close to Universal Life and one of his colleagues in Würzburg. The latter offered him a whole series of plots of land in an industrial area very close to Würzburg – in the village of Hettstadt with about 2000 inhabitants. The entrepreneur who had brought the project of a "community of the Sermon on the Mount" into the public eye had appeared in the press again a few days earlier and emphasized that the Christ-friends would by no means renounce this project, even though "initially, it cannot be built in a single place."

The relocation of the plans to the surrounding area was thus openly announced. And the mayor of the CSU village, Waldemar Zorn, a school friend (!) of the mediating Würzburg architect, initially welcomed the potential property buyers with open arms.

Until in November 1985, when one of "his" local councilors came up with the idea of asking the architect in charge of the project about his religious beliefs – a question that is not even permitted under the German Constitution. For a citizen who is dealing with the state in the broadest sense, neither an advantage nor a disadvantage may arise from his faith. (Article 3, paragraph 3 of the Basic Law). Which prayer book an architect has, who is negotiating the development of a building area for his clients, should therefore be of no interest to anyone on the side of the responsible municipality. However, the architect apparently recognized that a refusal to answer would have aroused the curiosity of those present all the more – so he truthfully answered the question: "Are you close to the Homebringing Mission?" with "yes."

From then on, everything changed. The already promised development of the building sites was suddenly postponed indefinitely.
Mayor Zorn, who previously, seemed to be particularly concerned that the citizens of Hettstadt sell their properties in the area in question to new citizens willing to move in, disappeared from the scene for several days – allegedly he had suffered a "bout of weakness." When he reappeared, he had undergone an astonishing about-face. He now

publicly warned against selling to the "sectarians" and without further ado, postponed the already promised development of the building sites indefinitely. He stated that he had not known anything about their religious affiliation – obviously a purely protective assertion to save his career. As stated, the mediating architect was his school friend – and the name of the Christ-Friends' architect was familiar to every newspaper reader.

The ambitious village Mayor Zorn had apparently tried to further his career shortly before, by bringing his community to the highest possible number of inhabitants, no matter how and with whom. The oversized building area that he had designated was still urgently waiting for buyers. There is much to suggest that Waldemar Zorn wanted to complete the long-awaited land sales and the associated development quickly before the local council got wind of it. When this plan failed, he had to very quickly change course – and howl with the church wolves in order to enable the continuance of his career.

By no means did he want to ruin things for himself with the Church. Waldemar Zorn, Kolping Brother (and later Kolping Diocesan Chairman) and cousin of a Catholic priest, namely saw himself as a village mayor by no means fully occupied – and in

1996 he was indeed made District Administrator of the district of Würzburg. Was this the "reward" for having acted in line with the Church?

Three years earlier, in 1993, after eight years of anti-constitutional stalling tactics, he had finally succeeded in driving the followers of the Nazarene out of "his" village. These had admittedly achieved considerable success through two court instances against the – in their opinion unconstitutional – behavior of the community. But the Federal Administrative Court in Berlin finally conjured up an alleged formal error that no one had noticed before – and everything would have had to start all over again. There was still no end in sight to the years of legal action. The constitutional state threatened to degenerate into a "state of legal recourse" – and the fallow plots of land were finally sold back to the municipality, which immediately carried out the development and commissioned a Catholic social welfare organization (!) with the building work.

When the terminally ill Waldemar Zorn was awarded the Pontifical Sylvester Order at the end of 2008, as Count Magnis had been years earlier, this act of expulsion was particularly emphasized by the Bishop of Würzburg, Friedhelm Hofmann, as Zorn's very own "merit." The press office of the

Ordinariate wrote about it: *The Bishop honored the disputes which the District Administrator had had with Universal Life during his time as mayor.* "Even as District Administrator you did not hide your Catholic roots, but made it clear that your political actions are oriented towards Catholic social doctrine.

Is that the practiced Catholic social doctrine – agitation and hate sermons up to the expulsion of people of different faiths, breach of law and character assassination?

"Eradicate Everything!"

In any case, it is in line with the Church to harm "heretics" wherever possible. The dogmas of the Vatican Church prescribe this, and that is how it has been practiced for centuries. In the collection of dogmas "The Teaching of the Catholic Church" by Neuner and Roos, Margin Note 352, which is still valid today, reads: *The Church has ... the duty ... to constantly watch over the salvation of souls with the greatest zeal. Therefore, it must remove and eradicate with painstaking care everything that is against the faith* – that is, against the Catholic faith. And all Catholics must help with this, especially those who, as "lay persons" (non-priests) admin-

ister a political office. In the Catechism of the Vatican Church, it expressly says under Number 899:
The initiative of lay Christians is necessary especially when the matter involves discovering or inventing the means for permeating social, political, and economic realities with the demands of Christian doctrine and life. Whereby the use of the word "Christian" here is fraudulent labeling.

But it goes even further. In the Catechism of the Catholic Church it says under Number 2242:
The citizen is obliged in conscience not to follow the directives of civil authorities when their demands are contrary to the demands of the moral order ... or the teachings of the Gospel.

Meant is the Gospel as the pope interprets it. The laws and dogmas of the Church thus downright **demand** that the elected politicians **disregard or override the Constitution** when the pope demands it of them. According to valid Catholic doctrine, Waldemar Zorn was therefore virtually obliged to disregard the Basic Law when the Church demanded it of him.

Pope Sylvester and Probably the Biggest Scam in World History

For this reason, Waldemar Zorn was also awarded the Pontifical Sylvester Order – as Count Magnis had before him.

Why is the Vatican award given this name? Pope Sylvester, a contemporary of Emperor Constantine at the beginning of the 4th century, was historically a rather insignificant figure, but almost half a millennium later, a major role on the chessboard of papal power politics was intended for him. At the end of the 8th century, a document appeared unexpectedly, most likely forged in the papal chancellery, which stated that Emperor Constantine had given half of Europe to Pope Sylvester as a gift and acknowledged him as being above the emperor.

Until today, this "Donation of Constantine" is considered to be probably the greatest case of fraud in the history of humankind, one of the most audacious forgeries ever to be written on paper – since it marked the actual beginning of the popes' secular power in the so-called "Papal States," which, for a millennium, has gone like a bolt right across the middle of the Italian peninsula.

So, one could conclude that whoever receives the Order of Saint Sylvester has effectively contributed to giving the Church as much secular power as possible and forcing the state to do its will – if necessary, even with lies and deceit. It is probably also "worthy of distinction" that a community refuses to let people gain a foothold who are displeasing to the Church.

Meanwhile, for the third time in a row, a project of the Christ-friends was abruptly stopped by the intrigues and smear campaigns of the churches: Dettelbach – Heuchelhof – Hettstadt. The events in the Lower Franconia village of Hettstadt reveal in an almost exemplary way, how strongly church and state are still meshed. This is why they should be examined more closely here.

Chicaneries Without End

Until his sudden about-face, Waldemar Zorn had still personally motivated landowners from the village to sell to the architect of the Christ-friends. Now, he invited some of the same citizens to the town hall to advise them against selling. In a letter, he justified this violation of the freedom of religion anchored in the German Constitution (which he even mentioned) with the sentence: "We warn against the sale solely for socio-political reasons." So, this is the constitutional understanding of many politicians when it comes to non-church persuasions: The Basic Law is there to be mentioned briefly if necessary – only to violate it all the more vehemently in the next breath.

Zorn explained to the *Main-Post* (Nov. 26, 1985) that he was "not prepared to offer a possible homestead to the Homebringing Mission." For this action he had "the legal approval of the Ministry of the Interior" in Munich. This last remark alone gives a deep view into the corruption between state and church, which is particularly pronounced in Bavaria.

Similarly as in the Dettelbach case, a situation had arisen in Hettstadt that only harms almost everyone involved: The property purchasers spent their money in good faith, believing that the development of the land follows as soon as possible. The property owners who have not yet sold their land cannot use it for agricultural purposes anymore, because the reallocation has already taken place and the routes of the new roads have already been laid out. The community, which was in urgent need of new citizens due to its indebtedness, is blocking itself. The situation benefits only the churches, which do not want to tolerate anyone they consider to be religious competition.

However, the settlement of the "heretics" could not be completely prevented: Some properties acquired by Original Christians were already developed, and thus, about two dozen houses could be built. You can recognize them in part by the fact that they have rounded building forms that are modeled on nature. As with many other projects, Gabriele proved her creativeness here, too, when she recommended to the architects at that time that they should try this or that. The result was houses without corners and edges, elegantly curved, with a slightly curved or even cloverleaf-shaped floor plan.

But the Franconian village Mayor Zorn (CSU) once again revealed all the pettiness and resentment of which he was capable. One would not think it possible, but the village council issued a special "design statute," according to which such construction forms were forbidden in the entire village area from now on. The elegant building designs of the Christ-friends were mocked as "igloos" and "nigger corrals" – until a court of law revoked the statutes after two and a half years – and the community had to be instructed by an independent expert that round buildings were an "invigorating enrichment" and were perfectly justifiable in the vicinity of the baroque city of Würzburg. Moreover, the overall appearance of the village was not uniform anyway, due to extensive war damage.

Every normal civil right, every matter of course had to be enforced in Hettstadt by means of legal action: For example, the permission for an information booth in the village, with which the Original Christians wanted to explain their view of things to the population. The legal process for such a permit took two years. Or the possibility of publishing an invitation to a meeting of the "Settlers' Community in Universal Life" in the Hettstadt Village Newsletter, like every other local association – this lawsuit took four years!

The village cut off a marginal strip of the still undeveloped building area, opened it up and built a new fire station there. Afterwards, a huge crucifix with an almost life-size corpse was erected – exactly opposite the houses of Original Christians that had already been built. For it was known that followers of Jesus of Nazareth appreciate the plain cross as a Christian symbol, but not the representation of the body of the suffering and dying Jesus, which was also unknown in early Christianity.

All Hell Breaks Loose in the Parish Hall

Of course, all these large and small pinpricks and chicaneries against a minority faith that were kept up for years needed some kind of justification. From the very beginning, these were provided by the church's slanderers. The first self-justification Mayor Zorn gave that his warning against Universal Life was solely "for social and socio-political reasons," came from the munitions depot of Count Magnis.

The Catholic sect commissioner is also quickly invited to Hettstadt and gives a lecture against the Original Christians in the Catholic parish hall.

> **Yesterday – Inquisitor: Persecution all the way to murder**
>
> **Today – Sect Commissioner/Sect Expert: Persecution up to character assassination**

The *Main-Post* (December 14, 1985) attributes an "often polemical manner" to the Count and states that in the parish hall "at times ... it was a veritable madhouse." The church representative Magnis and the politician Zorn are of one mind in accusing the Christ-friends of "undermining the welfare state": They claim that the latter allegedly pay their employees below the tariff rate (which is simply untrue) and thus enter into an "unequal competition" with "normal artisan businesses."

Apart from the fact that it is not understandable why an artisan firm should not be "normal" just because a part of its workforce is neither Catholic nor Lutheran – the real background of such a twisted "argumentation" is the need to move from a theological to a political level of polemics in the fight against "heretics." For, as stated before, according to the Constitution, a municipality may not discriminate against citizens on religious grounds – thus, the church and state obstructers simply work with false statements. The truth does not interest the slanderers: Of course the employees of companies founded by the followers of Jesus of Nazareth receive standard wages or more, in addition to considerable child allowances and meal vouchers.

Magnis summarizes his misleading and false allegations in another publication. In connection with Universal Life, he speaks of a "frighteningly great financial power," with which a group of "ice-cold economy careerists" is building an "economic sector" that is taking on ever-increasing dimensions." In the same breath, he paints a gloomy scenario: "In the event of a break-up of the sect, which is quite conceivable ... a community could incur the heaviest social burdens."

Now, what's supposed to be true? Are clever technocrats building a huge economic empire here – or are a few dangerous dilettantes on the verge of collapse? Apparently at this point, the count could not decide between two enemy images – or rather: caricatures of the enemy. But the modern inquisitor knows that anyone who is impressed by such suggestions, who allows them to bring him into a diffuse feeling of fear, will not even notice such contradictions.

Nor does he notice how dishonest it is, when the person who paints an allegedly threatening "break-up" scenario, simultaneously does everything possible to actually bring about such a "break-up," with his fight to destroy respectable citizens.

Who would ever think of referring such talk of an alleged "financial power" back to its originator: Which religious communities in Germany actually represent a "frighteningly large financial power," with billions of assets and billions in turnover – and, in addition, with billions in subsidies by the state? The churches, worth billions, get upset about a few medium-sized firms with a few hundred employees? Everything is exaggerated and stirred up against the Original Christians. Otherwise, the ordinary citizen could ask: What can anyone have against it, when respectable citizens establish businesses – and on top of that, if the principles of the Sermon on the Mount are applied there?

It is likewise absurd when Count Magnis demands in his pamphlet that "the legislature is called upon here to ... take the ground out from under the establishment of such totalitarian, political-economic theocracies." The only "theocracy," the last remaining absolutist monarchy in Europe, occupies the Vatican!

In his pamphlet, Magnis also presents the following thesis, which is later repeated a hundred times by church slanderers and politicians of various parties: "The group actually pursues political-economic goals." Incidentally, the National Socialist newspaper "Der Stürmer" (Sept. 12, 1940) made the same claim about the Jews: "The Jews are not a religious community at all, but an association representing economic and political interests." And Adolf Hitler had written in "Mein Kampf": "The Jews are not a religious community."

The thrust of the count's pamphlets is clear: The public, and above all, the politicians, are to be persuaded that this is not a question of faith or a religious battle, but a "danger" to the state.

This was, by the way, part of the "double strategy" of the scribes 2000 years ago against Jesus of Nazareth: Among the Jews, the Nazarene was demonized as "possessed by demons"; but toward the Roman-dominated public he was slandered as a "rebel" and a danger to the Roman state.

Waldemar Zorn's Campaign

Mayor Waldemar Zorn (1938-2008), who copied the majority of his "arguments" from Count Magnis, also takes a similar line. He accuses the followers of Jesus of Nazareth of "sealing themselves off," of wanting to found a "village within a village," even a "state within a state."
A "state within a state" – what Zorn imputes to the Original Christians is exactly what applies to the mainstream churches in Germany: They determine in an autocratic way what "their own affairs" are, in which the state does not have to interfere and for which state laws, for example in labor and collective bargaining law, have no, or only limited, validity. This leads, for example, to the fact that in the case of sexual crimes committed by priests against

children and young people, the state prosecution authorities are usually left out. (German: Carsten Frerk, "Kirchenrepublik Deutschland")

This would, Zorn continues, at least as far as the village is concerned, "totally destroy a Franconian village community, which has developed over centuries." Indeed, the "sect" – if he took the Constitution seriously, the mayor would actually not even be allowed to use this misnomer – represents "an absolute danger, even a lethal danger for this village of Hettstadt." They want "to establish their own community." That is pure incitement. As a person who is not entirely unintelligent, Zorn knows, of course, that there is a considerable difference between a political and a faith "community" – and only the latter can be the issue in this case. But he gives his listeners and readers the impression that it is one and the same thing.

It almost seems as if Zorn wants at all costs to make people forget that at the beginning, he was not at all reluctant to accept the new settlers with a non-church background. The eagerness with which he

> As a Reminder – Sect: A term of abuse used by the respective prevailing religious caste for all those against whom their Inquisition is directed.

rages against the new citizens, even undertaking extensive lecture tours against them all the way to Lower Bavaria, has almost medieval characteristics. During the time of the Inquisition, anyone who as a territorial ruler was suspected of sparing the "heretics" in any way, had to, as stated, immediately prove the opposite through a particular zeal for persecution – otherwise he himself was in danger of losing his lands and his position.

In the Middle Ages, as well as in our days, the Church wants at all costs to prevent Catholics or Lutherans from living peacefully with "heretics" for a longer period of time. Why? Because then they usually find that the allegedly so "bad" and "misguided" "outsiders" in matters of faith, are quite acceptable fellow citizens. Hettstadt is no exception.

Everyday harmony between "believers" and "heretics" – that must not be allowed, for that would refute the thesis that this "foreign" faith can produce only "evil" and "harmful" things – and therefore leads straight to hell. As such, it is probably no coincidence that Mayor Zorn, in search of

> **As a Reminder: The Lutheran pastor Haack wrote: If you are thinking Inquisition with me, you are right, of course.**

"catchy" slurs, takes offence at the "harmony." He claims that the modern-day followers of the Nazarene are exposed to an "enforced permanent harmony" that is "simply inhuman." "If there can essentially be nothing but harmony... then harmony is practically something deadly." (*TV Touring*, July 19, 1989)

The starting point for Zorn's absurd imputation that there is something like an "enforced harmony" among the Original Christians is presumably the title of the Original Christian company regulations: "Harmony Is the Life of the Enterprise." One would have to take the trouble to read through them: The Original Christian work regulations are based on the Sermon on the Mount of Jesus of Nazareth; there is no mention of "enforcement" anywhere. – But that's how it is: The truth-twisters have no idea about the reality. Apparently, they don't want to know anything about it, either, but simply invent something that they then trumpet with utter conviction.

Today, many years later, it can be said that the threatening backdrop, which church representatives like Magnis or politicians like Zorn have rhetorically constructed and painted with gloomy colors, has not materialized, neither in Hettstadt nor in any other community in which followers of

Jesus of Nazareth live – on the contrary: They get along very well with the population, and the villagers with them. But for several months and years, the poison of incitement and agitation usually does not fail to have its malicious effect.

The Master of Smear Campaigns

Friedrich-Wilhelm Haack repeatedly demonstrated his special talent in the unscrupulous invention of ever new untruths and distortions, the core discipline of the inquisitorial business. It was Pastor Haack who probably was the first to create the fairy tale of the aforementioned alleged "enforced harmony" of the Christ-friends. At a lecture in Marktheidenfeld in May 1987, he spoke of a "terrorism of harmony." Thus, respectable citizens are made out to be close to terrorism, without there being the slightest evidence of it.

In the same lecture, Haack also claimed that the announcement of the Kingdom of Peace through Universal Life is not found in the Bible; only the devil speaks of an earthly kingdom of Jesus. He apparently did not take note of the grandiose vision of the prophet of God, Isaiah. Or he rejects it just as the god of the underworld does.

The exaggerated self-confidence and zealous sense of mission of the "pastor" lead repeatedly to situations that are not without a certain discomfiture. When on October 8, 1986, the Original Christians organize a silent march through Würzburg to protest against their discrimination by church and state, Haack suddenly appears. He jumps back and forth in his leather coat in front of, and beside, the march, brandishing his camera, photographing the peacefully demonstrating Original Christians from all possible angles. He insults individual Original Christians, assigned (officially stipulated) to keep order, as "ruffian dwarfs," "secret police," "thought police," the entire demonstration procession as a "Nazi herd," "nothing but crazy people, right down to their toenails." He is visibly enraged that people of the 20th century are allowed to exercise their right to freedom of expression. *I'll finish you off,* berates the pastor, and, as stated before: *In the Middle Ages we would have treated you in a totally different way!*

In fact, in 1446, 127 Hussite followers were sentenced to march through Würzburg in a "penitential procession" before having to renounce their faith in a solemn ceremony.
A Christ-friend, who tries to calmly put him in his place, is yelled at by Haack: "You are on the verge

of a slap in the face! I'll throw you right into that fountain there!" At the closing rally in front of the Würzburg Residence, he tries, camera in hand, to push his way into a circle formed by the peaceful demonstrators. When he is prevented from doing so, he turns to a policeman: "Please help me, they want to hurt me." But this time, the state power does not respond in his favor – the police are satisfied with the peaceful and disciplined course of the event. A policeman rebukes the troublemaker: "That's not surprising. Why don't you leave these people alone first – or come with us! If you continue to behave in such an undisciplined manner and disturb the group peacefully gathered here, we will have to take you with us." Thereupon, Haack once again vents his anger on the bystanders: "You'll regret that! You're not doing your group any favors with this! Just wait, now I have enough material for more publications. Soon you'll have nothing more to laugh about."

Apparently, the material he collected was not very plentiful, after all. A short time later, the subversive pastor actually foraged for "material for further publications" in the trash containers of the artisan firm "We Are Here for You" in Würzburg, which is run by Original Christians. He is then asked to refrain from doing so.

Rabble-rousing in the Parish Hall

Haack was quickly involved in the unholy fight for the "Hettstadt Home Soil." He was invited by the local politicians of Hettstadt's town council to speak on January 4, 1988 in the Catholic parish hall, clouded with beer fumes and cigarette smoke. The Original Christians do not take part in the event – there are only a few standing in front of the hall, who present themselves as representatives of Universal Life and available for questions.

Haack immediately goes into high gear. He speaks of "massive attempts" to "conquer the grown village." He claims that he can ascertain an "increasing radicalization and aggressiveness of the Christ-friends." The prophetess is "completely unpredictable with her railroading decisions" – "a problem that psychiatrists should talk about more competently." The followers are "no longer capable of a rational consideration of things and are therefore unpredictable." Universal Life is "anti-democratic and dictatorial in its structure." A normal and tolerant coexistence with the village community would be "not at all possible due to the Christ-friends' ideology of faith, because they have blind obedience written on their banners."

Appreciation and flattery for the listeners, at the same time, disparagement and sarcastic mockery for the opponents – a simple and proven recipe of all demagogues. Haack describes the Original Christians as a "special species of people," who rather deserve "compassion," who represent a "potential for intensive pastoral care," and who would first have to become "mentally healthy." They are people with "rather low moral qualities," in whom "aggression is simply swirling," with whom one experiences a "maximum level of aggressiveness and abusive behavior toward others," who "express themselves caustically, aggressively and maliciously," who "talk big," who "spread disconcerting and disgusting insinuations" and who "constantly kick others in the shins." And such people wanted to "break into the village"!

In such a heated atmosphere, it takes a certain amount of level-headedness and self-confidence to register that this gesticulating and ranting pastor is actually only describing himself. Nobody dares to express this.

Now the pastor mocks the teachings of the Original Christians. The "newest crime of this group" is that they, "boldly, piously, happily, freely," use the term of a "thousand-year kingdom." This term is "burdened for us," which can "only be unpleasant," because: "With this term, 'thousand year kingdom,' no one thinks of a religious concept."

Does the Lutheran theologian reckon with the fact that the village population, predominantly of Catholic faith, does not know the Bible as well as he does? That no one has ever read the verses in which the "thousand years" are mentioned, for example, in the Revelation of John, chapter 20, shortly before the description of the "New Jerusalem," the "city on the mountain."

Then I saw an angel coming down from heaven, holding in his hand the key to the bottomless pit and a great chain. He seized the dragon, that ancient serpent, who is the Devil and Satan, and bound him for a thousand years:

Perhaps this particular biblical passage is one that theologians especially like to suppress because it is somehow so unpleasant – above all, in the ears of the institution, which itself is standing at edge of the abyss.

The "Inner Barbed Wire" Is Rolled Out

In this speech, Haack really pulls out all the stops; he blusters, mocks, flatters, frightens, and launches gloomy predictions – a rhetorical "masterstroke" of a negative kind.

A large part of Haack's speech consists of outright invectives toward those people who have bought land in a Lower Franconian village and now want to settle there. He thus acts like a military agitator who wants to prepare soldiers for war: As a rule, the opponents are first presented as inferior, as "subhumans" or the like, in order to suppress and prevent normal human interaction, if possible.

Haack's sentences become shorter and shorter at the end of his rant; staccato-like, he hammers into his listeners what they have to think and do: One must not "blindly submit to what is coming." Therefore, "we must do our utmost to set barriers here." "You can give the matter a decisive knock-out punch." Or: "Do nothing, then you have done nothing! Then one day, heaven will be shrouded over."

It seems strange how, at the end of the 20th century, a modern inquisitor uses medieval language in a village where people of Original Christian faith want to settle: It's as if he were threatening an interdict. In the Middle Ages, if a town was under a spell because, for example, it had given shelter to heretics, then heaven was "shrouded over": no masses, no funerals, no baptisms were allowed. ...

But there could still be someone sitting in the parish hall who thinks to himself: Where is the much vaunted love of neighbor?

An experienced inquisitor knows what people think. That is why Haack continues: *You do not have to have any respect for them ... There is no commandment for love and friendship or for the care and nurturing of those who want to kick me in the shins. ... You don't have to have anything to do with them.*

Jesus of Nazareth taught something quite different. Mind you: All this and even more is said by a pastor, who, then, in the Sunday worship service, may speak in his sermon about Jesus of Nazareth and about the commandment to love one's neighbor or even one's enemies!

Here, thresholds of aggression are deliberately lowered or completely removed from the listeners, and one can vividly imagine how several hundred years ago the audience listening to such inflammatory diatribes could be persuaded to attend a subsequent execution with satisfaction.

One ingredient is still missing in the poisonous soup being brewed by the hectically gesticulating agitator in the parish hall amidst cigarette smoke and beer fumes: fear. But he has by no means forgotten it: Haack paints the future of the "grown village" in dismal colors, in case "nothing were done." Because "they" are trying to "take over the village," to determine the "whole political fate of Hettstadt." They are people who "settle themselves in," who always "want more" until the whole village "is subjugated." "What we defend is our homeland... our village... ...our Hettstadt. And we are the ones being persecuted. They come here and want to steal and annihilate our home!"

Who would have thought it possible for a Lutheran minister to adopt the "blood and soil mythology" in such a way? One is reminded of the "German Christians," who in the 1930s, enthusiastically campaigned for the "national idea."

With all these threats, Haack continues, the people of Hettstadt are given a very special role – and now, a particularly diabolical move follows: The small village near Würzburg "is now suffering on behalf of many communities in the Federal Republic of Germany."

Haack repeats this twice more, so that everyone really gets it – and you have to imagine this: Not those suffer allegedly under this situation, those who are denied the move they had been promised, who are prevented from exercising their civil right to free choice of a place of residence, because, after all, they have to live somewhere – no: In a completely special and "invaluable" way, those suffer – so Haack insinuates – who are expected to live next door to "such people" in the future.

With a gloomy expression, Haack predicts that an "inner barbed wire" will cut through the village – but the one who is unrolling such a barbed wire fence in the village at this moment, and more so with every sentence, is the pastor himself with his barbed words and barbed sentences. One must consider that at this time the intra-German border still existed. A skillful inquisitor addresses all unconscious images and associations with which he can evoke fear and loathing.

The inquisitor had spoken – now, as in the Middle Ages, the prominent local figures were called upon to take a stand. Haack actually asked the local politicians present to "stand by" Hettstadt. Christian Will, a CSU (Christian Social Union) member of the Bavarian state parliament, then declared that "the politicians of both factions will not stand there with their hands in their pockets." A few days later, he will say in the district executive committee of the CSU: "Anyone who wants to undermine or even destroy our customs and social order should not expect that we will stand by idly and watch such goings-on."

"You Should Be Hanged!"

Just how much Friedrich-Wilhelm Haack has actually stirred up the villagers, how much he has succeeded in bringing deep-seated primitive reflexes to light, becomes apparent immediately after the event ends. In front of the hall, several people stand in silence, and name tags identify them as "Christ-friends." They deliberately did not take part in the "discussion" in the hall, but want to offer themselves unobtrusively as conversation partners for those who have still kept a clear head. But it seems that, at the moment, no such person is present. Instead, the Christ-friends standing there peacefully become the target of the inflamed rage of the crowd of visitors streaming past them: "Shoot them down!" "They should be put up against the wall – just as they are all standing, one after the other!" "You should be hanged right now!" "You should be burned!" An elderly woman spits contemptuously, and a man shouts, "Heil Hitler!"

The fourth of January 1988 in Hettstadt – a spooky spotlight is cast on the thin sheet of ice on which our democracy moves. In this case, however, no agitator of the people from the far right or far left has stirred up the masses, but an agitator of the people in a pastor's cassock.

Even days after January 4, 1988, the deliberately awakened "people's rage" continues. "Get lost, you pack of Homebringers!" "Homebringers get out of Hettstadt!" – these are the still rather printable versions of the exclamations that can be heard on the streets. "Let them die! I could run a knife into them," cries one woman. And a 10-year-old boy is insulted, kicked and threatened in the Hettstadt school as a "shitty Homebringer": "We'll make mincemeat of you!" In the days following the lecture, tools disappear from the construction sites of the houses of the new settlers, plastic foil windows are torn out or stacks of building blocks knocked over.

And still in the summer of 2009, a drunken youth screams in the middle of the night in front of a house inhabited by followers of the Nazarene: *Heil Hitler! You should all be strung up!*

The Mayor Continues to Incite

When at a press conference the Original Christians point out the growing readiness for violence in the village, Mayor Zorn and four town council members conversely accuse the Original Christians of "incitement of the people." Local politicians and church representatives flatly deny the incidents in front of the parish hall after Haack's inflammatory tirade. But the incidents are not only proven by affidavits of Original Christians and police statements, but also by a journalist of the local newspaper.

What happened here on this winter evening, not only in the hall, but especially afterward in front of the building and during the following days in the village, should have made every upright democrat reflect: How is such a thing possible, such a relapse into a stifling, unenlightened Middle Ages?

But Mayor Zorn and his companions did not regret the poisonous billows of smoke of the "people's rage" that had risen – after all, they had helped fan the flames themselves.

On the contrary, Waldemar Zorn feels vindicated by Haack's lecture; he gains the upper hand and still in January writes letters to the President of the Bavarian State Parliament, Franz Heubl, and to the Bavarian Minister-President, Franz Josef Strauß, in which he asks for "help to rescue our community." He urges the state to examine the loyalty of the Original Christians to the Constitution, because: "No sect has so far spoken out so clearly in favor of changing the social order." They are striving to "establish a state of their own."

That is how the Pharisees and scribes denounced Jesus of Nazareth to the state authorities, saying that he wanted to overthrow the emperor and be proclaimed king. The fact that the Nazarene said "My kingdom is not of this world" was not taken into account at that time – just as what the Original Christians emphasize again and again is not taken into account today – that the Kingdom of Peace is not an external state, but a group of people who open up the inner kingdom and live in peace with their fellow people and with nature.

Under all kinds of pretexts. the village mayor now tries to denounce to the authorities the followers of Jesus of Nazareth who live in the village: He expresses the supposition that the Christ-enterprises were not only founded "to employ their own followers here," but "to generate considerable financial means." Furthermore, he claims that people are not paid according to collective rates agreed to by trade unions, but "exploited to optimize profits." With "great probability," Zorn continues, there are foreign employees in these companies who "do not have work permits," thus, there may be "illegal employment."

There is nothing to any of these accusations, absolutely nothing – which is why the authorities cannot discover anything criminal. But Zorn goes one better: When representatives of the Original Christians accuse the community of Hettstadt of harming itself through the blockade, because it loses tax revenues, he publicly announces on January 20, 1990, that "up to this day" no Christ enterprise has paid even "a single German mark" in commercial tax.

Apart from the fact that with this he violated tax secrecy – with the blockade tactics of his village, he himself had ensured that there were few such businesses in the village. One artisan business called "We Are Here for You" was just being built up and therefore not yet in the profit zone; it was similar with two other small businesses – but all of them paid the otherwise accruing taxes in a correct manner.

Zorn, however, did not leave it at that. He presented himself to the Bavarian Ministry of Finance and lied like a trooper. He said that in his village there were "22 companies of the Homebringing Mission with up to 50 employees," of which "none of them pay commercial taxes." As mayor he had access into the documents and therefore knew that this was not true. The authorities thereupon ordered an extraordinary audit – not only in Hettstadt, but in the whole area around Würzburg, including the association of Universal Life.

Although the officials again found nothing – the scheming Kolping official Zorn thus started legal disputes about the non-profit status of Universal Life that were to last for many years. The fact that we know anything about these machinations today is due to the note of a conversation of an official from the Ministry of Finance, which came to light during one of the trials when the files were later inspected.

Universal Life later eschewed of its own accord the non-profit status, because the followers of Jesus of Nazareth did not want to receive any advantages from a state that discriminates against its own citizens at the instigation of the mainstream churches. Nevertheless, the state demanded substantial additional payments under contrived pretexts. Apparently this was an attempt to financially destroy the hated "heretics," as desired by the churches. As we will see later (Chapter 11), the Original Christians were finally able to repel this attack with united forces and under considerable effort.

A Mayor Should Abide by the Constitution

Meanwhile, Mayor Zorn continued to travel around the country, giving lectures, appearing on television and defaming the Original Christians in Universal Life.

The Original Christians simply could not believe that a mayor, who, as an official, is obligated to ideological neutrality, is allowed to cast aspersions on a minority in this way. Therefore, on July 12, 1993, they filed a complaint and, at the same time, an application for a temporary injunction against the mayor's defamatory statements. On August 11, 1993, the Administrative Court of Würzburg provisionally forbade Zorn from claiming that Universal Life is not a community of faith, but a "business corporation with widely ramified businesses and hard-hitting managers," an "economic organization with a religious cover," behind which is a "small group of profiteers who know every trick in the book;" this is a "sect" that wants to create a "sect-like village" and therefore represents a "danger" to the village – and some of its members are trying to create a "fear psychosis within the sect."

In its reasoning, the court explained that a mayor may not take part in an "ideological debate" and may not "forbid, oppose, reject or disparage religious convictions." This is dictated by the state's obligation to ideological neutrality and tolerance. The mayor had not succeeded in making any circumstances credible, "for example, practices contrary to fundamental rights, impairments of liberty or calls for acts contrary to fundamental rights," which could justify such an encroachment on the fundamental right of equal treatment based on an ideology. For a representative of the state, the word "sect" is also an inadmissible disparagement.

However, Zorn does not adhere to the restrictions of the court. Three times he insults Universal Life again in a similar way, for example, he tells *Der Spiegel* (March 14, 1994) that Universal Life is "deadly" for Hettstadt – and, three times, fines (5,000, 7,500, 10,000 DM) are imposed on him by the court – but it is not he who pays them, but the village treasury. Complaints against these fines up to the Administrative Court in Munich are dismissed, and the Würzburg Administrative Court also keeps to its decision in the main proceedings (February 8, 1995).

Without doubt, this was a success for the constitutional state. However, this decision applies only to officials in the exercise of their official duties. The

Main-Echo (August 19, 1993) put it in a nutshell: "As Mayor, Zorn will have to refrain from making a precisely listed series of statements in the future, but as chairman of the Kolping Family, as a CSU party politician, and as a private person, he may continue to repeat the accusations that he ... had made." Thus, anyone who is Catholic or Lutheran may continue to disregard the eighth commandment without scruples, just as the Church proclaimed as early as the Middle Ages: "Loyalty and faith need not be maintained toward a heretic, and the fraud committed against him is sanctified." The slander becomes particularly "sanctified" when it is uttered by a pastor in a cassock – because then, it is covered by the judiciary on the basis of "freedom of expression," interpreted in a way that is very friendly to the Church.

But religious neutrality is not easy to legally enforce even with regard to officials who play the guardians of the faith, as in the case of Hettstadt. In August, the head mayor of Wertheim, Stefan Gläser (CDU), "fears" that adherents of Universal Life want to acquire a second farm in Höhefeld, a district of Wertheim; he says there is thus the "danger" of an "infiltration" and of "dominating local events," because even clever people are "not immune" to "falling for" the organization. A far-fetched attempt at cheap propaganda – with only two farms it is supposed to be possible to dominate a whole village?! The Original Christians see here a parallel case to Hettstadt, which Gläser also refers to himself – but the Stuttgart Administrative Court refuses to forbid the head mayor from making these discriminatory statements: The statements were "not certain" and there was "no danger of repetition" – a strange statement considering that Gläser had refused to sign a cease-and-desist declaration and had publicly stated that he did not want to be "put off" and that one wanted to "intimidate" him. (The perpetrator always likes to make himself a victim.)

However, in the court proceedings, which took four months despite an urgent appeal, the head mayor denied that he had made the objectionable statements" in this way."
That was the only reason he got away with it – but the press obediently printed a press release from the city of Wertheim, according to which the court had "flatly rejected" the application for an injunction. According to the *Tauber-Zeitung* (January 29, 1994), the head mayor would "not be muzzled." Since the court had at least expressed the hope that the city of Wertheim would "in future ... avoid a disparagement of the religious convictions of the

followers of 'Universal Life,'" the Original Christians saw the purpose of their complaint fulfilled and waived a lengthy lawsuit on the main proceedings. But the Protestant-Lutheran Lord Mayor, who, according to his own statement, "is also engaged in an electoral office within the Church," continued undeterred to discriminate against the Original Christians.

On October 10, 1994, in a letter to the Minister of Social Affairs of Baden-Württemberg, Helga Solinger, he lamented the "systematic proliferation" through the region "by means of a non-transparent, multi-branched corporate apparatus." That a social service center of the Original Christians had "advanced far" and "competed" with other social service centers was a thorn in his side. Furthermore, he insinuated that Universal Life had "access to thousands of patient files" through a computer company run by the Original Christians – thus accusing the firm of betraying secrets!

The fanatical hysteria, with which Mayor Zorn in Hettstadt reacted to the settlement of Original Christians, apparently had a contagious effect on some colleagues. The fact that the discriminatory statements of an official were put under a judicial stop, at least in Hettstadt, brought the Original Christians only a very limited gain in the public sphere. This was ensured by the *Main-Post* journalist Tilman Toepfer, who announced in the regional section of the newspaper on August 14, 1993: "Temporary injunction prohibits criticism – a muzzle for the representatives of Hettstadt." In a commentary, Toepfer claimed that Zorn's opinions are "what critically thinking people believe" – more appropriate would be: have to believe. After Zorn had been sentenced to a fine for the first time for persistent slander, Toepfer remarked that Zorn, as a *private* person, was still allowed to say anything – but that would be "childish": "After all, the citizens expect mayors and local politicians to have their points of view and to represent them. There are more than enough 'neutral' politicians: zero profile, jumping on bandwagons and constantly checking the statutes." Thus, a mayor and a journalist not only succeed in downplaying a disregard of the basic rights of the German Constitution into a trivial offence, but in making it appear as something of a particularly "strong character."

A "Citizens' Initiative" Is Founded

Zorn's constant tirades against the Original Christian settlers probably served more to prove his own "orthodoxy" and his career advancement. The role of the "whip" against the new fellow citizens had long since been taken over by a "citizens' initiative against the plans of the Homebringing Mission-Universal Life in Hettstadt." In March 1988, shortly after Pastor Haack's slanderous high point in the parish hall, it appeared in public for the first time. Presumably, Haack, as an experienced "Initiative" founder, gave the decisive tip. Of all people, a Rhinelander, the engineer Hans-Walter Jungen, felt called upon to save his Franconian hometown from "destruction" by an "extreme group." According to the statutes, the initiative registered as an association, to which the wife and son of the mayor belonged as founding members, aimed at "... the prevention of the massive settlement of organizations and persons who belong to or are close to the 'Homebringing Mission-Universal Life' in Hettstadt." At the instigation of the Würzburg District Court, the following formulation was inserted before this: "... non-violent and within the means allowed by law."
Despite this addition, such an association's purpose, which aims to discriminate against people of

a particular community of faith, is unconstitutional. However, the Würzburg District Office, which was made aware of this circumstance and requested to withdraw the legal capacity of the association, did not react.

At first, the "work" of the citizens' initiative consists of copying the latest polemic articles in the daily press (for instance, a report on the lecture by Pastor Haack, of course, without attending ills such as "String-them-up" calls), distributing them in the form of "information sheets" and attaching them to the village notice boards. When the Original Christians also begin to affix articles there, the local council decides that all notices must be filed at the town hall with immediate effect. ...

In April 1989, the citizens' initiative distributed the minutes of a meeting of the Diocesan Council of Catholics in the Bishopric of Würzburg, mainly an accumulation of quotations from the writings of Count Magnis. The Catholics demand that Universal Life should not be called a "community of faith and religion," but an "economic group." "What we should be wary of," are, in their opinion: "indifference – naiveté – suppression – ... exaggerated liberality – retreat to the standpoint of religious tolerance."

As can be seen: Tolerance is rather a negative virtue from a Catholic point of view – after all, the non-Catholic should be "eradicated."

Then follows an outright call for a sales boycott: "Responsible consideration before buying from or selling to the HBM/UL: Should I give the business group the means to power that could be used to harm our community?"
This sales boycott, including completely groundless insinuations, reminds us of grim times. But what about the mainstream churches? How are the tax money and subsidies that they collect in millions from the common good used – always for the benefit of "our community"?

In any case, Hans-Walter Jungen does not refrain from spreading abstruse untruths in the exercise of his Catholic mission – for example, on January 16, 1989, when he, together with the mayor's son, Matthias Zorn, gives a lecture on Universal Life in Erlenbach near Marktheidenfeld. He repeats the false assertion by Magnis that Original Christians have "four to five hours of meditation duty" daily. Then Jungen even goes so far as to lie that at night, on the farm in Ruppertzaint, which is run by Original Christians, tomatoes from abroad, for example, from Holland, are delivered in big trucks and then sold on the market as farm-grown tomatoes "for good money." The company *Gut zum Leben* (Good for Life) immediately takes legal action against this damage to its reputation, with an affidavit stating that tomatoes from conventional cultivation had never been delivered. In the court proceedings, however, the main case is then declared settled, because Jungen denies having made this statement in the first place – although he himself admitted in a first protective brief that he had talked about trucks with tomatoes from Italy or Holland.

This was not the last case in which Jungen twisted and turned the truth or falsehood as it suited him, even in court. In 1993, the magazine *Stern* had quoted him with the words: "They are so dangerous because they keep seriously ill people from going to the doctor. Some sick people are driven to insanity." Because this is a malicious slander, *Stern* was ordered to recant and not to repeat it. But Jungen denied having made this statement. A few months later, however, in the appeal hearing against *Stern* (at which he personally was not prosecuted at all), he declared that perhaps one could have got the impression that he had said something like that, after all. Jungen at the first, or Jungen at the second – one of them must have been lying in court. However, a criminal complaint for sworn false testimony was dropped by the public prosecutor's office in Würzburg – saying that he might not have been able to immediately remember all these things (which took place only a few months before!)

Even when Jungen repeatedly claims in the press and on television in connection with Universal Life that he has received "murder threats" from there, he is still far from being called to account for this. After three years (!) of litigation, the Regional Court of Würzburg does determine that the correctness of the allegations has not been proven. But it does not condemn Jungen – because the Universal Life Association is not identical with the "followers of Universal Life," whom Jungen has named as the authors. It would not be the last time that a court, apparently in the absence of any other "escape route," would use this kind of hair-splitting to deny Universal Life any legal protection against slander.

The Hettstadt "Stab in the Back" Legend and Its Marketing

In this way, Magnis, Haack, Zorn and Jungen built up in a short time, a kind of "stab in the back" legend, which is willingly adopted by the media. The newspaper headlines already express whose side the gazettes are taking: "Conflict with sect fanatics has no end" (*Saale-Zeitung*, August 11, 1988); "Hettstadt Against Sect Planning" (*Münchner Merkur*, May 24, 1988); "Overrun by Purchasers – Sect Members Are Scrambling for Building Land" (*Nürnberger Nachrichten*, May 25, 1988); "Hettstadters Defend Themselves Against Sect" (*Saale-Zeitung*, May 13, 1987); "Homebringing Sect Behaves Radically" (*Main-Echo*, August 18, 1988); "A village Fights Against Universal Life" (*taz*, April 1, 1989).

The *Bavarian Broadcasting Company* also stokes the fire at regular intervals, for example, on February 2, 1989 in the program "Stations": "Hettstadt near Würzburg: Agitation and anger have ruled the village of 2,500 souls ever since the so-called Christ-State is being built here. At least, that's what the community of faith Universal Life wants." In reality, two dozen houses are being built, and the community of the Original Christians always emphasized that the "New Jerusalem" is emerging very gradually in the hearts of peaceful people. But the view of those affected did not interest the media at all.

This is the New Jerusalem, a settlement near Hettstadt in the vicinity of Würzburg, the television journalist Holger Lösch announces on Bavarian television on September 26, 1990. *For residents, so it is said, the end of the world can be experienced here as in an ark. The building contractor of this place is the so-called Homebringing Mission of Jesus Christ.*
How so? The community of faith doesn't own a single piece of land there.
In such programs it's mostly Zorn, Jungen and Magnis who talk into the camera: "I would say it's a terrible perversion of religion. ..."
Anyone who looks at the condemning doctrine of dogma and the trail of blood left by the churches over the centuries and compares this with the life of Jesus of Nazareth will very soon recognize who has perverted His teaching of peace and love for God and neighbor.
However, the case of Hettstadt becomes known beyond Bavaria's borders only at the end of 1992, when Pastor Wolfgang Behnk (see Chapter 8) replaced Friedrich Haack, who died in 1991, as the Lutheran Church's sect commissioner in Bavaria –

and discovers the church's influence on the media as a new field of work. On December 6, 1992, he is invited to the ZDF (a German public television station) women's program *Mona Lisa* – and in a film clip, the moderator introduces the desired manner of speaking: "The New Jerusalem should be created in the town of Hettstadt. Universal Life bought land here with huge financial means." Again, the same nonsense that one station takes over from another.

Some can do it even more primitively: "The sect Universal Life is spreading like an octopus there." (SAT 1, German TV, March 10, 1993); or Detlev Cosmann in the program "ZAK" of the *West German Broadcasting Corporation* (April 25, 1993): "And then New Jerusalem, the problem zone. A dozen sect houses, nothing more, so far. But it was meant to have been at least 86. ... And 1,500 to 2,000 sect members were supposed to have moved to Hettstadt to overturn the majority of the city council." Kamil Taylan and Ulrike Bremer from *Hessischer Rundfunk* in the television program "Diabolically Ripped Off" (June 22, 1993): *The sect Universal Life is taking over the country. It is building its own: The New Jerusalem ... In the beginning the new citizens were welcome in Hettstadt, but they isolated themselves. ...*

It is worth taking a closer look at this last sentence. Here, according to the principle of "Chinese Whispers" or "Telephone," a completely new story is already being invented: So now, the newcomers, themselves, are to blame, after all, they allegedly had their chance. Of course, that sounds better than: The local council stopped the development of the building lots and made sure that the new citizens were ostracized even before the first house was built.

A TV journalist from "Plus-Minus" (*ARD* – German public television channel, September 28, 1993) tells the television audience: "The promised land lies here … The sect Universal Life wants to build its New Jerusalem in the community of 2,800 souls … 300 Original Christians have already settled here." Which is already three times exaggerated – but who expects exact figures from a TV program that focuses on financial issues, anyway?

Even after the Original Christians had long since sold their building lots to the town (at the end of 1993), the *Hessian Broadcasting Company* still continues to expand the story: "In the Würzburg area, their disciples are in the process of buying up whole villages and undermining them." ("Underway in Hessian," February 1, 1994) This immediately finds eager imitators in its own house: "Most consumers are unlikely to be aware that behind this there is a real sect concern with a high-security farm, natural medicine clinics and a commercial center, just as little as the fact that the sect already controls entire villages near Würzburg." ("Trend," March 2, 1994)

Let us once again bring to mind whom this years long bombardment of public slander and mockery by the combined power of church, state and media, refers to: They are completely normal, peaceful people, whose only "offence" is that they want to distance themselves from the established churches and prefer instead to follow God, the Free Spirit, who comprehensively reveals to all interested people the teaching of love for God and neighbor through the prophetess and emissary of God, Gabriele. And it applies to the prophetess, herself, who brings His word, the eternal truth, to the Earth.

And in Hettstadt itself, the defamations show their effects again and again: An electrical box is sprayed with the slogan "UL Out!"; a young cherry tree in front of one of the Original Christian houses is broken off (after a letter to the editor from one of the residents of this house appeared in the newspaper the day before); at night, there is a storm of doorbell ringing and a half-empty beer bottle is hurled against a front door (after a fire department party).

The Truth Will Out

Nevertheless, a decline in media interest in Hettstadt could not be avoided, in the absence of new "sensations." The one who, in his pathological ambition, could hardly cope with this was Hans-Walter Jungen, who really enjoyed the role of nationwide "savior" from alleged Original Christian plans for world domination, who so gladly had led television teams to the houses and facilities of the Original Christians and who also offered passers-by a "financial tip" for the latest gossip. Who would still listen or pay attention to him now?

Together with the Protestant-Lutheran Pastor Mesner from the association "Citizens Watch Sects" (Chapter 7), he issued an invitation to a discussion event on February 1, 1996, at the Marienburg in Würzburg, with the topic: "Politicians, Stop Universal Life!" The main speaker was the Lutheran "sect expert" Wolfgang Behnk. Jungen insulted the Original Christian firms as a "pathological empire of companies" and called on the politicians present to answer the question: "How do the politicians intend to protect us from Universal Life?"

However, no one stood up who wanted to act as a muscleman in this "knock out the sect" game. The mayors present knew, after all, what the court had imposed on Waldemar Zorn in terms of constitutional neutrality – a brake that apparently worked, at least that evening. Which, in turn, shows that, despite numerous hair-raising verdicts in other cases, going to court is sometimes the only way for a minority to protect itself. A journalist from the *Main-Post* (February 3, 1996), however, did not care about such connections and wrote, listing the names of the elected officials present: "Politically disenchanted citizens are not born. They develop. ... Politicians talk a lot, but rarely give answers. ... On Thursday evening ... ...they didn't even take the floor. And yet there are still a few courageous citizens who take all the risks. ... These people have the right to be taken seriously by their representatives."

One could conclude from this populist tirade that the members of a religious minority have no right to be taken seriously by representatives of the people, journalists or judges, but solely their adversaries. And this is also how the *Main-Post* in particular reports on this topic.

Since the politicians did not want to play along (at least on this evening), a local Lutheran gave insight into his fascist thinking for the "sect" opponents present: He demanded of "the politicians": "Closure of the UL-owned kindergartens, closure of the UL-school, ban on membership recruitment, help for those who leave the sect, ... monitoring of the sect by the Office for the Protection of the Constitution and the appointment of a federal sect commissioner in the Ministry of the Interior." No one, least of all the journalists and politicians present, seemed to notice that with such demands, the fanatical Lutheran was more likely presenting himself and his cronies as an object of observation regarding anti-constitutional activities. ...

In any case, Mayor Zorn's career planning gained considerable "plus points" with the industrious agitation against the Original Christians. After he had successfully driven the Original Christian landowners out of Hettstadt and the self-inflicted blockade of the community development came to an end, he was made District Administrator of Würzburg in 1996 – and in 2008, as already mentioned, he was honored with the pontifical order.

A Bridge into the Future

For Gabriele, who wanted and wants to lead people solely to God, the Free Spirit – to God in us – who reveals the path of peace and love to a fulfilled life in God, who brings answers from the Kingdom of God to the great questions of humankind, and who gives people an understanding of a life in the Spirit of God, it was a very, very difficult time. In March 1988, in an interview, she said that all this had been announced to her in advance:

The Lord spoke of a modern persecution of Christians, in which spears, swords and lances are no longer taken up to massacre those of other faiths, but this time, with pen and paper. Thus, God spoke of the mass media, which in many cases is servile to the leaders of state and church, and in which is printed, unchecked, the untruths stated by these leaders. The Eternal One asked me thirteen years ago whether I wanted to endure this and much more for Him. I accepted the cross to carry it with Him – and have been carrying it for thirteen years already. I endure defamation, scorn and derision, disdain and malice. ...

To the sect commissioners and those who commissioned them, the institutions of the Catholic and Protestant Churches, who have poured their def-

amatory interpretations over me, and still do, who deliberately spread untruths, for often the falsities have already been clarified, I can only say:
Only when, from their heart and from their immortal being, they let God, our Lord in Christ, be effective and when in a few years, God has built up through them what He was capable of through His faithful ones and me, will I take seriously what they trumpet into the world.
Until they provide this proof, I will continue to carry the cross of defamation, and with many faithful ones, will continue to strive that the world be permeated and brightened by the Spirit of the Lord.

I will pray to God, our Father, and to our Redeemer, for my enemies as before, and I will ask: "Father, forgive them, for they know not what they do. They think they are acting against a person and they are acting against You. Have mercy on them, particularly when they enter into the soul realms and everything that they have done and caused becomes visible to them."

7. Attacks by the Church Against a Natural Medicine Clinic (1986-1997)

In the autumn of 1986 several Original Christians purchased the "Sanatorium Südspessart," located in a village near Marktheidenfeld called "Michelrieth." They remodeled it into a natural medicine clinic, which, until today, with its expert combination of natural and conventional medicine, attracts people seeking healing from all over the world. Life counseling talks are also offered. An important goal of the therapies is to activate the self-healing forces of the body.

It was a private sale, which meant that the village did not have to give permission, and even the church leaders, who usually have their ears everywhere, were totally surprised this time. But as soon as they learned that the people who had purchased the sanitarium were close to Universal Life, they pulled out all stops to stir up the villagers there against the "heretics."

On September 27, 1986, an article appeared in the local newspaper about the already accomplished sale of the sanatorium. And still on the same day, the seller, an eminent physician, received a nasty phone call from the village's Protestant-Lutheran pastor Wolfgang Bayer. In the traditionally Catholic Lower Franconia, Michelrieth and several of its small neighboring villages form a traditional Lutheran enclave, whose primary church is in Michelrieth, a village in the district of the town of Marktheidenfeld. And because the 27th of September was a Saturday, the pastor right away made use of the worship service on Sunday morning to stir up the villagers from the pulpit, saying: He is "very troubled, because the Homebringing Mission has bought its way in here."

One has to imagine this: Even before the residents of the small Spessart village could form their own opinion, they are already incited from the pulpit against the new citizens by the ecclesiastical authority. From the very first moment, the atmosphere is poisoned very personally by the man in the cassock who calls himself Christian.

The physicians of the new clinic responded to this unfriendly reception in their own way: They invited the Lutheran pastor as well as his Catholic colleague from Marktheidenfeld and the entire village population to an informational conversation on the very same Sunday afternoon. Those who didn't show up were the two clergymen. The Catholic priest had a message passed on: We will fight you. That is our duty. With this, he demonstrated that he was well versed in his Catechism. As already mentioned, in the official compilation of dogmas (Neuner and Roos, Margin Note 352) we can read:

... The Church ... must therefore with painstaking care remove and eradicate anything that is contrary to faith or in any way harmful to the salvation of souls ...

The clergymen do not follow the invitation; however, some citizens come who do not immediately react to the new situation with prejudices. So that even the last one understands what he is supposed to think, a few days later the "Clarifying Word" of the Würzburg deans is enclosed in the daily newspapers distributed in the village, a pamphlet full of distortions and slander (chapter 5). The highlight: The advertising sections of the newspapers know nothing about it! So how did this slanderous enclosure get into the daily newspaper? Apparently the clergymen used their connections to the women who deliver the newspaper. ...

But these are not the only relationships that one has at his disposition as a black-clad reverend. Three gentlemen from the district administration office suddenly turn up at the clinic and want to put a stop to the renovation of the building – although, as it soon turned out, all the documents and permits had been obtained. An inquiry reveals that the church had exerted the corresponding pressure. ...

Big Posse of "Sect Experts"

However, the conversion of the sanatorium into a natural medicine clinic could no longer be prevented. Then, the church leaders may well have thought, we'll at least continue to poison the local mood – and not only in Michelrieth, but in the entire town of Marktheidenfeld. At the end of May 1987, Pastor Haack from Munich and Count Magnis from Würzburg were invited to the Catholic parish hall of St. Laurentius in Marktheidenfeld. They brought along in their entourage two more "sect experts": Pastor Haberer from Nuremberg and Pastor Gandow from Berlin. Since Pastor Haack started in 1969, corresponding full-time positions in all German (Catholic) dioceses and (Lutheran) state Churches had meanwhile been installed.

> Yesterday – Inquisitor: Persecution all the way to murder
>
> Today – Sect Commissioner/Sect Expert: Persecution all the way to character assassination

Only visitors with a written invitation were admitted – not only because there was no interest in a discussion with Original Christians, the desire was to exclude them right from the start. Nevertheless, three Christ-friends managed to get into the hall and at least correct some of the defamations.

The person missing from the event was the head mayor of Marktheidenfeld, Dr. Leonhard Scherg (CSU); his absence was verbally abused by the organizers, because, unlike Hettstadt's Mayor Waldemar Zorn, he did not appear.

It was already this way during the Middle Ages: When the inquisitor came to the village, not only did the entire church congregation have to appear in the village church, but all dignitaries had to be present, as well. The inquisitor first spread lies and slander about the various religious dissenters, before he called on the people to denounce them. The countless lectures with which the "sect commissioners" of the churches misinform about "sects" up and down the country today resemble their medieval role models in every detail.

But this unfortunate "tradition" seems to be anything but embarrassing to the Church. Thus, shortly before his election as pope in March 2005, Cardinal Joseph Ratzinger declared in the *ARD* program "Kontraste": *But one must say the Inquisition was progress* ... .

And the Lutheran „sect pastor" Haack wrote, as mentioned: *If you are thinking Inquisition with me, you are right, of course.*

Back to Marktheidenfeld. The *Main-Post* (June 1, 1987) reported in detail and also with recognizable sympathy about the verbal abuses ("the greatest disgrace") of some visitors against the absent mayor and criticized that "far too often" questions had been directly addressed to the representatives of the Original Christians – probably because first-hand information could disturb the prescribed, one-sided reporting colored by the church.

On this evening, Pastor Haack insinuated that one must "set limits" against this "spiritistic sect" in its "will to implement ..." – whereby he very skillfully lowered the threshold for discriminating against a religious minority: Faith and religion were always "relative"; one could also "abuse" them – and if a "measure" against the newcomers "is not right, then a court will determine that." In plain language that means: The eighth commandment "You shall not bear false witness against your neighbor" does not matter to church representatives like Haack, likewise the spirit of the Constitution and the protection of minorities in a democracy – not to mention the commandment of neighborly love. As long as a court does not put a stop to them, (and the judges will think twice about this in view of the power of the Church), from their point of view everything is allowed.

He would like best, as Haack frankly says, if there was "somewhere still a piece of land where you can take land and build your temple and do your thing and not be hindered by the rest of the world."

A Lutheran pastor here unabashedly uses age-old xenophobic and fascist clichés. Who in the audience would know that a few decades earlier, namely, in the 1930s, the National Socialists thought out loud about the possibility of deporting all Jewish fellow citizens to Madagascar.

It is the same derisive speech in which – as already mentioned – Haack speaks of the "terror of harmony" and attributes the building of a Kingdom of Peace on this Earth to the devil – although the church Bibles often speak of the Kingdom of Peace. The Lutheran pastor has no trouble at all in denying his own Bible when it serves the persecution of heretics: "There is no mention of prophets and prophetesses in the New Testament." This is a brazen untruth – but it does not fit the concept of the modern inquisitor, who wants to mock a movement of faith that is based on the prophetic word of God that Paul mentions in 1 Corinthians (12:28), that God appointed prophets in the early churches. That Jesus, the Prince of Peace, announced the "Comforter" who "will guide you into all the truth" (John 16) – how else could this happen, but through the prophetic word? Or that Peter writes in his second letter (1:19): *We have the prophetic word made more sure. You do well to pay attention to it, as to a lamp shining in a dark place, until the day dawns and the morning star rises in your hearts.*

Catholic Horror Stories

Pastor Haack's Catholic Inquisition colleague, Count Magnis, also continued to stir up the mood against the Original Christians.
The big game hobby hunter demonized especially the vegetarian and – so literally – "life-endangering" nutritional teachings of Universal Life and presented as "proof" an "expert opinion" of a nutritionist, which the reader is already familiar with. (Chapter 3) However, this was the first time the followers of Jesus of Nazareth in the hall learned of this diabolical move.
But, not enough: According to the newspaper *Main-Echo* of June 1, 1987, Count Magnis also claimed that "some people had already died of

this dietary concept." A whopping lie! The followers of Jesus of Nazareth immediately called upon the judiciary system so as to have the Catholic persecution expert forbidden from spreading his mendacious opinions – which, in a temporary injunction, they initially succeeded in doing. But in the main proceedings at the Würzburg Regional Court, the modern inquisitor found a judge who was apparently loyal to the Church and who helped him save his neck at the last moment: He should simply put on record that he had not wanted to establish a direct connection between two deaths and the statements of Universal Life on the nutrition of people, and would not do so in the future. No sooner said than done – and the court case was quickly declared closed.

The fact that in those years, apart from exceptions, the judiciary system again and again gave the church inquisitors "administrative assistance," which was just barely legal, not only has to do with the religious education that Catholic and Protestant judges have gone through. Again and again, so-called "sect commissioners" of the churches were also invited to conferences by state academies of magistrates, and there, they were then allowed to cast aspersions on the religious "competition."

Regarding the alleged "deaths" caused by the dietary teachings of the Original Christians, we must look back again, into the year 1984. And likewise we find here an example of the unscrupulousness with which church representatives like Count Magnis manipulated the mass media in order to hatch and spread ever new mendacious stories.

Invented "Sensations"

On September 5, 1984, a report by the Würzburg *Germany Press Agency* correspondent Maria Speck appeared in several German daily newspapers, stating, among other things, that the city of Essen's "Sect Info" had filed a criminal complaint against the Homebringing Mission of Jesus Christ for negligent homicide following the death of a 42-year-old "sect adherent." It stated that "Obviously, the Christ healer had died due to the nutritional teachings propagated by the Homebringing Mission, according to which less and less should be eaten and drunk, in order to live like a 'divine spirit being.'" A downright lie.

As early as August 1984, West German newspapers spread similar reports, according to the *Bildzeitung Essen* (August 10, 1984): "Only fruits, grains, water – did a sect healer starve himself to death?" Here a "relative from Bochum" is quoted who is said to have stated: "Vlado died of malnutrition, lack of protein and fat." Heidemarie Cammans of the "Sect Info" adds: "A shocking example of where membership in sects can lead. We are bringing in the public prosecutor's office. ..." The *Westdeutsche Allgemeine* wrote (August 10, 1984): "Sect Info: Healer starves to death," the *Ruhr-Nachrichten*: "Sect member died of malnutrition," the *Bonner Express*: "Miracle healer starved himself to death for sect – 'Homebringing Mission killed him'" (August 11, 1984).

At this point, especially in view of the last outrageous insinuation, one must know that at this time, the Original Christians had hardly any experience with the press laws. But even if they had taken legal action against this outrageous lie – the slanderous sensation was already in people's heads.

What had really happened? Vladimir ("Vlado") P., who was born in Yugoslavia, ran a snack bar in Korbach in Central Hesse together with his wife and was active with the Homebringing Mission of Jesus Christ's prayer healers, died on August 4, 1984 of widespread tuberculosis, especially in the intestinal and peritoneal area. Until July 31, 1984, he had gone about his work as usual and had felt fine. Then he became ill, but initially thought it was a cold. When he arrived at the hospital, it was already too late. As the autopsy performed in Marburg showed, the tuberculosis had been encapsulated – otherwise it would have been found beforehand during the routine examinations that a snack bar operator has to undergo regularly.

And what about his diet? According to an affidavit from his wife, Vlado had been eating a totally normal and natural diet with sufficient amounts of nutrients until shortly before his death. He had already become a vegetarian five years before he got to know the Homebringing Mission. The "relative," who publicly attempted to blame the Homebringing Mission for his death, is a staff member of the "Sect Info" Essen! This allegedly "independent" institution is run by the Catholic Heidemarie Cammans and receives considerable public subsidies from tax monies. This employee is indeed distantly related to Vlado – she is the wife of a cousin of Vlado's wife. However, according to Mrs. P., she never visited her cousin in their home and saw him for the last time about eight months before his death – for about ten minutes! On this occasion, the woman had tried to convince him, "as if hysterical," that he was following a "wrong faith." ... Although she had had no contact with him at all since then, she claimed to the press that Vlado had lived on "water and grains" during the last months of his life – which was not true and which his wife also denied.

It is unbelievable, but true: In order to launch a sensational story against a religious minority in the tabloid press, the employee of a tax-subsidized reputation-damaging office even sacrifices the reputation of her own relatives! Imagine the unscrupulousness here, with which character assassination is inflicted upon a woman who has just lost her husband.

The Quotation Carousel Gathers Momentum

The Essen "Sect Information Center" even filed a criminal complaint against the Homebringing Mission with the public prosecutor's office in Kassel, stating that Vlado P. had "according to medical testimony, died from malnutrition, protein deficiency and fat loss due to the nutritional teaching declared by the Homebringing Mission. ..."

This serious claim is pure invention – every doctor knows that tuberculosis is not caused by a certain diet, but is an infectious disease.

But there is no mention of this in the notes of the Korbach hospital. They merely speak of an "extremely underweight condition" of Vlados, which is usually associated with consumption in its final stage. The charge, which was filed on the basis of a bold untruth, thus came to nothing.

However, the defamations made the rounds. The first newspaper reports were due to a press conference of the "Sect Info," at which Cammans presented her alleged "witness." The latter, in turn, was in contact with Count Magnis – and relied on "Sect Info" and Magnis. For his part, Count Magnis later repeatedly referred to the *dpa* (German Press Agency) report, which he had apparently helped to create himself – because the idea of the alleged "starvation" unmistakably bears his signature. **In this way, a veritable "quotation carousel" develops, which can be kept going for weeks and months with the help of gullible journalists.**

When a 55-year-old homeless and emaciated woman was found dead in a barn in southern Bavaria in the summer of 1985, the church-controlled tabloid press tried to blame this death on the Homebringing Mission of Jesus Christ – simply because long before her death, the woman had attended several public events of the Original Christians. The woman had remained Protestant until her death – but that did not interest the tabloids.

Magnis wanted to also use this invented sensation for his smear campaign against the *Naturklinik*. (Natural Medicine Clinic)

Unscrupulous damages to your reputation that keep going on and on! How do people fare, who advocate a peaceful world, peace between human beings, nature and animals, and who are then almost constantly insulted as "dangerous" outsiders? What is it like, especially for Gabriele, who brings to this Earth the wisdom of the heavens, the knowledge about the healing of the soul and the self-healing powers in the human being, when almost daily such and similar lies assault her? The soul knows about its divine mission and fulfills it day after day – but the person must come to terms with all this and endure it.

The teachings of wisdom from the heavens are indeed dangerous – namely, for the claims to power and hegemony of the cassock wearers of today. And these were also defended tooth and nail by the big-game, heretic hunter Magnis, with poison and bile, and with the entire arsenal of wickedness and malice that the Vatican institution has accumulated and practiced over all the centuries.

But when he himself later became ill, the same Count Magnis, who at every opportunity throughout the years had demonized Universal Life and the businesses founded by the Original Christians, as a pitiful old man, he asked to be cared for by an Original Christian nursing service. However, right up to his death (2004), he did not apologize for his evil slander. The Original Christians referred him to Catholic institutions. Why he did not choose this path of his own accord remains his secret. Did he know against whom he had fought all those years? Yet others also helped themselves to this arsenal of malice. The topic of health is very popular among church slanderers, because it literally gets under people's skin.

"Driven to Suicide ..."

On April 29, 1992, a sensational article appeared in the news magazine *Stern* with the headline: "Satanic Sects – They Preach Salvation and Lead to Ruin – Miracle Healers and False Prophets are More Popular in Germany than Ever Before." Among other things, the story of Michaela S. is described here, who used gasoline to burn herself to death. The journalists Daniela Horvath and Joachim Rienhardt claim that she "fell into the clutches of one of the most dangerous – in the opinion of renown experts – German sects: Universal Life. She had been treated several times in their clinic 'House of Health' in Michelrieth near Würzburg."

According to *Stern*, Hans-Walter Jungen from Hettstadt near Würzburg claims: "They are so dangerous because they keep seriously ill people from going to the doctor. Some sick people are driven directly into insanity," and *Stern* adds: " ... like Michaela S., who burned herself to death. ... The followers of such charlatans come in droves and not only to Universal Life." Under a picture of Michaela, it says: "Driven to suicide: Michaela S."

What had really happened? In 1988, the young woman had actually been to the *Naturklinik* for treatment, but had not at all concerned herself with the teaching of Universal Life. At first, the clinic had tried to help her with her difficulties, which obviously nobody had noticed before, but then, because she obviously had massive psychological problems, they referred her to a specialist for mental disorders. However, he had dismissed her as not suicidal. Shortly afterward, the suicide took place. Michaela's relatives had not noticed anything unusual that day and had a positive impression of her. In subsequent investigations, no blame was placed on the doctors who treated her at the *Naturklinik*. Rienhardt, however, based his defamations on a personal interpretation of the events, which an acquaintance of the deceased, apparently in search of a scapegoat, had passed on to church authorities, who then promptly passed this version on to the press.

The story is indeed a scandal – especially in the way journalists unscrupulously abuse the drama of a sick young woman to put the blame on a minority faith.

The Original Christians defended themselves this time – and were proved right, although nine months later. On January 11, 1993, in the second instance, the Higher Regional Court of Bamberg forbade *Stern* to make the allegations that Michaela S. had been driven to suicide and that sick people were driven to insanity. Furthermore, *Stern* is no longer allowed to report about Universal Life under the heading "Satanic sects."

Despite this success and a counterstatement printed in *Stern* (July 2, 1992) – the effects of such an article are devastating. Such publications serve modern Inquisition in ostracizing those of other faiths – with great success.

What so-called experts say is simply believed; what is then written in the newspaper is taken at face value and an enemy stereotype is built up in the minds of the populace, and this has consequences in all spheres of life. Following this article, a number of newspapers and newspaper publishers refused to accept Universal Life's advertisements. In a telephone booth in Kredenbach, a neighboring village of Michelrieth, an enlarged copy of the article was hung up a few days after its publication, with the inscription: "How long will you put up with this?"

The Bamberg court decision presumably led to the fact that since then, reputation-damaging people in the Churches package their untruths more cleverly and usually no longer refer to specific "cases," at all.

Among the members of every community of faith, as in society as a whole, there are suicides, crime and human error. In Germany about 12,000 people die by committing suicide every year, the majority of whom are Catholics and Protestants. The Catholic city of Würzburg, in particular, is statistically considered a "stronghold of suicide" – with up to 29 percent higher suicide rates than the national average. (*Main-Post*, July 3, 1999) Scientists attribute this to the "conservative, strongly Catholic milieu," which "makes life difficult, sometimes impossible, for those who leave" the Church. Every day, Catholics and Protestants abuse children, kill family members – but no newspaper reads: "Catholic caused family drama" or: "Protestant driven to death" or: "Member of the large Vatican sect commits suicide." With minorities, however, a connection is immediately fabricated – or, as in this case, is far-fetched.

Unconstitutional Slogans

Back to the *Naturklinik* in Michelrieth. There, the sexton of the Lutheran village church founded a special "citizens' initiative" against the followers of the Nazarene, which, however, for most of the time had hardly any members apart from himself. But at times, this was enough to bring the emotions in the village into quite a turmoil – albeit with demands that demonstrate a very strange understanding of democracy.

At the end of 1992, the sexton collected signatures under the motto: "No new building sites in Michelrieth – ... no further property transactions on a municipal basis with Universal Life – ... no 'Universal' local spokesman or councilor."
The zealous Lutheran (and also those who signed the petition) seemed to be unaware that all these

demands are unconstitutional, for a town is not even allowed to ask someone buying property beforehand what his religion is – nor may it reject a candidate for public office (for which, by the way, no supporter of Universal Life has ever applied in Marktheidenfeld until today) merely because of his faith.

The Lutheran sexton also presented plans on which all the houses that were occupied by "them there" were especially marked. People like him obviously lack any sense of injustice as to whose footsteps they are following, with such "blacklists."

In a flyer, the Original Christians reminded the people that 60 years earlier, signs had been put up at the entrance to German towns with the inscription: "Jews live in the following houses." And that in the 1920s, Nazi groups called for Jews to be forbidden from acquiring land, to be denied their civil rights – which later actually took place in the "Nuremberg Laws."

At least, the local politicians did not let themselves be taken in by the hysteria of the heretic hunters. The mayor of Marktheidenfeld, Dr. Leonard Scherg (CSU), attested to the Lutheran that his demands were contrary to the Constitution. During the following time, Dr. Scherg also remained a favorite bogeyman to fanatical representatives of the Church, because he acted in "too lax a manner" against "the sect," and, for example, did not prevent several followers of Jesus of Nazareth from being able to open a commercial center in 1992 in Altfeld, a district of Marktheidenfeld. Thereby, Scherg, who has nothing to do with Universal Life, merely upheld the Constitution. When in 1997 the Lutheran "sect expert" Wolfgang Behnk, who will be discussed shortly (Chapter 8), publicly accused Scherg of not having prevented the settling of enterprises by sympathizers of Universal Life, Scherg made it clear that here, too, the properties had been sold by private individuals and the city had had no opportunity to object.

Even the Deceased Are Still Persecuted

It is deeply shocking that people in the present time and in a free democratic constitutional state suffer from such character assassination campaigns – only because they are not Catholic or Protestant. The persecution mania against the followers of Jesus of Nazareth even goes so far that not even deceased Original Christians are tolerated in "Lutheran" territory. As late as 1986, immediately after the acquisition of the clinic by Original Christians had become known, Pastor Bayer and his church council changed the cemetery statutes of the Michelrieth cemetery, which is operated by the Lutheran Church, and determined that from now on "solely Lutheran and Catholic burials should be permitted" there. The family of the 46-year-old Michelrieth citizen Irmtraud M., a former Protestant who died of cancer in August 1988, was the first to be affected by this: For the burial they had to go to neighboring Altfeld, where the nearest town cemetery is located. For the denominational "God's acre" in Michelrieth, the medieval heretic laws immediately apply, according to which "the remains of heretics" have no place there!

Also the Original Christian Aloisia S., who died at the end of 1991 at the age of 68, was not allowed to be buried in Michelrieth. In a press release, the Original Christians pointed out that logically, Jesus of Nazareth would also have no chance to be buried in Michelrieth – after all, He was neither Protestant nor Catholic!
And that, by the way, would also be consistent.
In his story of the "Grand Inquisitor", Dostoyevsky has the "Grand Inquisitor" say this to Christ: *Perhaps it is Thy will to hear it from my lips. Listen then: We are not working with Thee, but with him [with the adversary of God], that is our mystery.* And at the end he sends the returned Messiah out of the city: *Go, and come no more.*

Modern Inquisition Needs Modern Technology

In the meantime, the Lutheran pastor in Michelrieth had died. In the eyes of some of the Lutheran church superiors, his young successor had apparently acted too weakly against the "heretics." Therefore, the neighboring dean of Lohr, Michael Wehrwein, made sure that the village of Michelrieth with 500 souls temporarily got a second pastor, Michael Fragner – a completely unusual occurrence – who should primarily deal with the controversy over the "sect." Thus, in a series of television appearances, the new inquisitor Fragner immediately complained in a theatrical manner that the village had been almost completely bought up by the "sect." (This was no such thing.) As a result, church-affiliated journalists were only too happy to pounce on the small village and set up their cameras, preferably directly in front of the clinic entrance, so that neither employees nor patients could go in and out without being filmed.

What church authorities – also in relation to the state – presume to do, in fact, unfortunately, can still presume to do, is unbelievable: Fragner set up an Internet site especially for his attacks. For this, he took the name of the village instead of using the name of the church community, that is, he misused it – an obvious impertinence, because according to the law, the political communities always have first access to village names. Fragner now used this website as a campaign platform against Universal Life, where he accumulated all the available ammunition of poison against these dropouts from the churches.

Even the medieval Inquisition was always based on a preferably comprehensive "data collection" of denunciations, informers' reports and interrogation protocols, which were passed on in copies everywhere in Europe, even as far away as the American colonies – so that it was almost impossible for heretics to escape the meshes of this network by fleeing. It is only logical that the modern Inquisition of our days continues this "work" by means of computer technology.

When after only three years, Pastor Fragner left the parish of Michelrieth to take up a parish post in the district of Würzburg, he by no means ceased his activity as a compiler and postman of vilifications, but continued it – still under the village name! – from his new place of residence.
Universal Life then called upon the town of Marktheidenfeld to take legal action to reclaim the In-

ternet address, which looked like an official parish address, from the Lutheran Church. But in an extremely narrow vote, the city council voted this down by a thin margin in February 2005. Apparently, the narrow majority didn't want any trouble with the Church, even though it had obviously put itself in the wrong. And the court, called upon later by some local citizens, did, indeed, rule that the city could reclaim the site – but that it could not be forced to do so by court order. Thus, the rights of a minority for protection against discrimination fell by the wayside once more.

> **Inquisition:**
> Persecution and eradication through lies, slander, discrimination, torture and murder of all those who do not submit to the prevailing religious caste.

The Consequences of the Incitement

The fanatical opponents of the Original Christians, in association with the reputation damaging people in the Church, had achieved one goal in the Michelrieth area, as well, at least for a time: the incitement of a part of the population. This can be clearly seen in individual reactions.

In the years 1987 to 1989, for example, the *Naturklinik* was repeatedly the target of telephone terrorism. The calls were mostly made at night; in some cases, the caller knew the extension numbers and reached the rooms of completely unsuspecting patients. "You should all be killed," he said; "you should all disappear"; "you should all be gassed," etc.

Children in the neighboring village of Marienbrunn were forbidden by their parents to play with the children of Original Christians. On their way to school, children of Original Christians were called "sect pigs," knocked to the ground and kicked.

At the beginning of 1993, a stone cross made of red sandstone which Original Christians had erected in Kredenbach on the grounds of an Original Christian farm, was knocked down with an axe; a wooden cross erected in the same place as a reminder was also damaged.

In the night of September 5, 1994, 60 bales of straw were set on fire in the fields of the same farm – that night, a "boozy" and merry CSU beer party was held in nearby Esselbach, opposite the Original Christian school.

This and other things were obvious consequences of the church smear campaigns against fellow citizens, whose sole "offence" was to have the wrong prayer book … .

Politicians Before the Cart Of the Church Slanderers

Politicians also took part in the smear campaign against the *Naturklinik*. At the beginning of December 1996, a former clinic patient is presented at an event of the SPD (Social Democratic Party) in Wertheim-Höhefeld.
She reports "experiences" she had five years earlier during a stay at the clinic: During a treatment, she had become "woozy," she felt "observed" (which is certainly desirable for a clinic with regard to the well-being of its patients), someone wanted to imperceptibly "co-opt" her. It is odd, however, that for a long time after her stay, the woman had spoken only positively about the clinic. A "drop-

out counselor" had "helped" her to break away from the "sect" – whereby she was never active with the Original Christians in any way, hardly anyone even knew her or had contact with her! One can well imagine how an inwardly unstable person first reacts euphorically to something new, but also can very easily be "convinced" of the opposite again. And one can only wonder how a democratic party and the media can talk up such unspecific and nebulous accusations into a kind of "drop-out report." Carla Bregenzer, a member of the state parliament for the SPD in Baden-Wurttemberg, is in charge of this issue. She can be described as the "spokesperson for sectarian policy of the SPD state parliamentary group" and apparently wants to make a name for herself with this topic.

At this point, church "experts" such as the Bavarian sect commissioner "Pastor" Behnk already handed over a part of their defamation work to compliant politicians. At the end of 1994, Behnk had given the impression in the town of Kreuzwertheim that Universal Life preferred to listen to cassettes rather than receive medical treatment. It is not surprising that even government agencies include such slander in their reports – for example, the state government of Schleswig-Holstein in a "Report on the Activities of Sects" (1995), in which it is said about Universal Life: "Newly revealed healing methods are taking the place of conventional medicine." Or in Berlin, where in 1997 there is speculation: "For the believing follower there is the potential danger that in case of illness he will seek specialist medical treatment too late or not at all, in order not to expose himself to the suspicion of a lack of steadfast faith."

With such false assertions, one wants to discredit the medical institutions run by Original Christians as well as the Original Christian healing through prayer and faith, both of which are offered completely independent of each other. Original Christians may repeat ever so often that they also use conventional medical methods in their clinic and that they expressly point out with every healing by faith: "Attending this event does not by any means exclude a visit to a doctor or alternative practitioner" – and in spite of this, the false assertions are deliberately repeated.
In 1999, the Administrative Court of Würzburg also determined there were no grounds for these defamations:
Inquiries of the court at the government of Lower Franconia, subject area human medicine, regarding the naturopathic clinic operated by the community of faith Universal Life, did not result in any findings

that indicated a danger to patients. According to information from the government of Lower Franconia, there are also no known individual cases in which a late or delayed consultation of a physician has led to endangerment of life and limb of individuals. ... Purely naturopathic therapies are applied in only 10 to 15% of cases. This fact demonstrates that the followers of Universal Life also make use of healing methods recognized by conventional medicine. The theoretically existing possibility that a credulous follower of Universal Life could in practice actually forego medical help and therefore put his life in danger must therefore be regarded as speculation.

One might add that the greatest danger to which a follower of Universal Life is subjected is the ecclesiastical character assassination that is spread about him and his faith, and the defamations that have been ruthlessly spread, without considering the damage this causes to respectable citizens.

8. The Modern Inquisitor Wolfgang Behnk (1991-99)

At the end of 1990, when Pastor Haack died at the age of only 55 years, Bishop Scheele of Würzburg honored his "merits":
For the Catholics of the Bishopric his death was a "painful loss." With "rare clarity, he had recognized the emerging extreme ideologies as a challenge for all churches of the apostolic creed," as the Episcopal eulogy is reported in the Catholic *Volksblatt* (March 15, 1991). And in the *Evangelisches Sonntagsblatt* (March 31, 1991) the "expert" is also broadly honored: "Countless youth, as well as adult women and men owe to Pastor Haack's well-founded work of clarification that they have not fallen victim to groups that selfishly exploit their religious longings to the detriment of the person."
What, for example, may the countless men and women have thought about this, who had been abused by priests and pastors as children or young people?

Through his high church council, the Lutheran bishop of Bavaria, Johannes Hanselmann, had long before informed a Protestant fellow citizen who criticized the sect commissioner that the state church council was "very grateful to Haack for his service." And through a church council, Hanselmann later also had Haack's successor and his "committed service" honored – for the latter should indeed make every effort to reach and even surpass his predecessor's level of vilification.

Wolfgang Behnk, 42, Protestant-Lutheran pastor in Gerbrunn, a suburban parish of Würzburg, became Haack's successor. Thus, he already knew the activities of Universal Life. However, when he was appointed Haack's successor in June 1991, hardly anyone had any idea how ambitiously he would strive to outshine his predecessor in intensity regarding the unscrupulous work of persecution. On the contrary: The rather cool Northern German is at first markedly relaxed and communicative. He appears without notice at the House of Universal Life, allegedly to "make contact," and then tells the *Main-Post* that he does not want to act like his predecessor, who for many was "too polemic" and who was often "stingy with facts" – no: His style would be "argumentative and dialogical"; he wanted to "openly seek dialogue with the groups and movements," because he was "no inquisitor"; he practiced "tolerance," and did not want to "aggressively demand agreement or threaten with deprivation of salvation," but merely "provide help for the formation of judgment, show facts, but the judgment has to be made by everyone himself." He stated that the Protestant Church wanted to "convince by its faith and by actions that follow from it, not by institutional or state power."

Whether Behnk actually meant this honestly, or whether it was all just a socially acceptable lie from the start, is anyone's guess. In any case, to familiarize himself intensively with his new "field of expertise," he first spent several months in the extensive archives of his predecessor, who had died shortly before. Since science teaches that no energy is lost, everyone can vividly imagine that his "spirit" could have still been more or less physically present. Moreover, Behnk could hardly escape the "constraints" and expectations of his regional church.

A modern inquisitor can do his dirty work with kid gloves or even with the truth, just as little as his colleagues in the Middle Ages. And that was exactly what he had been chosen for.
Thus, it came about that with his first public appearances, following his official inauguration in December 1991, Wolfgang Behnk thoroughly gave lie to his own announcements regarding a "change

of style." Again and again, he came up with particularly pointed, even malicious formulations, which he literally hammered into his listeners – be they journalists or churchgoers.

Who Is Afraid of Selfless Love?

In December 1991, for example, Behnk published an article in the *Münchner Merkur* (December 16, 1991) under the heading "Guru Made Rich Booty." According to Behnk, Universal Life is a "sect" that tries to "draw young people into its nets." He therefore warns against "letting oneself be impressed by the cordiality of the sect members: This friendliness is a hard-hitting investment that will be reclaimed with interest and compound interest."
"If I see someone who is friendly, he can't be so bad." – spontaneous perceptions and the emotional ability to judge were suspect to inquisitors at all times – and they still are today. After all, they could lead to people encountering "heretics" or "witches" in an unbiased way – and in the end, even feel compassion when they fall into the clutches of the inquisitor.
In the past, the inquisitor would have said: If someone seems particularly friendly to you, beware: it could be a witch or a sorcerer who wants

to cast a spell on you. Today, the modern inquisitor says: They just want your money.

Moreover, Behnk has obviously not found anything concrete that the Original Christians could be accused of – no violations of the law or the like – so he resorts to such ominous threats. And like many of his predecessors, he uses catchy images of the enemy: "Sects" are "like a poisonous mushroom: seen from the outside, they are beautiful, but if you bite into them, you recognize the poison."
"The Poisonous Mushroom": This was the name of a "Stürmer book" published in 1938 by the National Socialist hate paper *Der Stürmer*, in which "German youth were to be taught knowledge of Jewish things." Even though the persecution of Jews in the Third Reich cannot be compared with the persecution of religious minorities today, the analogies in the argumentation to damage reputation are frequently astounding.

Behnk namely combines the inflammatory slogans of Haack and Magnis into a new hostile image of Universal Life, which, detached from reality, he continues to expand and, with unrestrained polemic, gets into the media during the following weeks and months: Universal Life is a "financially strong artificial religion," "a totalitarian organization built up with admirable legal finesse," which is led by a woman" (here follow insults of such a low standard that we will not repeat them), "who, with her revelations ... has built up a merciless system of self-redemption, which leads people seeking help into dependency."

All those who know Gabriele are appalled – how a pastor who calls himself Christian can turn the truth upside down to such an extent, and has no inhibitions about publicly defaming Gabriele, a selfless, compassionate woman of integrity, in such a way.
And how does Gabriele react? She answers by writing the following in a publication of the Original Christians:
Someone who judges has already condemned himself; he has become his own judge. Between Mr. Behnk ... and myself there has never been one single face-to-face encounter. And we have never exchanged a word with each other, either. His assertion ... does not touch me.
With such and similar slanderous speeches his predecessor, "Pastor" Haack, has already argued and tried to provoke me. He did not succeed. And neither will Mr. Behnk succeed, because I know who sent Mr. Haack and Mr. Behnk, and I know where Mr. Haack went and where Mr. Behnk will go.

With Mr. Behnk, you can clearly recognize the inspirer. His arguments and defamations are very similar to those of "Pastor" Haack, whose manuscripts and notes he studied for a long time. ... They have tried to sully me with all the colors of the Catholic and Protestant Churches, primarily with the substance of the color of both institutions: black. I have not defended myself – and I will not defend myself – nor have I let myself, and will not let myself, be provoked, no matter what is poured over the work of the Eternal. With the power of selfless love, I have overcome ... "Pastor" Haack. With the power of selfless love I will also overcome Mr. Behnk.

Dear reader, if you wish, pause for a moment. What do you understand by "selfless love"? Perhaps you are thinking of the love that is also spoken of in the Bible of the churches: Love is patient and kind, it bears all things, hopes all thing, endures all things, is not envious. ...
And how did Wolfgang Behnk react? Instead of thinking about himself and his character assassination attacks, he took up Gabriele's words and tried to use them against her, by imputing that in this case "overcoming with selfless love" could only mean "leading to death." – How did he come up with such thoughts? Because Pastor Haack, whom

Gabriele had included in this sentence, had died. So the pastor was obviously afraid of selfless love – perhaps, because he does not know it? Or was he merely concerned, in the old inquisitor manner, to immediately use everything that flows out of the mouth of a "heretic" against them again? Be it as it may: Radio stations like *Bavarian Broadcasting* or *Antenna Bavaria* willingly took up the pastor's odd "logic" and described Gabriele's statements as a "death oracle" or even "death curse."

We will see shortly who actually delivered a "death oracle" of himself at the time. ...

The Church Describes Itself

As with the modern inquisitors that have appeared so far, Behnk's accusations against the Original Christians are also brimming with projections: "Merciless" – what about the world of thoughts of Behnk himself? And what about the attitude of his church founder, Martin Luther, toward his fellow human beings, for example, the peasants, Jews, the so-called witches? The founder of the allegedly "Christian" Lutheran Church "mercilessly" spouted whole tirades of hatred against dissidents, for instance: "Therefore, let everyone who can smite, slay and stab!" against the peasants, or: "Such a despairing, evil, poisonous thing it is with these Jews who these 1400 years have been and still are our plague, pestilence and all misfortune."

"Financially strong" – that is without doubt the Lutheran Church; an "artificial religion," too, if one considers how far it has distanced itself from the original Christianity and how many pagan ideas it has adopted, beginning with the "expiatory sacrifice" that had to be offered to an allegedly "cruel God" in the figure of Jesus of Nazareth.

And the "legal cunning" – Behnk himself applies this by formulating his cumulative load of insults, vilifications and untruths so cunningly that they just barely pass as "expressions of opinion" with the mostly Catholic or Lutheran judges.

Someone who feels exposed by criticism, but absolutely refuses to change, fights in his neighbor exactly what he still is himself – that is his projection. *Who* has been leading "people seeking help into dependency" for centuries? *Who* then draws "young people into his nets" by already subjecting infants to baptism – thus forcing them into a system from which they can escape only under the threat of "eternal damnation"?

But how many people are capable of seeing through these connections straightaway? How many can still let themselves be lulled by "tradition" and be impressed by solemn demeanor, by rituals, ceremonies and vestments, and by the socially acceptable lies of alleged "experts"? How many are still convinced that a pastor or priest cannot lie, nor deliberately and maliciously disparage his neighbor?

The reader now has, if he wants, a key in hand with which he can correctly assess the further flood of reproaches and mendacious opinions that is only partially passed on here. Whereby the cited vilifications are always only the tip of an iceberg – an iceberg that is still, even after years, drifting through the ocean of public opinion and on which countless media representatives and politicians still run aground.

The distortions and lies that Behnk and his ilk have spread over the years through all available channels continue to haunt the Internet, and through church and state film distributors, reach even the last student in religion classes.
Thus, the incitement propagates underground, even if it appears only sporadically in the daily press. How many decades will it take, until minds are free of it again, and are able to form their own, impartial picture?

"Death Oracle" – a New Dimension to Damaging Reputation

Back to Wolfgang Behnk and his campaign against the followers of Jesus of Nazareth. The insinuations, speculations, mendacious opinions and projections continued.

He claimed, for example, that in Universal Life "any critical ability is excluded, and the formation of conscience is no longer possible." Perhaps he reckoned with the fact that only the fewest people know that the religious founder of his own church, Luther, denied the human being not only the ability to be critical but even simply denied his free will – and thus, the possibility to follow the voice of his conscience. As already mentioned, according to Luther, the human being is either predestined by God for evil or for good. Incidentally, Behnk wrote his doctoral thesis on precisely this central teaching of Luther's, so he knew it very well.

Behnk also used every opportunity to portray the followers of Jesus of Nazareth analogously as dangerous, unpredictable, "crazy" outsiders. When on April 19, 1993, 81 people died in Waco, Texas (USA) when the ranch of the "Davidians" was stormed by the police, he had no scruples exploiting the tragic events that had played out in the USA for his campaign against Universal Life. He had the following report distributed via the *Protestant-Lutheran Press Agency*:

A mass suicide such as that of followers of the Davidian sect in Waco, Texas, is also possible in Germany, according to the Munich sect commissioner, Pastor Wolfgang Behnk. "This danger exists as soon as people move into the sphere of influence of a closed ideology in which any ability to criticize is excluded and the formation of conscience is no longer possible." ...
If the ideology of the sect is permeated with apocalyptic expectations of the end time and there is a psychological dependency on a leading figure, the possibility of mass suicide is given as soon as the sect leader sees her- or himself in a hopeless situation. ...
"If suicide is demanded as the last consequence, then everyone, like the lemmings, follows her or his command without criticism." In this context Behnk warned against the group "Universal Life," which wants to establish a "Christ-State New Jerusalem" near Würzburg."

And yet, Wolfgang Behnk knew the Original Christian writings – he had studied them extensively and therefore knew very well that suicide is out of the question for a person who has accepted the teachings of the Christ of God through Gabriele. The Original Christians and everyone who knows them and the Original Christian teachings were stunned: What drives a person who calls himself a "Christian," indeed, even a "pastor" and "pastoral worker," to take such action against his fellow human beings? – The answer comes from history: Since the beginning of time, the caste of priests has been the enemy of the prophets of God.

Incitement on Prime Time ...

The mass media were not interested in the truth – they reacted immediately, eagerly took up the "sensational news" that wasn't one, and sent droves of sensation-hungry journalists to the area around Würzburg to take a look at the "Waco in Lower Franconia."
A film team even rented a helicopter to film a farm inhabited by followers of the Nazarene. According to their own statement, they had received the determining tip-off from Pastor Behnk.
A modern inquisitor not only invents slander – he also makes sure that it is spread widely. Behnk actually succeeded in advancing new dimensions of damage to reputation that even his prede-

cessor had not yet achieved. He had created the death oracle himself that he wanted to impute to Gabriele – and with that, he promptly made it into the television channels, namely, nationwide.

What came of this could be seen for example in "ZAK" (*WDR*, April 25, 1993). There, the moderator talked about the "pathetic deaths" in Waco, and in the same breath, about Universal Life. A very similar approach was taken by *Pro 7* ("Die Reporter" May 9, 1993), where even the murders of Charles Manson's gang (1969), and the mass death of the "Peoples Temple" in Guyana (1978) were shown, before the Original Christian establishments were brought into the picture – and Pastor Behnk appeared in the picture at the end of the clip.

An inflammatory article in the local daily press is bad enough – a nationwide evening television program – and these were only two examples of several – with sensational, frenetic sequences of pictures and somber background music has an even stronger effect on the subconscious. In contrast to a newspaper, a text spoken quickly to this can hardly be reflected upon; often, only fragments of associations and prejudices remain.
One has to imagine this: Upright citizens, who have never done anything wrong, are put on the

same level as mass murderers, criminals and mass suicides by means of suggestive pictures.

... and Its Effects

How did the people fare, peaceful fellow citizens, who were literally besieged on this farm for days on end by TV journalists with camera teams from all over Germany, who wanted to film with wanton sensationalism the "Waco in Lower Franconia" – which did not even exist?
How do people feel in a house, in a company, when they are suddenly asked: Is it true that among you the next mass suicide is imminent?
How do people feel when a helicopter suddenly roars low over the property? What is it like for the animals living on the farm – horses, cattle, chickens, cats, dogs – that are totally frightened and terrified, and want to flee in panic?

What is it like for people who can no longer move about freely and without concern because they constantly have to reckon with the next attack? How do mothers feel who no longer dare to leave their homes with their children without fear of being pursued or harassed by journalists and camera teams – accompanied, of course, by sect commissioners? Even at night, they were no longer safe from being stopped in their vehicles and immediately subjected to the harsh glare of headlights.

The rabble-rousing at prime time, which kept up for months and years, did not remain without effect on many viewers, as well, who then wanted to vent their fears and aggressions, stirred up by such broadcasts, on the followers of Jesus of Nazareth.

After such a program, that very evening, a man calls the rooms of a meeting place of the Original Christians in Nuremberg, where an event is taking place, and shouts into the receiver: "Get lost, you pack of swine!" The next day, a passer-by who is offered a flyer from Universal Life in Munich is outraged: "I saw the program and I hope you burn soon!" The most scurrilous insults are to be heard on answering machines of Original Christians and read on faxes. Original Christians are insulted in public as "pestilence" (Ingolstadt), as "fascists" (Berlin), "worse than Hitler" (Darmstadt), as "gang of criminals" (Marktheidenfeld). It was said that they were "similar to the Davidians in Texas," that they should be "forbidden," "gassed" (Frankfurt) or "locked up in prison," "shot" (Würzburg). There is a bomb threat in the House of Universal

Life in Würzburg (December 28, 1993). In Tübingen, a woman goes to the market master with an article in which Behnk is quoted and demands that the "UL stand" must be "marked accordingly." In Lower Franconia, village inhabitants are insulted by neighbors because they shop "from them."

At least just as characteristic of the effect of the films are the statements of less raving contemporaries: for example, customers in Christ-enterprises, who "can't believe at all" that "this nice shop" is also part of it. Others understand the programs as a call to take the law into their own hands: In Darmstadt, a showcase of Universal Life is torn out and dragged away; in Singen, a showcase is smeared; in Arnstein near Würzburg, car tires are punctured in front of the houses of Original Christians; in Michelrieth, antennas are bent, and lamps in the yard of the Original Christian school are smashed.

What weighs more heavily, however, are the unspoken thoughts, the prejudices fixed in people's minds, the effects of which can be retained for years. In order to reinforce these, some of the inflammatory broadcasts are spread until today via church and state media offices, shown in schools during religious instruction or, (as in Würzburg) recommended to students studying pedagogy.

The Perpetrators See Themselves as the "Persecuted"

When the Original Christians do not let themselves be intimidated by such television broadcasts and partly refer to them in flyers and denounce the church affiliation of the radio stations, some of the journalists promptly present themselves as "persecuted": In their residential area, a small village, they complain in a lachrymose voice that flyers were distributed in which they are labelled "rabble-rousers." Today's inquisitors and their henchmen are extremely sensitive. The fact that through such actions (and this is the sole reason why they are made) they could get an inkling of what they are doing to others, does not occur to them.

Thereby, the fraudulence of such church inflammatory slogans has long been proven. Around the farm, which at the time was vilified as the residence of potential suicides, a flourishing oasis of life has developed during the years that followed. Original Christians have put into practice an agricultural concept from the Spirit of God – peaceable farming, out of respect for nature, without manure and slurry and without any chemicals. Hedges stretch for kilometers through a previously completely bare, dead agricultural landscape. Forests, field trees and shrubs, wetlands and stone biotopes provide habitats for hundreds of animal species, including many endangered birds, butterflies or bats. Here, peace reigns among people, nature and animals. A unique nature reserve has been created, a Land of Peace, whose concept has received worldwide attention and imitation, among others places in Africa.

But a person whose profession is to damage reputations will not admit that his defamations had and still do not have the least to do with reality – especially since with his sensational reports in the media he gets a lot of exposure. For him, what he is doing to his fellow human beings with this is hardly worth thinking about – not only to those whom he pillories, but also to those whom he thereby prevents from forming their own opinion. Wolfgang Behnk reacts all the more sensitively when it comes to his own person. When during the summer of 1996, Original Christians distribute flyers in his residential area, requesting that his neighbors appeal to his conscience regarding his character assassination activities, he pulls out all stops to defend himself against the "smear campaign." The *Protestant-Lutheran Press Agency* is prudently silent about the actual background as such – the Protestant-Lutheran mud-slinging against a minority.

Incitement on All Television Channels

In any case, the highly influential inquisitors use all channels – the Original Christians, on the other hand, usually only have the distribution of flyers as a countermeasure to reach the public. Behnk and his colleagues of calumny can be seen everywhere, from the *ARD* "Tagesthemen" (July 2, 1996) to the *SAT 1* "Frühstücksfernsehen" (October 12, 1994) – and only rarely do they fail to point out Universal Life as a "particularly dangerous sect." On almost all talk shows, from Hans Meiser (April 12, 1994, March 4, 1996), Ulrich Meyer (October 11, 1994) and Jürgen Fliege (December 14, 1994), to Bärbel Schäfer (February 20, 1997) and Arabella Kiesbauer (September 10, 1998), the Original Christians are given a raw deal.

And regardless of whether the Sun Templars die (1994), the AUM sect undertakes an attack in the Tokyo subway (1995) or 50 "Heaven's Gate" followers commit suicide in California (1997) – Behnk is always on hand on these occasions to give an oracle about a possible mass suicide of the Original Christians. In order to protect himself legally, he makes a seemingly dismissive statement at the beginning: "I do not want to claim that a mass suicide, as in the USA now, is imminent among the Wittek believers," he says, for example, to *Stern* (April 10,

1997). But then he does say so, after all: "But the UL leadership may conceivably be drifting towards a point that can no longer be controlled. ..."

Tabloids like the *Nürnberger Abendzeitung* (April 12, 1997) willingly place something like this in their headlines: "Mass suicide? Frankish sect out of control." Even *Stern* is only too happy to take over the enemy image used by the pastor, who so virtuously plays with the fire of the audience's emotions, and *Stern* concludes from this that Universal Life is "Germany's most dangerous sect." Which Behnk then promptly picks up again and spreads further: "... according to *Stern*, the most dangerous sect in Germany!"
Thus, a classic "quotation spiral" is again underway, which is very popular among rumormongers of all kinds. But nobody masters it as well as the modern inquisitors: I set something into the world and afterward plead "not guilty," referring to the media, which kindly took over my smear campaign.

In the afore-mentioned *Stern* article of April 10, 1997, Behnk claims about Universal Life, among other things: "They are playing with fire in a dangerous way, because they stir up end-time fears and skillfully build up enemy images. It is as if one checks out an explosives shed with a lighted fuse."

Yet it is Behnk himself who is busy stirring up fears and building up enemy images.

In connection with Universal Life, it is enough to constantly speak of a "sect," of "danger" and "perilousness" – with this, the Original Christians are constantly in the pillory. Today character assassination – and tomorrow?

Gabriele was repeatedly made the main target of the hateful attacks. Spurred on by the constant ranting tirades of the Lutheran sect commissioners Friedrich-Wilhelm Haack and Wolfgang Behnk, numerous sensationalist television journalists tried to lie in wait for her, even in front of her private home. And this, often for days on end, so that Gabriele was rarely able to leave the house without being accosted. Since the journalists could not see into the living quarters from the street, they drove their broadcasting vans into a small side street, and used a telescopic arm to pan the camera over the entire garden in order to film into the living quarters. Gabriele fled into the cellar

> **As a Reminder – Inquisition:**
> Persecution and eradication through lies, slander, discrimination, torture and murder of all those who do not submit to the prevailing religious caste.

hallway to protect herself from this brazen harassment.

It has always been a special species of people who cling to the network of priestly arrogance, both against the prophets in the Old Covenant and in the present time. Another example shows how "honestly" public television stations then "report": Because the house of Gabriele was too modest to suit the journalists, a large and representative house on the same street was filmed without further ado – and then presented in a program as the "house of the prophetess." "Outrageous," any normal citizen would say – but the radio and television stations, protected by the state and paid for by the citizens, apparently could afford to defame people and brand them in public.

Damaging Reputations with a Montage of Quotations

In order to find out which of his mendacious opinions were well received and which less so, the persecution expert Behnk frequently traveled to the villages of his adopted home in Bavaria and received invitations countrywide from Lutheran parishes.
During the Middle Ages, it was always a great event when the inquisitor came to the town or village. In our days, his modern successors usually find well-filled parish halls and expectant faces.

For his appearances, Behnk usually armed himself with a wealth of transparencies, onto which he had copied single sentences from the writings of Universal Life, to then project them onto the wall with a projector. With this, he wanted to suggest to the audience: "Look here, everything is documented and real!" However, the sentences immediately before or after, which often make the meaning clear and understandable in its context, had been omitted.

Only two examples are listed here, which show how unscrupulously and insidiously the inquisitor proceeded:

Stillness of thought: In the book "Cause and Development of All Illnesses," which Gabriele received from Jesus, the Christ, through divine revelation, toward the end, a "morning alignment" is printed, with which, for example, an ill person can attune himself for the day. Now, sick people are more likely than healthy people to fall into brooding or pessimism, and to torture themselves with negative thoughts and thus waste valuable life energy. At the end of the meditative text, they therefore receive the following advice in this context: *"Talk little and think even less! Speak only when it is essential! Have noble and good feelings. Ennoble yourself!"*

Behnk takes out only one single sentence ("Talk little and think even less"), but withholds the entire context, for instance, that in many books and writings Original Christians are again and again encouraged to think about their lives and about their share in the events of everyday life – and he now presents this in such a way as to give the impression that in Universal Life one is generally kept from thinking.

Again a malicious projection, because it is the churches themselves that want to keep people from thinking, especially about the contradictions between the teachings of Jesus of Nazareth and what the churches have made of them. In the Lutheran Church, for example, a great effort is made to conceal Martin Luther's cruel image of God as an alleged punishing and arbitrary God, who is supposed to have predestined some of His children to eternal damnation. Luther also stirred up hatred against Erasmus of Rotterdam in a most hateful way, because the latter valued human reason highly.

We also find similar things in the Vatican Church. In April 2013, according to Radio Vatican on April 20, 2013, Pope Francis prayed at an early mass in the Vatican Guest House Santa Marta:
May the Lord deliver us from the temptation of "common sense." ...
And in one of his books he wrote:
The worse thing that can happen to a person is that he let himself be led by the will-o'-the-wisp of reason. (*Welt am Sonntag*, April 14, 2013)

Disassociation: During the Gulf War of 1991, the Original Christians published several so-called Extra Editions, in which they called for peace and abstention from violence and indicated that Jesus of Nazareth was a pacifist. They disassociated themselves from all governments and rulers that call themselves Christian, but have bombs dropped on their fellow human beings. Behnk, deliberately misleading, now picks out the phrase "We disassociate ourselves" without mentioning the background of the war and concludes from it that, on principle, the Original Christians flatly rejected fellow human beings of a different faith and especially state institutions.

Behnk's numerous colleagues, the "sect commissioners" of the more than 20 other German regional churches and dioceses (along with the state and semi-state "experts") – all gladly adopted the mendacious misrepresentations of their colleague from Munich, and still do.

The thrill of the hunt does not let go of a "heretic hunter" so quickly; it can become an addiction. So one evening at dusk, Behnk, showed up unannounced, and with camera in hand and a companion at his side, in front of the farm near Würzburg. The same farm, which a few years before, had been stamped "Waco of Lower Franconia" through Behnk's subversive activities. There, he pretended to want to "visit" Gabriele. Or he appeared as a pastor in Gabriele's birth place in Bavarian Swabia, in order to "inquire" from her closest relatives about Gabriele's deceased parents – apparently with the intention of spying out any kind of "dark spot" in their past that could possibly be exploited for further defamation.

As mentioned, the consequence of this is that Gabriele can no longer visit her closest relatives and the grave of her parents. Her relatives do not want this, because they finally want to be left in peace from the constant hostilities and conversations on the part of uninvited "guests."

So, what Gabriele brought to this Earth as spiritual treasures was not only mocked and dragged through the mud – little by little, every private point of reference on this Earth was also spoiled for her. How did she get through all this? One can only repeat: She could endure it only because she was and is linked with the power of the All-Highest – and because she knew and knows: The word that is given through her comes from the heavens. Who could endure such slander and torment if they did not know and were deeply convinced: It is God, the Eternal, who speaks; it is His Son, Christ, and the Cherub of divine Wisdom.

But the prophetess and emissary of God, in addition to her task of bringing the eternal word of God, the Free Spirit – God in us – in all its facets to this Earth, was repeatedly forced to deal with the filth of the ecclesiastical aggressors, with their evil mendacious opinions and insidious attacks. In the 1990s, the church attacks reached a highpoint. Behnk, inspired by his predecessor Haack, agitated with the concentrated media power of the Lutheran Church and the Vatican Church behind him – and all this, against a small group of people of peaceful disposition. There were times when Universal Life had its back to the wall.

Everywhere in the world military armaments are upgraded; wars are incited, in which millions of people are murdered; people live in the greatest misery; countless die of hunger; the planet Earth is mercilessly plundered; the brutal slaughter of our fellow creatures, the animals, takes on monstrous proportions. Into this time, God, the Eternal, through His prophetess and emissary, once again brings the message of love, of peace, of freedom, of the unity of all life. People who feel addressed by the teaching of love for God and neighbor from the Kingdom of God join together to live the teaching of peace in everyday life, step by step. And what happens? The mainstream church concerns, which have wrongly attached the label "Christian" to themselves, attack her and expose her to decades of merciless smear campaigns.

Paul:
Whatever a Person Sows He Will Also Reap

In this situation, while the modern inquisitor was bringing one untruth after the other into the world against the word of the Free Spirit and against the Original Christians, Gabriele herself took up her pen and wrote a long letter to Pastor Behnk in February 1986. Her statements at that time could have been very informative, not only for the Lutheran theologian Wolfgang Behnk – if he had only let them fall into his heart. They also reveal the background of the fight of the church slanderers against the newly resurgent Original Christianity, which, to this day, characterizes the fight of the caste of priests against the Free Spirit. And quite incidentally, the reader learns some details about the specific effects of the smear campaigns on ordinary minds. Gabriele wrote, among other things:

Dear Mr. Behnk,

The statements in this open letter are not intended as a reckoning with you – I am not entitled to do so – but only as clarification and to set things straight. The reckoning takes place through the law of sowing and reaping, of which Paul spoke: ... "Do not be deceived: God is not mocked; whatever a person sows, he will also reap."

As a pastor you should also adhere to the analogous words of Jesus: ... "Whatever you do to the least of My brothers, you do to Me." ...
Do you want to be mocked, discriminated against and ridiculed? Do you want lies to be spread about you and your family? ...
Do you and the regional bishop, Mr. von Loewenich, want your children and grandchildren to be verbally abused of being "sectarian pigs"?

For many years I have studied the behavior and the content of the lectures of the sect commissioners and their accomplices, and have reached the conviction that many sect commissioners became unscrupulous, that is, they got rid of their conscience. ...

Anyone who has gotten rid of his conscience has no feeling for his neighbor, either. He attacks his neighbor thoughtlessly, without questioning whether what he says corresponds to the truth or not. Someone who is rid of his conscience also has no sense of shame and demands that his slander be admitted as expressions of opinion. ...

It is the greatest nonsense, in view of 700 to 800 Original Christians living in communities, to claim that they would infiltrate the state and form an economic empire. 700 to 800 people can neither infiltrate a state nor be an economic empire. Whoever believes such things can no longer be helped. ... No community can infiltrate the state anymore. It has already been infiltrated by the Catholic and Protestant Churches. ...

Mr. Behnk, you should be ashamed of deceiving your fellow human beings in such a way and leading them up the garden path. Those incited by you then pick up cobblestones, for example, and throw them into the windows of the Original Christians. In the end, it's not those incited by you, but you, the agitator, ... who throws the stones by way of those you incited. ...

Those who were stirred up by you were probably also the ones who set fire to the hay, the food of the animals, in the fields of the Original Christians. ... Signs of the Original Christians and crosses without a corpus were desecrated and destroyed by the agitated people. ... The death threats against Original Christians, which were caused by you and your employer, are your work – by way of the agitated people. Some of the people stirred up by you yell at children from Original Christian families: "You sectarian pigs." ... The list could go on and on. ...
If I were a self-proclaimed prophet, I would have given up long ago. After all, who would gladly and

joyfully allow him- or herself to be pelted with the dirt of the church institutions, of their accomplices and the press misguided by you? I would have planned something else for my life. But what I had planned for my life was thwarted by the Spirit of prophecy, by God, the Absolute. He took me out of the purpose I had for my life – with which I was very satisfied – and put me in this office, which has brought me as a human being only privation, austerity and also suffering through the lies of the sect commissioners. ...

Although you are ever so very afraid of selfless love, I wish you selfless love from my heart. For what is not, may yet come to pass.

In the Spirit of God
Your sister Gabriele Wittek

Behnk also replied with an open letter, whereas he had no trouble finding a daily newspaper right away that printed extracts of it: the *Münchner Merkur* (February 13, 1996). Behnk called on Gabriele: "Turn back, Gabriele Wittek!" And further: "Obviously you want to muzzle criticism by imputing to the critics every imaginable evil up to murderous intentions." It would be "terrible demagogy" if Gabriele were to "denounce him as an instigator of murder."

Intent to murder? Instigator of murder? The passage from Gabriele's letter, to which Behnk obviously refers here, is also printed above. The reader is welcome to reread it – and will find that Gabriele did not attribute this to Behnk at all, but that through his work of incitement, he caused *others* to make death threats. And an instigator of death threats is still something different than an "instigator of murder." But the modern inquisitor is not at all interested in a truthful account.

It is similar regarding two further statements by Behnk, which he repeats in this letter of response and which is still being circulated today: "... in nearly 100 lawsuits brought against him by the community, it has been decided again and again that his criticism is factually substantiated," and that his accusation that "the UL is totalitarian" has been "confirmed by the court."

And again, he stated an untruth – there were no "nearly 100 lawsuits" – here, Behnk simply counted dozens of identical criminal charges, which had been once filed against him, as individual "lawsuits" in each case, which juristically is nonsense. And the next false statement: The courts did *not* precisely "confirm" in terms of content what Behnk is in the habit of spreading about the followers of Jesus of

Nazareth – instead, they merely determined that such statements are just barely permissible within the framework of freedom of expression.

"If They Have Persecuted Me, They Will Also Persecute You"

But, apparently, a modern inquisitor can't do otherwise: As soon as he opens his mouth, he succumbs to the compulsion to twist or misrepresent something. Jesus of Nazareth was apparently confronted with this phenomenon. We are reminded here of what He said to the scribes of His time:
If God were your Father, you would love me ... Why do you not understand what I say? It is because you cannot accept my word. You are from your father the devil, and you choose to do your father's desires. ... He does not stand in the truth, because there is no truth in him. When he lies, he speaks according to his own nature, for he is a liar and the father of lies. But because I tell the truth, you do not believe me. Which one of you can prove that I am guilty of sin? (John 8:42 ff.)

Gabriele again took up Behnk's method of peddling mendacious opinions – which courts had confirmed for him as being just barely admissible

– and giving the impression that they were confirmed facts, when she answered Behnk:

My life belongs to the Spirit of God, whom I honor. And you? As it seems, Mr. Behnk, you are a person, a pastor, who reveres court rulings in order to make devastating things out of them. ... Mr. Behnk, we should stop corresponding. You rely on "expressions of opinion," which you prepare for defamation purposes. I rely on God, on the Ten Commandments and the Sermon on the Mount. Let's wait and see. Another world will either let your support collapse or mine.

Among other things, in his response Behnk had been annoyed by the fact that his home address was given in the first open letter. Gabriele did not leave this unanswered either:

You state that in the open letter to you your home address was mentioned. Perhaps you can thus appreciate a little of what we Original Christians have been enduring for years. Everything that I mentioned is merely a pale reflection of what we had and have to endure for years through so-called sect commissioners, their employers and their accomplices.
As stated before: If someone touches your family ever so slightly, you cry out. But what would you say

if for years the agitated press was to appear again and again in front of your house with a camera to take pictures of your house? ...
Your associates have drawn up a map on which the homes of Original Christians are marked. And this map is circulating in the surroundings of Würzburg and has even been shown on television. And you cry out when your address is given. What would you say if your children were accosted by incited children in the school buses and, as has already happened, also beaten up?
In our further publications of our open letter, we will omit your address. We just wanted to show you how painful it is when, like us, you are publicly pilloried with your name, house and address.

Since Pastor Behnk was still not yet willing to think about his actions against people of other faiths, Gabriele wrote to Behnk's immediate superior, the High Consistory Dr. Hartmut Böttcher, in April 1996, to ask him why he allows representatives of his church to organize veritable manhunts. When the latter did not react, she wrote to him again and described at least to some extent how she had personally fared for twenty years as a result of the church's smear campaigns and what effects this has had on her family – for example, that not only was her husband put under pressure, but that another member of her family also lost his job in a church-oriented facility.

Gabriele wrote:
For almost 20 years the dirt of the Protestant and Catholic Church has been processed and thrown at me by church heretic hunters in the guise of "sect commissioners." Nothing, but absolutely nothing at all corresponds to the truth. All their neurotic suspicions are cleverly packaged expressions of opinion, which they present to the untrained ear as truth. None of their sordid suspicions are proven. You can't prove anything against me either, because I've done nothing wrong. I gave and still give the message of God to my fellow human beings, just as many instruments of God, whom the Eternal One called His prophets, have done. Here, too, the words of Jesus of Nazareth apply: If they have persecuted Me, they will also persecute you. ... Cleanse my last name from the dirt of the two church institutions. ...

If one or the other of these letters – also sent to the regional bishop and to the synodal members of the Bavarian Lutheran Church – had an unexpected effect on the conscience of one of the church representatives, at any rate, he took care not to admit this. To the outside world, all regional bishops – whether they were called Johannes Hanselmann,

Hermann von Loewenich or Johannes Friedrich – covered up the actions of their commissioned persons and even called their machinations "pastoral care." As a sign of special esteem, Behnk was even promoted by his superiors to the church council. But after all the effort that Gabriele took with the theologians who stalked her, at least one day, no one will be able to say that he hadn't known about all this.

So that the Black Transmitter Stays Black: Blackening Original Christians

Meanwhile, the modern inquisitor Behnk, with his extensive arsenal of distortions and false statements, continued to go into action and blacken the Original Christians and their facilities to the media, the authorities and politicians. A zealous sect commissioner also takes care of the details – the "heresy" must be fought and eliminated, even in seemingly minor details. When, for example, in the summer of 1996, the firm *Gut zum Leben* broadcast commercials for its products on *Bavarian Broadcasting*, Behnk immediately called the station to stop the further broadcast of the commercials, claiming that the company was a "sect" that, in addition to selling bread, invited customers to come to the events of Universal Life. The state broadcasting company then cancelled the commercial for a week, until it could be convinced that it had been taken in by a lie: Nobody is being proselytized at the company's market stalls. Behnk, of course, knew this – the city of Munich, in response to an inquiry from the CSU regarding a market stand, had clearly determined this.

But Behnk was far from satisfied: He wrote a letter to the chief executive of the broadcasting company, which promptly resulted in a renewed cessation of advertising. The essence of the false accusations in this letter is a montage of quotations taken from a letter written by an Original Christian to Pastor Behnk: The Original Christian had asked Behnk how he would react, for example, if one said publicly about his wife that she was being "unscrupulously and chillingly exploited by her husband. That she is not capable of her own opinion and is therefore, in extreme danger of committing suicide": for exactly this is what Behnk spreads again and again about the Original Christians. Behnk, however, simply left out the introductory sentence ("Would you remain calm and composed if I were to publish the following in the press?") and pretended that the Original Christian had actually insulted him and his wife in this way.

This is a cold-blooded slur on one's reputation: to take the exposure of one's own guilt as the springboard for the next lie. Incidentally, in his letter to the director, Behnk himself indirectly calls his own behavior "criminal" – by labelling those who spread such "family hate" against his fellow people – as it allegedly happened to him – as "criminal."

Only with the help of the courts was it finally possible, after a year had gone by (!), to get the broadcasting company to adhere to the concluded contract. But for his part, Behnk now persuaded the broadcasting company to air a report on the day of the rebroadcast of the product advertising, which counteracted the advertisement:
Against its will, the Bavarian Broadcasting Company must broadcast a commercial of a totalitarian sect. BR spokesperson Mr. Tief said that the station had been ordered by the Munich Higher Regional Court to broadcast the spots of the advertiser Gut zum Leben. Behind it is the sect Universal Life, which, according to the Protestant-Lutheran sect commissioner, wants to make people seeking help dependent and take from them their freedom to criticize and develop their own conscience.

As it was in the Middle Ages: Anyone who doesn't follow the instructions of an inquisitor,

has to justify himself – otherwise, he will inevitably come into the line of fire. The fact that such business-damaging behavior does not fit into the 20th century and into present-day contract law, and therefore, cannot be repeated had to be reestablished by a court order.

The *Bavarian Broadcasting Company* has learned nothing from this. Just how unscrupulously a public television station throws all principles of fair journalism overboard, if the churches want it this way, was demonstrated by an environmental journalist in the program "Weeds" (January 13, 2003). Under the topic "Environment and Magic," "Power Places" in Catholic monasteries became famous; even the Far Eastern "Feng Shui" was praised as "Chinese-Bavarian harmony" – but then, the moderator and the "sect pastor" Behnk talked about Universal Life with a series of sweeping condemnations without any factual content ("extremely dangerous," "power-obsessed" etc.). That the people concerned were not heard is almost a matter of course for *Bavarian Television*.

A "Pastor" as Job Killer

When it is about harming religious "competition," a sect commissioner like Behnk does not shy away from destroying jobs.

In May 1997, he succeeded in getting an article about the computer company run by Original Christians, *EDV für Sie*, published in the professional journal *Medical Tribune*. Among other things, this small company looked after 400 medical practices in Lower Franconia – on behalf of the Hanover-based software company Medi-Star. Under the telling headline "Can psycho sects spy in the practice of EDP (electronic data processing)?," the *Medical Tribune*, explicitly quoting Behnk, now spread the suspicion that the EDP experts could misuse data from the medical practices for proselytizing purposes – for which there were no indications whatsoever!

Now the usual media deception game began: Behnk soon took up the suspicion, which he himself had raised, as ostensible news from "independent" third parties, and spread *Medical*

Yesterday – Inquisitor:
Persecution all the way to murder

Today – Sect Commissioner/Sect Expert:
Persecution all the way to character assassination

Tribune's accusations as a press release from the Evangelical-Lutheran regional church in Bavaria, not without hypocritically adding:

The Bavarian sect commissioner of the Evangelical-Lutheran Church, Wolfgang Behnk, welcomed the work of clarification of Medical Tribune. Behnk emphasized that the matter affects not only the medical profession, but particularly the patients. After all ... UL is "Germany's most dangerous sect" (Stern), which based on court decisions, can be called a "totalitarian" organization, through which those seeking help are brought into spiritual, psychological and material dependence. ... The concern expressed by the Medical Tribune about possible "computer espionage" by a psycho-sect must ... be dealt with using appropriate protective measures.

In an interview with *Antenne Bayern* (May 25, 1997), the "pastor" made himself even more clear and explained what he meant by the nice sounding term "protective measures": "... and here, the medical profession should consider whether they want to let such organizations have access to personal patient and billing data."

Behnk had indeed miscalculated the reactions of the physicians – the overwhelming majority of them trusted their long-standing colleagues and would have liked to use their services even longer.

But the media avalanche set off by Behnk's subversive work snowballed the software company in Hannover, which terminated the contract with *EDV für Sie* with a heavy heart due to the church-induced public pressure. Ten employees lost their jobs.

The attempt of the EDV company to at least receive compensation from the magazine *Medical Tribune* and the Lutheran Church for this scandal failed; apparently, judges in high places were friendly with the Church. The courts summarily classified the spreading of such rumors as "expression of opinion." Could it be that many judges are involuntarily afraid – (Of what, actually? – Can it be, of "eternal hell"?) – if they have to decide against the Church?

Another Way to "Earn" One's Daily Bread ...

The destruction of "heretical'" jobs is probably one of the "special moments" in the daily work of a modern inquisitor. What the daily "work" otherwise looks like can be surmised from the following incident, for which a witness vouches:

In a large southwest German city, a lecture in the city hall on "holistic medicine" has been announced, and the presenters will be doctors from the *Naturklinik* Michelrieth.

The day before the lecture evening, a telephone call is made to the official in charge of renting the city hall. A Mr. Behnk is calling. He wants to "warn" the city that behind the lecture is a "dangerous association," Universal Life. He stated that the Bavarian state government has also essentially confirmed this to him.

But Behnk is out of luck in this case: The official had, by chance, received a publication of the Original Christians through his secretary, in which the relevant report of the Bavarian government – which, by no means confirmed Behnk's defamations – was printed verbatim. (Chapter 10) However, the official was more disturbed by the unpleasantly fanatical and agitated manner of the church representative than by this lie. He described later how much this unfair procedure had upset him.

When the official did not give in to the church representative, Behnk tries to intimidate him. He now demands to speak to his supervisor, the head mayor. But the city was not to be put off – the lecture took place.

When you look at the multitude of cases in which the Original Christians were denied halls or halls were canceled (Chapter 12) – mostly with no reasons given – you can only guess in how many cases such a procedure was more successful.

In another case, Behnk went berserk in public against a city leader who was insubordinate to him. In July 1997, during a lecture in the Church of the Resurrection in Lohr am Main, Behnk publicly complained about the mayor of Marktheidenfeld, because he had not prevented a settlement of Original Christian firms in the Altfeld district. When the mayor clarified that the plots of land were sold privately and that under current law the town had no possibility to object, Behnk retaliated again in a letter to the editor. In order to present the politician's alleged inability to implement church wishes in a bold manner, he praised the "informative" and "proper" prevention of the settlement of the Original Christians in Heuchelhof, a district of Würzburg – sect commissioners love such campaigns! The mayor then announced a disciplinary complaint against Behnk to the Lutheran Church, which, as expected, came to nothing.

Farmers Defamed as "Enemies of the Constitution"

The Departments of Agriculture of Aschaffenburg/ Karlstadt and Würzburg were close to the church line when they rejected the applications of two Original Christian farms for subsidies, within the framework of the *Bavarian Cultural Landscape Program* in March 1998. They referred to a "fortified democracy" and to the fact that, according to court decisions, "Pastor" Behnk was allowed within the framework of freedom of opinion to spread with impunity the alleged psychological, material and spiritual dependence of the Original Christians. Tilman Toepfer of the *Main-Post* (May 8, 1998) put it this way: "The agricultural departments now argue that the totalitarian structure of UL forbids any support. ... The principle of equality does not go so far that the state has to finance its enemies." In *Focus* (26/98) could be read: "Bavarian authorities doubt the loyalty of Universal Life to the Constitution. ... The principle of a fortified democracy does not require 'handing over the state to its enemies.'"

Why "totalitarian structure of UL"? Why doubt "the loyalty of Universal Life to the Constitution?" Why "handing over the state to its enemies?" From where does that come? All that has nothing to do with the truth. In a constitutional state, are church, state and media allowed to freely invent and spread defamatory allegations to the detriment of law-abiding fellow people?

Of all people, the farmers who – unique in Germany – not only fulfill all the requirements of certified organic farming, but also plant hedges and practice three-field farming, in which every field is allowed to lie fallow every three years in order to recover – these farmers, of all people, should no longer receive money from the state. Isn't that absurd?

Yes, it is absurd. But the corruption of church and state makes it possible. Thus, organic farmers who have done nothing wrong can become "enemies of the state" overnight – only because a Lutheran pastor has had his mendacious opinions approved by the courts as "permissible expressions of opinion." And because the democratic state is anything but "fortified," quite the contrary, too cowardly to vigorously stand up to the unconstitutional marginalization demands of the mainstream churches.

On the other hand, where ecclesiastical organizations are concerned, the same ministry is extremely generous. For years, the Ministry of Agriculture granted subsidies in the millions to an association called "Catholic Village Helpers," although there was no "proof of use," as the Bavarian Court of Auditors criticized. In total, the scandal, which was uncovered only in 1999, resulted in more than 20 million marks in fraudulent subsidies and evaded taxes.

But state organs do not always succumb to pressure from the official churches. On April 14, 1999, the Würzburg Administrative Court overturned the rejection notices from the agricultural authorities by pointing to facts, which the authorities must have known long before:
That Universal Life is demonstrably "not an object of observation for the protection of the Constitution." That there are "no indications that internal organizational principles would be transferred from the area of community life to the state sector." That "the Bavarian authorities currently have no factual evidence of politically motivated efforts by Universal Life against the free democratic basic order."

These court decisions, however, did not make a big splash in the media – it is a lot more striking when a "pastor" delivers his damnation verdict from the media pulpit.

Police Protect Slanderers

Many of Behnk's "colleagues" used his prefabricated quotations collages, for example, the Würzburg sect commissioner Alfred Singer, in order to run down the Original Christians in public or at carefully selected events. Other colleagues willingly took up the vilifications and added new ones – such as a pastor from Northern Germany, who in 1993, at the Protestant Church Congress in Munich, spoke up at Behnk's lecture as if on order and claimed that he knew someone who had had to contribute his entire inheritance to the Homebringing Mission and who was now no longer allowed to have any contact with his children. There never was and never is such a thing among Original Christians. Nevertheless, Behnk replies that he receives similar reports of experiences "again and again." When Original Christians present called upon the "contributor" to name names and to provide evidence for this accusation, the audience greeted this with laughter. When the Original Christians then called the police, to at least have the personal identity of the denouncer determined, this was theatrically described by the church representatives present as an "attempt at intimidation" and "restriction of the free expression of opinion" – and the *Protestant Press Service* spread the news with feigned indignation that the police had reacted "to a cue from a sect." (In our government, only one party is allowed to give such "cues": the Church!) The police did indeed come and take down the personal data of the defamer – but the Original Christians did not receive them. A few days later they were allegedly "untraceable." The Church can therefore be reassured: The police is still in line with them! When two years later, the name of the pastor became known by chance, it was far too late for any clarification of the incident. When Wolfgang Behnk retired at the beginning of 2014, the Lutheran Church Newsletter once again expressly praised him. He was "the man who pulled out all stops."

One can only agree with that: In fact, he pulled out all stops to persecute and defame innocent people, to incite journalists and media representatives against them, with the result that people lost their livelihoods.

9. An Original Christian School? That Cannot Be Allowed! (1986-2011)

Original Christians, followers of Jesus of Nazareth, consider it important to carry out the education of children in the meaning of the Free Spirit – God in us – on the basis of the Ten Commandments of God and the Sermon on the Mount of Jesus of Nazareth – without being bound to a denomination, without dogmatic constraints, without a hierarchical priesthood, without rituals and ceremonies. So in the mid-1980s, they began to build corresponding private educational facilities, first a nursery school and a kindergarten. Furthermore, a private ideological school was planned. In Germany, there are numerous private schools that are founded to offer children alternative educational concepts – therefore, it was nothing unusual.

From the beginning, however, it became clear that such establishments were a thorn in the side of the Church. The mainstream churches have always regarded the education and instruction of children and young people as their very own domain.
In the case of one kindergarten, the authorities had little possibility to refuse approval, as the legal requirements regarding qualified personnel, etc.,

are not too difficult to meet. However, a campaign was immediately launched by the Church when the Original Christians opened their first kindergarten in Würzburg: The Würzburg representative of the *Evangelische Pressedienst* published an almost full-page article in the Catholic *Fränkische Volksblatt* (February 1, 1986), in which he reported in detail about "personnel links" between the association "Kindergartenland e.V." and the Original Christians.

One would like to ask: Yes – so? Since when does every person have to be either Catholic or Protestant-Lutheran? But in the Catholic city of Würzburg, this was enough to start a cheap campaign against those who think differently: Look at what the "heretics" are up to!

The Würzburg Social Affairs officer is actually offended by the fact that he was left in the dark about this connection (whatever he wants to imply with this) before the provisional operating permit was granted – although the city has no more business being concerned about the "prayer book" of the operators of a kindergarten than it does with that of parents and children – and although this would not have changed the slightest thing in the legal requirements for granting the permit!

According to the *Volksblatt*, the government of Lower Franconia then found fault with the fact that the kindergarten was "surrounded by busy main roads in an industrial area." The fact that the building in question – a one-storey building – is located in a protected, green courtyard, shielded from the surrounding streets by multi-storey buildings, is not only concealed by the *EPD* (Evangelische Pressedienst) journalist: he also presents a completely misleading photo, in which he does not show the kindergarten, but an adjacent parking lot with a garbage container and empty bottles. And at the end of the article, he bluntly calls on the readers to boycott the kindergarten – because, otherwise, they might get the idea to send their children there, given the lack of kindergarten places in this part of the city: "If the Kindergartenland-Kindergarten at the Europastern (a traffic junction), which is so controversial within the administrative bodies, were to officially start operating, interested Grombühl parents would probably have to ask themselves a few questions." What questions? Whether they must fear reprisals from the Church if they enroll their children in an institution officially branded as "heretical" by the Catholic newspaper?

School Application in for the Long Haul?

In this case, they were spared the decision. The Original Christian parents very soon found other locations for their kindergartens outside the city. And still in the same year, (on October 24, 1986) they applied to the responsible authorities for permission to establish a private ideological school. This possibility is expressly provided for in both the Basic Law and the Bavarian Constitution. But the government of Lower Franconia, on the instructions of the higher authority, the Bavarian Ministry of Education and Cultural Affairs, in fact, flatly rejected this first application in the summer of 1988.

The Original Christians made use of their right to look into the files – and were astonished to find that the government of Lower Franconia had, "in reaching a decision" largely based itself on an "information" file of the Episcopal Ordinariate of Würzburg! However, the only official reason given was that the organizational "stability" of Universal Life was not sufficient for running a school.

This rejection is a scandal – especially when one is aware of two events that took place simultaneously on September 5, 1988: On the same day that the Ministry of Education in Munich issues the instruction to the government of Lower Franconia to reject the school application of the Original Christians, the government of Upper Bavaria, also by order from "above," approves another application for the establishment of a private school: a church school. The applicant is the "Integrated community" in Walchensee. Here, the procedure is exactly the opposite as in the case of the Original Christians: The Ministry of Education even revokes a rejection notice from the Government of Upper Bavaria. Bishop Stimpfle from Augsburg had personally campaigned for this application – just as, in the reversed case, Bishop Scheele from Würzburg had campaigned against the Original Christian application.

Therefore, one knows who in Bavaria is really "in charge" of political decisions, especially in the area of education: the Catholic bishops! A Catholic school is immediately approved – an Original Christian school, however, is rejected with spurious reasons and under pressure from a bishop.

But the Original Christian parents are not intimidated. Some of them travel to Munich with their children and find the Minister of Education Hans Zehetmair in his office building. However, he reacts insulted and leaves the room. The Original Christians once again experience what it means to have a church-influenced public against them: Normally, such actions with children are positively received by the press. But the *Bild-Zeitung* (September 6, 1988) prints a headline about the event: "Sect children occupied ministry office – abused by their radical parents for political action." The "sect specialist" Pastor Haack is quoted as saying: "It's good that the ministry did not allow the school to operate."

And once again, the Original Christians are left with only the legal path. But that costs time and money. Since certain conditions must be fulfilled in advance, as a prerequisite for the approval of the school: The teachers must be available; they must be paid, but they can work only once the school has actually started. The school building, which was acquired with a bank loan that was not easy to get, stands empty until approval is granted, however, it must be maintained.

The representatives of the school association *I Help You* have to wait two more years under these difficult circumstances for the first hearing. And lo and behold: On August 16, 1990, the Administrative Court of Würzburg decides that the government of Lower Franconia is obliged to grant the

Original Christians the license to operate a private elementary and secondary school! There was "no room for a discretionary decision by the authorities in the given constitutional situation." The state is not only obligated to religious and ideological neutrality, it is also forbidden to "carry out a quality examination of the religious and ideological content, to favor certain denominations or to assess the faith or lack of faith of its citizens." The fundamental right to equal treatment (Article 4 of the Constitution) protects "not only the mainstream Christian Churches, but also all other religious and ideological communities and groups."

In these proceedings, the Original Christians had presented an expert opinion by the religious scholar Professor Hubertus Mynarek on the question of whether Universal Life was an ideology in the meaning of the Constitution. According to Mynarek, there can be no doubt about this: In Universal Life "all structural elements that belong to an ideology are consistently and logically derived from the supreme principle of existence." Mynarek also confirmed in his expert opinion that Universal Life is a community of Christian ideology.

The result of the court case is an embarrassment for a state that had disregarded the principle of equal treatment of all citizens in front of everyone. But those who now assumed that this state would carry out an apparently long overdue correction of its attitude towards a minority of faith, saw that they were misled: The Minister of Education and Cultural Affairs Zehetmair went on holiday a few days after the Würzburg judgment and announced that one must first wait to have the grounds for the judgment in writing before granting permission.

The new school year begins in September in Bavaria – and the physical conditions for a provisional start of school were available! Even the *Main-Post* (August 21, 1990) shook its head in disbelief over such indifference towards the rights of respectable citizens: "The struggle of these people against the windmills of state and church is not yet over. ... And nobody really understands the reason for it anymore." Also the request of the followers of Jesus of Nazareth to Prime Minister Max Streibl (CSU) to "exercise his authority" in favor of a minority goes unheard. When Minister Zehetmair takes part in a conference in Würzburg shortly before the start of school, Original Christian parents and children stand in front of the Hotel Rebstock to speak with him and to reaffirm their determination for their own school. But Zehetmair escapes through the back exit.

Stalling Tactics and Chicanery Until the End

The Bavarian Ministry of Education and Cultural Affairs does not grant a school permit, but rather appeals – a pure stalling tactic, since the authorities had no new arguments to present. This was confirmed just under a year later, on July 24, 1991: The Administrative Court in Munich confirmed the initial verdict. A major role in the appeal hearing is played by the beliefs of Universal Life, which are laid down in the books of the Inner Path and in the comprehensive work of revelation "This Is My Word – Alpha and Omega." On the basis of a detailed report on the beliefs, the thinking and living of the Original Christians, the court reaches the conclusion that the objection of a "lack of stability" – a mere pretext of the ecclesiastically influenced authorities – is not valid, and that therefore, the prerequisites for operating a school are fulfilled.

But the Original Christians are meanwhile familiar with the corruption between church and state and their prevention strategies. Still in the courtroom, they apply for the judge to grant permission by means of a temporary injunction to put a stop to further delaying tactics.
This indeed proves to be necessary. The new school year starts on September 12th without a

permit. The government of Lower Franconia lets it be known that it is still waiting for a statement from the Ministry of Education. The written grounds for the decision have not yet arrived.

The children, who were already looking forward to their new school, will have to go to the regular schools once more. But some of the parents let their children stay home because the permit they are legally entitled to should arrive any day. When the authorities now threaten to impose fines, the children attend school, but some refuse to participate in the lessons; they want to go to the Christ-School. Instead of apologizing for the shenanigans of his authorities, the head of a department of the government of Lower Franconia complains about the "massive psycho-terror" to which his authorities are being subjected – and this, only because the parents campaign for their constitutional rights by legal means.

It was not until September 23, 1991 that the wait came to an end: The Bavarian Administrative Court issued a temporary injunction to permit the school to start operating without delay.

For almost five years, the Original Christians had to fight for something that usually drops into the laps of church applicants: their own school. It is called: Private School *"Learn with Me"* in Universal Life. It is the first and, until then, the only private ideological school in Germany – because other private school supporters usually justify their applications preferably with pedagogical reasons.

Apparently, the authorities who were under pressure from the church leaders had not expected that parents close to Universal Life would get through the years of financial drought, not to mention the nervous strain.

However, the echo in the press already gives an idea of the extent to which this breakthrough infuriates the mainstream churches. There is talk of it being a "cadre factory for the community of faith"; in the *Rheinische Merkur.* (July 30, 1991) Werner Thiede, theologian and co-worker of the "Protestant-Lutheran Central Office for Questions of Ideology," stirs things up against the new school even before the first day of operation: The teachings of Universal Life are "dangerous" for children, and stories about elves and gnomes are "questionable ideological elements." Doesn't the state have, asks Thiede, "a mandate to protect still underage schoolchildren?"

He does not speak of a mandate of the state to protect the constitutionally guaranteed right of parents to decide on the education of their children themselves, within the framework of the law. The parents themselves have to fight for this before the courts, against the corruption of state and church.

A School with a Family Atmosphere

The fight was to continue. First, however, the school is opened in Esselbach (Main-Spessart district) in a former clothing factory, which was lovingly renovated by parents and friends of the school and which offers the children an atmosphere in which they can feel comfortable. Grades are given only in the higher classes. The teachers are informally addressed on a first name basis and attach great importance to targeted individual support and social learning: Older pupils help younger ones, and everyone takes on smaller tasks in turn, such as tidying up, cleaning and washing up.

Great importance is also attached to a good contact with the parents, who are always well informed and actively participate in shaping and supporting school life, especially the joint celebrations. From the very beginning, the school, which is open to all children in the surrounding area, offers all-day care with a common (vegetarian) lunch, language electives, study groups and leisure activities. Later, a music school is added – all this, at a time when the expansion of all-day care was by no means a topic of general discussion among politicians concerned with cultural and educational policies, as well as teachers and parents. Special emphasis is placed on early vocational orientation opportunities: regular internships in firms of the pupil's choice, where they can familiarize themselves with the tasks of working life.

The pupils are taught according to the curricula customary in Bavaria; this is regularly checked by the authorities without any objections ever having been determined. On the contrary, after unusually frequent and also unannounced visits, the Bavarian education authorities now repeatedly praise the "informality," the "eloquence" and "maturity" of the pupils.

Ever since the school was officially approved, the relationship between the authorities and the school administration quickly returned to normal, despite the initial difficulties. The responsible school authority then even protected the private school from improper attacks by the church and its accomplices.

Behnk Blows the Horn for a Witch Hunt Against the School of the Original Christians

This is what "Pastor" Behnk must also experience when he calls for a witch hunt against the school. Immediately after he assumed office at the end of 1991, he claims that Universal Life is a "sect" that tries to "draw young people into its nets."
Mind you, this is what the representative of an institution claims that baptizes children as infants, thus co-opting them lock, stock and barrel – and, at that, according to its teachings, in perpetuity.
According to a newspaper report at the end of 1994, Behnk then implied to his listeners in Kreuzwertheim that "the school of Universal Life is against the Constitution, because Article 2 of the Basic Law, which guarantees the free development of personality, is disregarded there." He wanted to substantiate this with the goals of Universal Life, "which" – as he claims – "involve the reduction of all individuality, all family and personal ties, ultimately, of the personhood." "It is particularly questionable to expose children to a system of 'depersonalization and desocialization.'" (*Main-Echo*, December 17, 1994)

Just a reminder: Martin Luther, the founder of his church, denied the human being any kind of free will. The human being is thus degraded to the puppet of an allegedly arbitrary and cruel God. More "depersonalization" and less "free development of personality" is simply not conceivable.

In August 1994, when the school association announced the expansion of the primary school to an elementary and secondary school with nine grades, Behnk seethed: "This is not an education suitable for children, but ideological indoctrination." Behnk simply states this in his usual slanderous manner – without any reference point.

But it can happen to a particularly zealous modern inquisitor that he stumbles over his own feet in overzealousness. In April 1994, Behnk had apparently warmed up his predecessor Haack's good contacts among the Bavarian CSU politicians and provided three CSU members of the state parliament with his defamations. Christian Will (Würzburg), Karl Freller (Schwabach) and Markus Sackmann (Roding) submitted an extensive inquiry to the Bavarian state government regarding "The Spread of Sectarianism in Bavaria; here: Homebringing Mission – Universal Life." One of the questions asked also concerned the school: with what legitimization was it established and whether state supervision is possible?

Quite apart from the fact that the entire catalogue of questions already is a basically unconstitutional request for investigation against respectable citizens: The questions asked, also allow an insight into the obvious intellectual limitations of representatives of the people who are servile to the church. Every attentive newspaper reader was aware of the court case that compelled the state to approve the school. And that a private school is also subject to state supervision is part of the basic knowledge of every politician concerned with education and culture.

The government's answer to the second question was correspondingly brief, and like all answers, it was made public at the end of February 1995.

As an approved private elementary school, this ideological school is also subject to state school supervision, which very carefully ensures that lessons are given in accordance with legal requirements. So far, no irregularities have been found.

Such sober, exonerating answers run like a common theme through the entire 16-page report, in the formulation of which six Bavarian ministries were involved. **According to the government, there is no reason to monitor Universal Life through the Federal Office for the Protection of the Constitution; nor are there any "findings about right-**

wing extremist publications or activities … At present, there is no evidence that from the basic religious attitude of 'Universal Life' efforts against the free democratic basic order are being pursued, especially against human rights." But that is exactly what Behnk had claimed about the school! The report also stated that there are "no indications that … Universal Life wants to transfer the inner-organizational principles from the sphere of community life to the state sphere." And, there is also no evidence of "reprisals against drop-outs."

"The State Is Not the Beadle of the Sect Commissioners"

The Bavarian state government's report on Universal Life proves to be a boomerang for the Lutheran sect pastor – and a rehabilitation of the Original Christians.

But the modern inquisitor still has the press. A few days after the publication of the state government's report, the *Katholische Nachrichtenagentur* (Catholic News Agency) reports:

The sect commissioner … Wolfgang Behnk has once again warned against the group "Universal Life" and accused it of "unconstitutional, anti-democratic ideology and practice." Behnk vigorously opposed the Bavarian Ministry of Education and Culture's statement that there is no indication that UL endangers democracy and violates human rights. ... Behnk presented Minister Zehetmair with a total of 20 "documents," which in his opinion do indeed provide "massive factual evidence" for a threat to democracy through "Universal Life."

These "documents," however, were merely the well-known defamations and distortions that Behnk always resorts to on such occasions.

Minister Zehetmair, on the other hand, emphasized that the state is bound to ideological neutrality – and therefore the state is not "the beadle of the sect commissioners." How much must the modern inquisitor Behnk have harassed and annoyed a conservative minister before he made such a statement?

But the Church has a lot of staying power, when it comes to persecuting those of other faiths. Werner Thiede now expresses the "hope" in the substantive service of the *EZW* (8/95) (Protestant Central Office for Worldview Questions) that "now the Bavarian Ministry of Education and Cultural Affairs will subject the school of UL to a renewed examination, which is oriented toward the criterion of constitutionality."

The Bavarian school authorities react to this pressure, which certainly does not come only from this one church office, by carrying out an additional, particularly detailed visitation of the school without prior notice. However, the result is again positive – in particular, as already mentioned, the "informality," the "eloquence" and the "maturity" of the pupils are emphasized.

However, this does not prevent Behnk from again demanding the closure of the Original Christian school at the beginning of 1996, because the courts had allowed him to express the opinion that this school was "unconstitutional." A modern inquisitor with his limited and basically misanthropic thought patterns is apparently hardly able to cope with the fact that in a constitutional state, the authorities cannot take such a step on the basis of the mere opinion of a pastor.

The difference, above all, is that the representatives of the authorities were on site several times and gained a personal impression from their own experience. The modern inquisitor, however, never set foot in the school. He condemns it to "eternal damnation" purely theoretically and with intellectual bigotry on the basis of church doctrines that condemn anything that deviates from them. He thus hides a complete lack of factual knowledge behind pretentious pseudo-sociological slogans. He vilifies, so to speak, at large, by twisting the teachings of Universal Life as he sees fit and then transferring to the school this distorted image drawn up by himself – and thereby exposes the school as well as the parents, children and teachers to character assassination. And his persistent attacks show their effect.

Politicians Are Stirred Up

When Minister-President Edmund Stoiber (CSU) went to Lohr in February 1996, two Inquisition henchmen sat in the front row and asked him whether he "finally wants to take on as vigorous action against Universal Life as against the 'Scientology Church' or whether Bavarian sects enjoy special privileges." According to a newspaper report, (*Main-Echo*, February 2, 1996) Stoiber "regretted" that the action against the school had been defeated in court, although "everything possible" had been done to prevent the founding of this school. The report continued: "The fight must be continued, he did not consider the judgments as 'facts for all time.' Stoiber wants to take action against the private elementary school of the sect 'Universal Life' with all means at his disposal."

You have to imagine this: A Minister-President – who is required to abide by the German Basic Law and the state's duty of neutrality and who swore to uphold precisely this in his oath of office – regrets that the Free State of Bavaria unfortunately had to abide by law and order, although the intertwining of sect commissioners and politicians had done everything possible to prevent the founding of this school! With this, a Bavarian Minister-President placed himself above the law, above the Constitution. To whom did he want to justify himself?

Encouraged by this, Behnk made another push to close the school, this time at the Bavarian Ministry of the Interior, because he is apparently banging his head against a brick wall at the Ministry of Education and Cultural Affairs. Zehetmair had previously declined with thanks an invitation to visit the school personally:
The results of the school visits are known to the State Ministry and are not doubted here. The Ministry ... knows that the exercise of its office is in the best hands with the responsible government of Lower Franconia.

Behnk manages to get the responsible department head of the government of Lower Franconia to visit the school personally. But the result is, in turn, not to Behnk's liking: **"The building and the other factual requirements ... are to be evaluated very positively. ... Pedagogically, very attractively designed classrooms are characterized by a comfortable atmosphere. ... The students in all grades make a cheerful, friendly and disciplined impression. The information provided by the school administration was given willingly and without reservation,"** thus, the government report.

Minister Zehetmair is now attacked by his own party. At the forefront, CSU politician Markus Sackmann, who correctly states about himself: "The fact that this association can operate an elementary school with state subsidies exceeds the legal understanding of the Roding CSU delegate Markus Sackmann." Because this "understanding of law" obviously has a strong Catholic bias. "The ministry does not dare to tackle the matter," Sackmann states; Minister Zehetmair obviously shies away "from an offensive confrontation with dubious religious movements." Sackmann submits a motion to the Bavarian Parliament's committee on education and culture for a renewed inspection of the school. The SPD aptly speaks of a "motion of no confidence" by the CSU against the government of Lower Franconia. Freller (CSU) accuses the SPD of "keeping silent" on the topic of "sects."

That's how it is with the Inquisition: Anyone who does not join in the attack on the "heretics" becomes suspect himself.

The school *"Learn with Me"* then invites all members of the Bavarian Parliament to the school – but no one comes. The Ministry officials, however, arrive again, examine the probably best-investigated school in Bavaria one more time, let themselves be shown the exercise books and determine: **"In the preparatory documents, the exercise books and in the lessons, no indications could be found that constitutionally questionable contents are being conveyed."**

By now, at the latest, it would have become clear to an unbiased observer that Behnk, with his warnings of alleged dangers of the Original Christian school, is acting on a purely ideological-theoretical level (and thereby also twisting the facts), while practical investigations on the spot produce the opposite results each time. But church-indoctrinated politicians are not interested in findings or facts, they want to distinguish themselves by means of the

> Sect: A term of abuse used by the respective prevailing religious caste for all those against whom their Inquisition is directed.

"sect" hunt to the predominately Catholic electorate. On behalf of these politicians, Behnk prepares an "expert opinion on the unconstitutionality of the elementary and secondary school of the organization 'Universal Life,'" which is presented in June 1997 at a public hearing of the CSU faction, and then circulated within the state government – and that, without the Original Christians having access to this church document!

At this CSU hearing, the Lutheran sect commissioner Kurt-Helmuth Eimuth from Frankfurt is also permitted to present to the audience his abstruse theses on the alleged "endangerment of children in sects," especially and allegedly in Universal Life. In contrast to the ministry officials, he, too, has never seen an educational facility of the Original Christians from the inside, let alone spoken to one of the children. In November 1997, Behnk again demands the closure of the school by stating that the inspections by the state school authorities that have thus far revealed no objections proves nothing at all.

> Yesterday – Inquisitor:
> **Persecution all the way to murder**
>
> Today – Sect Commissioner/Sect Expert:
> **Persecution all the way to character assassination**

Strauß-Daughter Incites Against Original Christian School

The area of responsibility of Minister of Education Zehetmair, who cannot readily be pressed into such a scheme, is divided at the next cabinet reform in 1998; the area of schools is taken from him; he remains in office as Minister of Culture and Science. Now, the daughter of the late CSU Minister-President Franz-Josef Strauss, Monika Hohlmeier, responsible for schools and the new minister, immediately adopts a completely different tone: She is "very negative" toward the school of the Original Christians and works closely with the "sect commissioners" on this issue.

On October 28, 1996, Hohlmeier, at that time still State Secretary with Zehetmair, claimed at the *Frauen Union* in Herzogenaurauch that Universal Life "systematically seals itself off from the outside" and pursues "in a rather aggressive way economic and also political interests." ("That's how it's described," she said – but by whom?) The school of the Original Christians, she added, "is a thorn in our side."

Apparently, the minister believes the church functionary Behnk more than her own officials, who –

in contrast to the latter – have known the school for years. However, the minister did not respond to repeated invitations to get to know the school herself. Every time it is about people of other faiths, the Catholic lady seems to "forget" her oath of office, which would obligate her to ideological neutrality.

At the same time, it becomes known that nuns in a Catholic school in Auerbach (Upper Palatinate) had torn out sex education pages from a biology book with their own hands. They are apparently close to the Catholic "Work of Angels" and make the children afraid of the devil. In the kindergarten, the children are threatened with imminent death if they are not well-behaved; anyone who talks while eating is locked into the storeroom. Here, the Ministry of Education and Culture becomes active only when parents protest. Some of the nuns are no longer employed and the kindergarten director is dismissed. An Original Christian institution would probably have been closed immediately, at the very slightest incident of this kind, not to mention the resulting media campaign. But here, where, for once, actual (and not only imagined) grievances are present, nothing is heard from Behnk. Why is that?

Never Be Seen with "Heretics"!

Meanwhile, the constant inflammatory slogans of cassock wearers and politicians are not without effect. How does a mother feel when her child comes home from school crying and asks: "Mom, what's a sect pig?" Some children were insulted with these and similar words, especially at the beginning, after school had started – at the bus stop, for example. And how do children feel when they are ostracized in the village because some parents forbid their children to play with the "sect children"?

A child usually believes what he is told. When a child is told: "You're a sect pig," most children tend to think: "What's wrong with me that they say such things to me?" But it can also turn out differently: Children who have grown up in an atmosphere of respect, esteem and goodwill, who also have a good relationship with their parents, can also emerge strengthened and take with them the question: "What kind of people are they, who do and say such things?"

This is the great opportunity an educational institution has that does not indoctrinate or drill children and young people, but whose goal is to help young people learn to think independently and develop the positive abilities in them.

Apparently, that is exactly why it is fought so bitterly by church representatives – and also by politicians who adopt the ecclesiastical propaganda of lies.

Thus, in 2011, the then Bavarian Minister of the Environment, Markus Söder (CSU), suddenly refused to personally present the private school *"Learn with Me"* with the award of an "Environmental School in Europe," as is normally the case with all winners of this award.
The school received the certificate by mail, but was not invited to the official award ceremony, as had been customary during previous years (the school was awarded three times in a row before). When asked by telephone, it was explained, because it was the school of the Original Christians – that is why it was not invited by the Bavarian Minister of the Environment.
What was not mentioned on the phone, but could be read in the press: That Minister Söder – a Protestant! – had shortly before traveled to Rome for a private audience with Pope Josef Ratzinger and had received a black rosary as a gift from him. ...

This discrimination of the Original Christian school on grounds of faith was also repeated during the following years with subsequent ministers – because the school *"Learn with Me"* is one of the prize winners year after year. And again, it is the children who suffer most. Year after year, they participate with enthusiasm and joy. But the Bavarian Minister of the Environment, who should actually be glad of their great efforts, does not want to see the children there. He should be ashamed of himself!

In this way, children and young people are taught at an early age a bitter lesson about the constitutional reality in a country where in many cases, the "horseman" Church still directs the "steed" State in its direction. But at a very early age, they also learn not to make themselves dependent on the external approval of church and state "authorities:" We have supported the cause of nature and of the animals. If the minister wants to acknowledge this, he can, but if he does not want to acknowledge it, that's his business.
And precisely this inner freedom is why the cassock wearers fight the school in such a way. ... The concept of this school has become so successful that it has found numerous imitators in Africa known as the "Sophia Schools."

10. "End-Time Apostles" or: God Gave Warning in Time (1985-2000)

"And God said…," so it is written again and again in the scriptures, from Abraham onward, throughout the times. The Eternal, All-One God, who is the love, did not and does not speak through priestmen. He gives His eternal word, the word of truth from the Kingdom of God, solely through His prophets, through enlightened men and women, who at all times have proclaimed His message of love, peace and unity and pointed the way to our eternal homeland. He is the speaking God, who does not forsake His human children, who sends His messengers, the bearers of His word, to us to bring the eternal truth in the words of the respective time.

Today, the Kingdom of God has been giving revelations for over 45 years, through the great teaching prophetess and emissary of God, Gabriele, giving us human beings the fullness of divine Wisdom for all spheres of life. And He, the Eternal, also clarifies; He admonishes and warns. Out of love for His human children, He has shown the correlations in countless revelations through Gabriele, and since the 1970s, has repeatedly issued warnings in the following sense: If humankind continues to treat nature and animals in this way, then, according to the law of cause and effect, hard times and upheavals will inevitably come upon humankind.

The question is: Why has the majority of humankind not heard about this? And what upheavals, disasters and suffering could have been prevented or mitigated if people had heard the word of the eternal Creator 45 years ago and taken it seriously? At that time, many things would still have been possible; at that time, the course could still have been changed.

Many years later, such warnings were also voiced more and more frequently by scientists, and today hardly anyone denies that planet Earth is facing a climate disaster caused by humankind itself.

The admonishing words from the Kingdom of God were not heard and were not accepted, because narrow-minded, conceited representatives of the mainstream churches slandered the bearer of His word, the prophetess of God, persecuted her with modern Inquisition methods, and buried and fought His word of truth with mockery and derision.

The helping hand of God, which He gave us with His warnings and admonitions, was spurned. His word was ridiculed, and on top of that, twisted and abused, thus renewing the defamations of the prophetess of God and the followers of Jesus of Nazareth.

And why? Because the eternal word of the Free Spirit, who lives in every ensouled human being, exposes once and for all, the official churches with their dogmas and rites, with their wealth, their power and influence in politics and society, with their priestmen, as alleged mediators between God and human beings – and makes them utterly superfluous.

The Falsified Reports of the Priestmen

During the years before the turn of the millennium, the disparagement of the followers of Jesus of Nazareth as "end-time apostles" or "end-time disciples" was especially popular among the heretic hunters.

Already in 1985, the Würzburg *Caritas* employee and qualified psychologist Alfred Spall claimed in the afore-mentioned "expert opinion" on the meditation courses offered in Universal Life (Chapter 3) that young people were deliberately frightened, in order to demand from them a "total decision for the Homebringing Mission": "Then grim prophecies are given ('the world is burning, there are wars, conflicts ... an end is not in sight'; '... hard times will come for the world ...')."

This is sheer nonsense – the "disasters" are not mentioned at all in the meditation texts that Mr. Spall apparently had. And how can one be urged to make a "decision" for a community of faith if one cannot even become a member of it?

Decades later, the concept of "fake news" is discussed in public, the fake news that demagogues and populists put into circulation to confuse the people. But this is nothing new – it is an ancient phenomenon. The priestmen and their accomplices have been masters of this for thousands of years.

When the cassock wearers decades ago mocked those giving warnings as "end-time disciples," they distracted from the fact that it is they themselves, who bear a large part of the blame for what is approaching humankind, because they did not teach the people the love for creation. God, the Eternal, gave timely warnings through His prophetess Gabriele – but through their defamations, the cassock wearers prevented these warnings from reaching countless people.

Neither Gabriele, the prophetess of God, nor the followers of Jesus of Nazareth ever received an apology for the barrage of malice and contempt to which they were exposed for years, because of their unfortunately all-too justified indications of the threatening overload of the planet Earth and the impending climatic disasters. Instead, today, when climate change and its devastating consequences can no longer be denied, the mainstream churches suddenly act as if they have always been nature protectors.

The Churches and the "Business with Fear"

In 1988, the deacons of both Würzburg mainstream churches took up the topic of the "End Time" (Chapter 5). "We Christians," they claim, "have always lived in the end time. ... That the end time is beginning only now contradicts Holy Scriptures. ... That business with fear, which has often been done in the history of the Church with apocalyptic dates and times" – which expressly do not exist in Universal Life! – "we Christians reject."

The "business with fear" is again a projection of the churches: They are the ones who have been generating massive fears for nearly two thousand years, namely, of an alleged "eternal damnation," which has not the slightest thing to do with God, who is eternal love. Until today, innumerable credulous people all over the world are intimidated with this fear – and asked to pay.

"Eternal damnation" continues to be an integral component of the doctrine of both mainstream churches. Still today, for example, the Catholic dogma is valid that: ... *no one remaining outside the Catholic Church, not only pagans, but also Jews, heretics or schismatics, can become partakers of eternal life, but they will go to the eternal fire prepared for the devils and his angels, unless before the end of their life they are joined to it (the Church).* (Neuner and Dupuis, Margin Note Number 1005)

A Diabolical Gambit

Count Magnis also sees the "heretics" already burning in hell. With his slanders he stirs up the fire in advance. In one of his writings in March 1988, he attributes to Universal Life the announcement of a "world holocaust, in which all the undertakings, establishments and people not belonging to the 'Christ-State' ... will be destroyed."
Magnis knows very well that in Universal Life something completely different is taught: Survival in the time of upheaval has nothing to do with belonging to some group or other or even a company. Someone who does not know Universal Life at all, or only from a distance, can be very close to God and do the right thing at the right moment. Conversely, a supporter of the Original Christians can be just as affected by disasters as other people are – especially if he has merely listened to the teachings, but hardly put them into practice in his daily life. It is not for nothing that the Bible (Mt. 24:40) says: *Then two will be in the field; one will be taken and one will be left.*

The assertion of the church inquisitors that according to the teachings of Universal Life, only its followers would be saved is wrong, and nothing more than a diabolical gambit. Warnings from the

Spirit of God, which are issued to all people, are thus purposefully falsified and rendered implausible. What is an urgent problem for all of humankind is presented as the "psychological problem" of a few "end-time apostles" who want to make themselves important.

The further assertion in Magnis' writing that in Universal Life the "total destruction of the planet" is taught is also a mendacious distortion. This is also wrong – the Earth is purifying itself from the destructive excesses of human civilization, from the negativities of this world – the "world" in this sense will therefore pass away, but not the Earth.

The So-called "End-Time Disciples"

The church "sect experts" now zero in on the new topic. When in 1988, Pastor Haack held the annual meeting of his "parents' initiative" in Würzburg, as he had done for years, the press reported: "According to Pastor Haack, doomsday mania and psychological terror are more and more part of the arsenal of sects. With young people ... the motives... are mainly curiosity and boredom, but also deficits in orientation, the escape from the real world into an illusory one, as well as fear of the future and uncertainty."

You have to read it twice, to grasp the absurdity and perfidy of this statement. The institution, which as the centuries-old ruler of the western world is itself responsible for the disorientation and insecurity of many people, closes its eyes to the impending dangers – and then accuses those who want to point out these dangers of "escape into an illusory world." The law of projection also applies here.

In a divine revelation, Christ, the Co-Regent of the heavens, illuminated this behavior of the churches through the prophetic word in 1991:

Many years ago I again admonished through My instrument. Especially those who were and are in the Christian religions and call themselves Christians accuse those who spoke of the so-called end time: They are so-called end-time disciples who want to stir up the people, to build up an external power structure through fear and the like.

Who was servile to them? He will be with them today.

My children in all the world: There is no turning back! The floods are rising. The conflagrations are getting bigger and bigger. Famines, disasters, wars and the like are already alternating.

Inquisition on All Channels

The Lutheran pastor Wolfgang Behnk, the successor to Pastor Haack, succeeded in also bringing the topic of "End-Time Disciples" to television – for his most important strategic innovation was to include as many TV stations as possible in his campaign to damage reputations. Already on December 6, 1992, the women's program "Mona Lisa" *(ZDF-TV)* addressed the topic: "Between Religion and Ecstasy." The moderator denigrated Universal Life, of course, with the obligatory "only they" untruth:
"They believe in rebirth and in the imminent end of the world. Only they, the chosen ones, will survive the chaos in the New Jerusalem." Let it be repeated: There was never any talk of the Original Christians as the "chosen ones."

It quickly became clear that making fun of the "end time" should continue to play a major role in the Church's defamation repertoire. Finally, the year 2000 gradually came into view. Behnk himself pronounced it:
"Many people are particularly susceptible to the promises of salvation at the 'magic threshold' of a new millennium." (*Augsburg Allgemeine*, February 7, 1992) Or:

"Behnk expects a further increase in new doctrines of salvation until the turn of the millennium." (*Evangelische Sonntagsblatt Bayern*, February 21, 1993)

The "End-Time Apostle" Martin Luther

However, it is a great hypocrisy that Behnk, of all people, a representative of the Lutheran Church, accuses others of stirring up fear of an imminent "end of the world." It was Martin Luther, who – in contrast to the Original Christians in Universal Life – tried to calculate exact dates for the approaching end – and, three times at that! For the years 1532, 1538 and 1541, he respectively announced the "end of the world." Once again, the cassock wearers project their own mistakes onto others.

So that negative associations retain their effect, they have to be refreshed from time to time. As soon as something terrible happens – such as the mass death of Davidians in Waco (1993), the death of the "Sun Templars" in Switzerland (1994), the poison attacks in the Tokyo subway (1995) or the suicide of the group "Heaven's Gate" in California (1997), Behnk immediately takes advantage of this to prophesy an allegedly threatening "mass suicide" among the Original Christians (Chapter 8).

For anyone who has even the slightest sense of

ethics and decency, it is completely incomprehensible, how a pastor, who calls himself Christian, can constantly spout such mendacious opinions in public. This behavior is probably comprehensible only if one knows that behind the cassock wearers are the forces of the Baal system.

Defamations Bring Ratings ...

Behnk now appears more and more frequently on television, and he prefers to mix different religious groups, embellishing his descriptions of alleged facts, more and more. On October 12, 1994, in the "Morning Magazine" of *SAT 1*, for example, he explains:
So, the Jehovah's Witnesses, like Universal Life, are an apocalyptic end-time group, who with great alarm paint the end from which only they will be spared. ...

Anyone familiar with the media landscape knows that "new" topics usually do not come from just anywhere. One imitates the topics at the neighboring station that could bring "ratings." After a certain point, Behnk and other professional modern inquisitors don't even have to pull strings anymore – the topic becomes a sure thing.

And anyone who thinks that the stations do new research in each case is mistaken. For public broadcasters especially, financed by all citizens, ethical standards or their own broadcasting regulations play almost no role in this context – for these say that minorities may not be discriminated against.

But cassock wearers sit in all editorial offices and on all radio councils. And they make sure that minorities of faith that are unpopular with the mainstream churches do not fall under the law regarding the protection of minorities, and that they can be vilified at will.

If foreigners or disabled people are ostracized, protests are at least still made. In the case of non-church communities of faith, however, virtually all stations and editorial offices listen to church commands and discriminate without restraint.

On February 2, 1996, the topic of "Universal Life" appeared on the program "Heute-Journal" (*ZDF-TV*): "On these hills above Würzburg the sect community Universal Life wants to survive the coming apocalypse. ..."

... into the Last Living Room

It should be repeated here that the centuries-old ecclesiastical term of insult "sect," alone constitutes a severe discrimination. The viewer immediately "knows" – and this is intended – how he has to classify the whole thing, through which eyeglasses he has to consider it; the further wording of a contribution then merely serves to underline and "confirm" the prejudice. Moreover, the persistent "demonization of sects" distracts from the fact that the mainstream churches themselves are the largest sects in the truest sense of the word, because they have separated from the original teaching of the love for God and neighbor of Jesus of Nazareth.
Programs against Universal Life (often mixed with other communities of faith) are now broadcast in Germany at ever shorter intervals.

God, the eternal Creator, admonished and seriously warned what was to come. His word was ridiculed. Here is a small selection of the defamatory remarks:

- *Pro 7* – "Die Reporter" (March 19, 1996): "Storms, springtides, earthquakes. For religious fanatics, surely the harbingers of the apocalypse. At the turn of the millennium, visions of the end-time are booming worldwide ..."

- *Focus-TV* – "The Trumpet of God. About the businesses of the Universal Life Sect and the powerlessness of the authorities" (May 24, 1998): "Revelations announce the imminent end of the world. The exclusive offer to the disciples: Universal Life provides lifeboats for the Apocalypse."

- *Pro 7* – "Arabella"(September 10, 1998): "Universal Life – so ... is the name of this religious community, which ... probably also works with such doomsday scenarios, with death and ruin and sin, which I have already heard a few times now, for example with the Mormons. Am I getting it right?" (Original words of Arabella Kiesbauer questioning a "dropout")

- *ORF* – "Report Special" (March 8, 1999): "The area around Würzburg is the preferred settlement area of Universal Life ... in the eyes of the followers, the area here is the only one that should survive the prophesied end of the world somewhat unscathed."

The moderator emphasizes that the Apocalypse in the Bible – "theologians nowadays have to emphasize this quite often" – "is not to be understood as a prophesy." Then they let the Lutheran "sect expert" Michael Fragner speak, who, on his own Internet site, abuses the municipal name of a village in the district of Marktheidenfeld, and gathers together all attainable defamations against Universal Life.

Thinking for Oneself Is a Matter of Luck

In the war of "modern" Inquisition, television provides the big guns, with which the brains are "bombarded." But, as "ground troops," so to speak, the written word also fulfills an important task. A whole army of journalists, who have apparently "successfully" gone through the official church religious education, takes over the church defamation patterns against religious minorities with almost euphoric enthusiasm.

With it, in view of the ominous "millennium," one can captivate readers, achieve scary and sensational effects – and make a name for oneself. One's own reflection and examination, conversations with those concerned, principles of the rule of law and Constitution – all of these are secondary. Many think and act in this way because greed for sensation is more important to them than to deal with what God, the Eternal, really says through His prophetess.

Here, too, are a few examples:

- Holger Reile (among others, *Südkurier*, January 5, 1995): "'God's prophetess stirs up the fear of catastrophes in her followers: the 'end time' is imminent: earthquakes, epidemics, volcanic eruptions and finally, the deluge. The survivors – according to the 'Trumpet of God,' of course, the UL members – then found the ... Kingdom of Peace."

- *Main-Echo* (May 26, 1995): "Other sects make headlines with disaster scenarios: ... the community Universal Life ..."

- *Wiener Basta* (June 1995): "Redemption from all evil is hoped for through nature disasters. Afterward, the followers of the 'true world religion' can rejoice in a ... Kingdom of Peace."

- *Fränkische Landeszeitung Ansbach* (November 11, 1995): "Thus, the sect commissioner of the Protestant-Lutheran Church in Bavaria, Pastor Wolfgang Behnk, describes 'Universal Life' as an 'extreme apocalyptical worldview community'."

- *Frankfurter Allgemeine Zeitung* (January 1, 1996): "According to Keden's view, the alleged revelations from Gabriele are also shaped by doomsday ideas ..." (Pastor Joachim Keden is the sect commissioner of the Lutheran Church in Rhineland).

- Uwe Birnstein (*Das Sonntagsblatt*, February 2, 1996): "Inevitably, images of the Davidian farm in Waco come to my mind, where sect guru David Koresh and his followers entrenched themselves – and killed themselves." (The Lutheran theologian Birnstein visits the area around the Original Christian farm "Terra Nova" accompanied by the Inquisition accomplice Hans-Walter Jungen.)

- *Solothurner Zeitung* (September 25, 1996): "Sect advisor Toni Wirz of the 'Schweizerisch Beobachter' points to the exclusivity of 'Universal Life': The community of faith refers to being the only chosen ones who can prevail before the Great Last Judgment. An unmistakably sectarian trait."

- *Abendzeitung Nürnberg* (April 12, 1997): "End-time visions are part of the standard repertoire of the self-named 'instrument of God' ... Sometimes she warns of a poisonous cloud, a nuclear war or a deluge. And again and again, the year

2000 is given as the point in time of the great disaster.

(The reader knows meanwhile that this is a sheer lie – the readers of the evening newspaper did not know that.)

- *Kirche + Leben*, Münster (June 2, 1997): "The members of 'Universal Life' count themselves among the survivors of an end of the world, brought about by disasters."

- Holger Lösch (*Zeit-Punkte*, 4/97): "Universal Life also frightens its followers with threats of the end time, while at the same time promising 'lifeboats.'"

- *Frankfurter Neue Presse* (October 8, 1997): She (Gabriele) "prophesies the 'end time' to her followers, from which they can, however, protect themselves as members of the sect – especially if they bring all their capital with them into the association." (A new variant of a mendacious opinion – and a new projection: The Roman Catholic trade in indulgences sends its regards! The new defamation immediately makes the rounds.)

- *Offenbach-Post* (November 6, 1997): "With its end-time incantations, the sect induces its members to give up all their possessions to it."

As these few examples make clear, the churches obviously have an immense influence on the mass media – even if this is very rarely made the subject of discussion in these media.

Thus, for instance, on December 29, 1997, in the weekly magazine *Focus*, an article appeared with the headline "Millions for Missions." Therein one could read:

Never before have the churches exercised so much influence on the media as today. ... For their 'media zeal, the church princes' ... spend 'almost as much money as for the preservation of their places of worship and church facilities.'

Focus mentioned an amount of 300 million German marks annually.

In Germany, the churches have their own journalism schools, radio stations, press agencies, publishing firms, printing shops, newspapers, magazines and TV production companies.

And on January 17, 2015, the German daily newspaper *taz* wrote about the influence of the churches in the media: *The Catholic and also the Protestant Churches enjoy unique privileges in this country ... No other social lobby is so favored.*

How do people fare when articles about their faith appear weekly, even daily, and programs are broadcast, all of which are defamatory and distort the facts, or boldly make up lies in public? You can still write a letter to the editor of a local newspaper or hand out a flyer – but what do you do about a prime-time TV show that flickers over the screens all across the country? At that time, television was the dominant medium everyone used and relied on; the Internet and the like were still in their infancy.

And how did Gabriele, the prophetess and emissary of God, fare under this barrage of lies and slander? Through her, God, the All-Wise One, had warned humankind in time. But now, these warnings were obscured by a cascade of mockery and imprecations. And the calamity on the planet takes its course almost unchecked. To a large extent, the devastating consequences of this go on the debt account of the mainstream churches. If the churches had not used their media power to ridicule the word of the Christ of God in public and thus prevent the warnings of the Spirit of God from being taken seriously, many things could still have been prevented or mitigated.

The Scapegoat Has Long Since Been Found

So that the zeal of the journalists does not slacken in reproducing and spinning his stories, Pastor Behnk speaks out here and there, this time in the *Süddeutsche Zeitung* (February 4, 1998):
With a view to the approaching turn of the millennium, Wolfgang Behnk has warned of the increase of self-destructive actions in sects and psycho-groups. The evocation and "conjuring up" of "end times" entails much aggressive potential, said Behnk. Especially groups such as the Jehovah's Witnesses and Universal Life, which predicted doomsday scenarios, are at risk.

This, too, should be read twice. On the one hand, it once again reinforces the assertion that it is not the crises looming on the horizon that are the problem, but those that point to them. On the other hand, something like a classic scapegoat theory is prepared between the lines: If it does come about – then we already know who is to blame: Of course, not the churches, which have been throwing sand in the eyes of the people for centuries, and which, with their contemptuous interpretation of the words "Subdue the Earth," have given people carte blanche to exploit nature. Instead, it is those who "conjured up" the disasters! In superstitious times, (and they do not seem to be over yet) in stormy seas, people ultimately sought the "guilty party" on the ship, in order to throw him overboard.

And as for the "aggressive potential" that the modern inquisitor Behnk imputes to others: On behalf of his regional bishops, Johannes Hanselmann (until 1994), Hermann von Loewenich (1994-98) and Johannes Friedrich (from 1998), he himself constantly sows discord in the country, creating and fomenting prejudices and ostracizing people.

"Under the Spell of the Apocalypse"

The closer the year 2000 approaches, the more the suspicions and imputations increase:

- Hugo Stamm (*Tages-Anzeiger* Zürich, October 10, 1998): "Sect specialists warn that the one-sided concentration on apocalyptic developments and end-time delays could lead to a longing for death."

- Behnk's colleague Bernhard Wolf from Nürnberg also stokes the same fire: "In view of the coming turn of the millennium, obscure sects like 'Universal Life' ... and some others are eagerly taking hold of such [sic!] prophecies, wanting to stir up an end-time atmosphere and fears – in the name of Jesus."

In truth, it is the churches that are constantly stirring up fears and aggressions against dissidents. In any case, the articles in the press turn out as desired:

- *Kieler Nachrichten* (December 29, 1998): "End-time fanatics feverishly await the year 2000 ... One of the best known end-time sects in Germany is the Würzburg group 'Universal Life,' whose members ... are preparing for life after the Apocalypse."

- *Frankfurter Neue Presse* (December 30, 1998): "End-time prophets are in great demand ... the turn of the millennium is giving a further boost to the end-of-the world prophets in the western world, and in the course of the year 1999 we will have to brace ourselves for a lot more. ... (Universal Life) is establishing small or larger businesses ... in order to make its members capable of survival and equip them for the expected disasters of the transition period."

Again, this comes through: The problem is not the state of the world – the problem is created by those who talk about it. And hints and warnings that should have been valid for everyone are simply reinterpreted as the selfish "survival training" of a "sect." The plans of the church slanderers are working out.

- *Bild am Sonntag* (January 17, 1999): "Is there Going to be a Big Bang? The dangerous predictions of the death cults to the turn of the millennium." Universal Life is also "included" here.

- According to the *Abendzeitung Nürnberg* (April 20, 1999), hospitals are preparing "emergency plans" for December 31, 1999 – "because many gurus could call upon their followers to commit suicide."
Immediately, Pastor Wolf (who may have launched the article himself) is again on hand and mentions Universal Life as one of the groups "that play a role here." The caption under his portrait reads: "Wants to Remove the Fear of the Apocalypse: Pastor Bernhard Wolf."

So, the dangerous "heretics" have frightened the good citizens without reason. The Church comforts them again. And meanwhile, Mother Earth must continue to waste away.

And Then?
Besides Defamations – Nothing!

Then, when the year 2000 actually dawned, the "Big Bang" in the religious scene, so eagerly predicted by the church "experts," completely failed to materialize. No mass suicides far and wide, no disappointed doomsday disciples who had sold everything and now were forced to go on living – none of that.

But this did not really bother the "experts." When other communities of faith predict something that does not happen, they are mercilessly ridiculed and mocked. But when the "dark forebodings" of the cassock wearers that are celebrated in the media do not come true, then they simply turn back to business as usual, trusting in the short memory of the people – and invent further modern Inquisition methods to take action against their dissident fellow human beings.

11. State and Justice Department Under the Thumb of the Church

As we have seen, church inquisitors repeatedly used their massive influence in the mass media to slander the Original Christians in Universal Life and to make them look ridiculous in the eyes of the public.

After the followers of Jesus of Nazareth had begun to build up businesses and social services in the spirit of the Sermon on the Mount, the church representatives considerably expanded their destructive machinations: They then exerted pressure on politicians, authorities and courts in order to harm the Original Christians as much as possible, and to make every effort to hinder them in the pursuit of their constitutionally guaranteed rights as citizens.

The priests and cassock wearers have had thousands of years of practice in this. Just a few examples:

- It was the priests who incited the rulers of the Israelites against the prophets of God, in order to imprison, expel or murder them. In the Bible of the churches, for example, the bitter lament of God's prophet Hosea is handed down: *"As robbers lie in wait for a man, so the priests band together."* God's prophet Jeremiah was declared a traitor to the people at the instigation of the priests and thrown into a mud pit to starve, from which he narrowly escaped. But later he was stoned to death – just one of many.

- It was the caste of priests of that time that blackened Jesus of Nazareth, the greatest prophet of God of all time, with the Roman occupation power. They defamed Him, the Prince of Peace, as an alleged leader with political motives, thus bringing about His cruel murder.

- It was the priests, who in 331, led Constantine to ban the meetings of all "heretical" movements deviating from the Roman Church – such as the Marcionites or Montanists, who were oriented toward early Christianity – to confiscate their properties and destroy their meeting houses.

- It was the priests who achieved the fact that in 380, with the stroke of a pen, Emperor Theodosius abolished the freedom of belief in the Roman Empire, which had still been partially practiced until then, and made Catholicism the sole religion still allowed. Even then, state inquisitors (investigating magistrates) and denunciators (secret agents) were used to combat "heresy." To have a different faith was considered "high treason" and was punished with death.

- It was the priests who, in the 6th century, incited the Eastern Roman Emperor Justinian against the Arians, that is, the "heretical" vandals and Ostrogoths, whose peoples were radically exterminated.

- In 1215, it was a pope – Innocent III – who, under threat of excommunication, obligated all the rulers of the Occident to fight the Cathar "heretics" in their country.

- Pope Honorius III extorted from Emperor Frederick II (1194-1250) cruel laws against the "heretics," which included a kind of collective punishment (no public offices) into the second generation.

- In 1477, the Dominican monk Alonso de Hojeda used moral pressure to force the Spanish Queen Isabella to establish the terrible Spanish Inquisition.

- The former Augustinian monk Martin Luther called on territorial rulers to persecute and kill the Anabaptists. From the pulpit, preachers of both denominations urged sovereigns to persecute the "witches."

- And when in 1933, the National Socialists in Germany began persecuting Jehovah's Witnesses (who refused military service), both Catholic and Lutheran princes of the Church welcomed this. Lutheran pastors were even asked by their church leadership to denounce the religious minority to the state authorities.

- After the Second World War, both churches, despite their obvious involvement in fascism, presented themselves as "resistance fighters." They resumed their fight against everything that was not church-related and achieved in almost all German federal states the fact that in addition to the church "sect commissioners," state "sect observers" were also appointed.

These are just a few examples, highlights in an unbroken grim historical chain of persecution of dissidents on the basis of the Baal system, the adversary of the Free Spirit – and this, always under abuse of the name of God, the Eternal, and His Son, Christ. (This is described in detail in the book "Das Kettenopfer.")

Why should it be any different today? Here, too, just a few examples. We have already seen what representatives of the churches were able to achieve:

- that the purchase contract for the District Hospital Dettelbach was rescinded by the authorities;

- that the Original Christians received no chance from the Würzburg City Council to establish an industrial area in the district of Heuchelhof;

- that the village of Hettstadt (district of Würzburg) refused to carry out the already promised opening (electricity, water connections, etc.) of building lots purchased by Original Christians;

- that Original Christian parents had to fight in court for years to gain a permit for a private school;

- that an agricultural office refused to grant state-guaranteed subsidies to Original Christian farmers;

- that the *Bavarian Broadcasting Company*, a public corporation, refused, after a signal from a "sect commissioner," to broadcast a commercial for the business *Lebe Gesund!*

In 1995, when the Bavarian Minister of Education, Hans Zehetmair, angrily exclaimed: "The state is not the beadle of the cult commissioners" (Chapter 9) – he confirmed precisely this ecclesiastical pressure which was and is being exerted on him and on many others. This statement, which unfortunately remained an exception, confirms the rule: In many cases, with few exceptions, the state and politicians are all too willing to let themselves be hitched to the carts of the Church Inquisition of our days.

Federal Government:
The Public Pillory

Many citizens also consider statements made by government agencies to be particularly credible – and all the more so, the higher up an agency is positioned.
It is all the more alarming, when this power is abused by official government agencies to well and truly pillory communities of faith in the spirit of the churches, for instance, in public "warnings."
Thus, **Cornelia Yzer** (CDU), State Secretary in the Federal Ministry for Family Affairs, claimed on August 3, 1993, that the Federal Government had "findings" regarding Universal Life, "which indicate

possible dangers for the personality development and social relations of young people."

This was in response to a parliamentary question by **Ursula Schmidt**, an SPD member of parliament (and later Federal Minister of Health) from Aachen, who apparently wanted to make a name for herself with the "sect" issue. What these "findings" of the government precisely consisted of and where they came from, Mrs. Yzer could not, or did not want to, reveal, not even in court, where the Original Christians filed a suit for an injunction against this slander.

The Administrative Court of Cologne (March 29, 1995) could not, however, agree to an injunction – not because the judges assumed the truth of this allegation, but because they assumed that the State Secretary would not repeat the statement, which, incidentally, as they said, was "not particularly defamatory," anyway.

In her reply, Yzer had announced, among other things, "the creation of information material aimed at specific target groups," which in normal language amounts to: a state "sect report." A short time later, the Federal Minister of Family Affairs, **Angela Merkel** (CDU), daughter of a Lutheran pastor and later chancellor, also personally announced this. She tells the public that "Occult practices are booming among young people." And, "negative consequences of membership can be dropping out of school and vocational training, radical personality changes, alienation from reality, conflicts with parents, partners, friends and children."

The *Bild-Zeitung* (September 13, 1993) even gives the whole thing a headline: "New Gurus Endanger Our Children." No church "expert" could have more crassly formulated this all-round attack, in which the "Homebringing Mission of Jesus Christ" was also named, than the minister sworn in to ensure the equal treatment of all citizens.

What the later chancellor overlooked, however: The full-bodied announcement (174 pages) listing all potentially "dangerous" groups had a tactical disadvantage. The communities of faith thus branded as heretics were not willing to let themselves be publicly pilloried by the self-appointed state inquisitor. Through an indiscretion, the intended text got into the hands of the groups attacked – and triggered a wave of lawsuits.

On the one hand, the pages directed against Universal Life proved to be outdated (hence, the title "Homebringing Mission"), as they were largely based on a text that the Berlin Youth Senate had published as early as 1988.

On the other hand, they were teeming with false statements about the Original Christian teachings.

For example: Allegedly, the souls that had not found their way back to God by the end of time (when the material Earth passes away) would be "destroyed" – whereby the concept of an eternal damnation expressly does *not* exist among the Original Christians, but rather, it is taught that all souls will sooner or later find their way back to God. Or they stated that negative thoughts are supposed to be "suppressed" – in truth, the opposite is taught: Negative thoughts should by no means be suppressed, but recognized, analyzed and worked through. At the end of the text passages from a church encyclopedia about "sects" are inserted – without any reference! – in which, among other things, "healing methods" are mentioned, "which indiscriminately are used in place of conventional medicine." A downright lie, when one knows that, for instance, in the Original Christian *Naturklinik*, conventional medical methods and medicines are also used for a large part of the treatments.

The danger of "alienation from reality," which **Angela Merkel** attributed across the board to non-church religious orientations, had apparently affected her own ministry.
The Original Christians brought action against being included in the "report" – because, according

to democratic conventions, they would have had to be heard beforehand, at least regarding the assertions. The Administrative Court of Cologne (December 20, 1993), in expedited proceedings, at first actually ruled in their favor. But in August 1995, the Higher Administrative Court in Münster denied them legal protection and referred them to a main proceeding that would have taken many years – the "expedited proceedings" alone, had already dragged on for two years! The judges in Catholic Münster even considered the assertion of the alleged suppression of orthodox medicine by early Christian healing methods to be not entirely far-fetched – and thus, simply ignored counter evidence and affidavits by doctors of the *Naturklinik* which proved the opposite. The judges paid more attention to the claims of church "sect commissioners," which the ministry presented in great numbers for its defense.

When "collecting data," ministry officials did not even shy away from downright espionage, which in a democratic state is actually reserved for the constitutional protection authorities: They asked the Würzburg criminal investigation department for "information" about Original Christian physicians. The Criminal Investigation Department – a clear violation of the Data Protection Act – willingly provided information; however, as was to be expected, nothing useful came of it.

Nevertheless, Merkel's successor (from 1994) **Claudia Nolte** (CDU) was still unable to publish the report because of other proceedings – and finally gave it up entirely in favor of a parliamentary *Enquetekommission* (commission of inquiry) set up at the instigation of the church. That the final report of this inquisition commission (French "enquête" and Latin "inquisitio" have, not by chance in this case, the same root word) did not turn out to the satisfaction of the churches, was not due to the "committed Catholic" Nolte – as she herself said – who shortly before her appointment as Helmut Kohl's youngest minister had defended the Church against the accusation in the magazine *Tango* (October 13, 1994) of excessive wealth: "The Catholic Church is certainly not an economic power ... With these insinuations against better knowledge, the intent is to undermine the authority of the churches," thus, Claudia Nolte. (For more details on the wealth of the Church see, for example, Carsten Frerk, "Violettbuch Kirchenfinanzen.") Youthful naiveté or deliberate stultification of the people?

Rhineland-Palatinate:

Minister Calls for Denunciation

We could also ask this of the Rhineland-Palatinate Minister of Social Affairs **Ulrich Galle** (SPD), who in 1993 called on the people of Rhineland-Palatinate to denounce all non-church religious activities throughout the state – "to makes it easier ... a reply card is enclosed." When Original Christians then reacted to the defamations of the *Hessian Broadcasting Corporation* with a comparison of the current church defamations and National Socialist defamations against the Jews from the early 1930s, the CDU faction leader **Hans-Otto Wilhelm** considered an argumentative discussion on this topic to be completely superfluous and got annoyed: This is "completely intolerable," the state has become a "romping place for such groups" – and Universal Life is even missing from Galle's "brochure on sects."

Minister Galle made up for the "lapse" in March 1994 by publicly "warning" against Universal Life: It was conspicuous by its "totalitarian claim," was "against the Catholic and Protestant-Lutheran churches in an extraordinarily aggressive way" and tried "to achieve political influence by founding political parties (Urdemokraten – Original Democrats)." (There was only one local councilor who was associated with Universal Life in a single Franconian village!) An inquiry at the ministry revealed that they had no documents whatsoever of their own there – they simply took over the assertions of the Catholic sect commissioner Christoph Bussen (Diocese of Speyer), which he made at the same time in Rhineland-Palatinate (March 24, 1994) – not without adding the impudent false assertion that in Universal Life not only the consumption of meat but also the use of medicines is "forbidden." All physicians and patients of the clinic and medical practices run by Original Christians can testify to the contrary – but for a Catholic theologian, only prohibitions count; he obviously cannot imagine anything else.

The church news agencies eagerly took up all these untruthful assertions again – and the well-known quotation carousel was again set in motion. An appeal to the courts again proved to be unsuccessful: The Administrative Court of Mainz (June 8, 1994) objected to the Original Christians not having credibly shown that the ministry would repeat its statement – although the ministry had declared during the trial, that it was still necessary to warn against Universal Life. The Higher Administrative Court in Koblenz, however, decided (August 8, 1994) that Universal Life could reasonably be expected to engage in main proceedings lasting several years.

Galle's successor in the office of the Minister of Social Affairs, **Rose Götte** (SPD) even went so far as to issue a public warning about the market stands of the company *Gut zum Leben*, which the *Evangelische Pressedienst* immediately circulated. And in May 2002, Götte's successor, Minister of Labor **Malu Dreyer** (SPD), later Prime Minister of Rhineland-Palatinate, also considered the "business activities" of the Original Christians in Frankenthal to be "very problematic." Nor did she give any evidence or justifications; she relies solely on the mendacious opinions of the church. It seems that the Rhineland-Palatinate government's dependency on the church is not based on slip-ups by individuals, but has a system, to wit, straight through the parties.

The consequences are accordingly: What a state government announces is simply parroted at the local level. Hardly anyone there tunes into their own common sense.

The example of the city of Überlingen shows the effects of governmental denouncements in Germany, where, unfortunately, subservience to authorities still exist: In October 1994, head mayor **Klaus Patzel** refused to continue renting municipal spaces to Universal Life with the "reasoning" that he "examined all the … available sources of public knowledge, especially a publication in the magazine *'Stern'* as well as "information ... from other German states" – meant was, as one inquiry revealed, the state Rhineland-Palatinate. (Poor Germany, if it thinks it has only church "sources of knowledge" at its disposal.)

Schleswig-Holstein:
Federal Cross of Merit for Hounding "Sects"

That is why the Original Christians did not become reconciled to the "Report ... on the Activities of Sects in Schleswig-Holstein," which the state government published in 1995. Not only because the long known and refuted untruths from the mentioned church encyclopedia were again copied there: The "aspired Christ-State" should become "political reality," or "newly revealed healing methods" were to "replace conventional medicine." But also because experience shows that a mere mention in a state report, no matter how insubstantial, is quite sufficient to stamp a religious community as leprous in the eyes of many citizens and authorities. And that is quite obviously the aim of such publications.

Although the Original Christians again seek expedited proceedings, the Administrative Court of Kiel allows itself half a year – and then rejects the application with the "justification" that the plaintiffs had not taken direct action against the publishing house that acted as the editor, but directly against the state government – a pretext that is obviously far-fetched. The court was not interested in the fact that the government also sent the report on request. In March 1996, the Original Christians then are compelled to make a compromise before the Higher Administrative Court of Schleswig: The state government is allowed to publish further editions, but must, however, refrain from the (above mentioned) worst defamations.

What such a state government is brewing from the poison cupboards of the church inquisitors is, however, not just any one insignificant report among many. The extent to which authorities and politicians then rely on exposés that have been produced in such a way can be clearly seen in a sample contract that was presented to all exhibitors at an Esoteric Fair in Lübeck in the middle of 1996: "The organizer must ensure that exhibitors who advertise for sects, which the federal or state government warns against do not participate in the event. ... Reference is made to the printed matter ... of the German Parliament." In Lübeck, a municipal (!) "representative of the Youth Welfare

Office for Sects and Psycho-cults," Eberhard Arent, ensured a strict ecclesiastical course.

Typical for the servility to the church of nearly all German government agencies with regard to non-church minorities is what the "sect commissioner" of Schleswig-Holstein, **Hans-Peter Bartels**, later military commissioner of the German Federal Parliament, had to say in February of 1996 at a planned conference in North Frisia on the subject of "New Religious Movements and Psycho-cults." Even though the subtitle "Soul Devourers Are Coming?" only poorly disguised by a question mark, can hardly be surpassed in terms of polemical propaganda, SPD politician Bartels takes offence at the fact that the "controversial sects" are allowed to introduce themselves: He categorically rejects "offering sects a platform at all."

In plain language: The "heretics" should not be allowed to defend themselves – after all, they were not allowed to do so in Inquisition processes during the Middle Ages, either!

Defamation Attack in the Dead of Night

Berlin is particularly zealous in the persecution of religious, that is, non-church, minorities. In the German capital, which should actually be a role model for other cities with regard to the rule of law, the Lutheran sect commissioner, Pastor Thomas Gandow, has the state authorities fully under control. Here, in the city of corruption scandals, one can also observe the personnel intertwining of state and church.

Just one example: The Senator for Family and Youth, who published the first Berlin "Sect Report" in 1994, was **Thomas Krüger** (SPD) – a Lutheran pastor, later president of the German Children's Emergency Fund and still later, head of the Federal Agency for Civic Education.

The "education" that he imposed on the citizens in this first Berlin "Sect Report" was – as to be expected under these circumstances – purely church-inquisitorial.

There were several objections to this report from groups that were pilloried in it, among them one from the Original Christians in Universal Life. They resisted the fact that in this report from 1994, a series of suspicions about them were simply compiled – after all the groups listed in the introduction had been presented with skillful insinuation as "monsters," as "anti-democratic and socially incompatible."

But the Berlin Higher Administrative Court rejected an urgent application to prohibit the city of Berlin from naming Universal Life, and provided a reasoning that was sheer mockery: The community of faith is not prevented by such a report from "continuing its activities, such as it believes to be right according to its faith."

That is approximately so, as if one would afterward say to a craftsman, whom one had innocently pilloried during the Middle Ages and thrown all kinds of rubbish at him: "You are now welcome to continue to offer your craftsman services."

In order to make such lawsuits completely superfluous in future – one doesn't not want to listen to the groups anyway – Kruger's successor, **Ingrid Stahmer** (SPD), tricks the courts and publishes the next "Sect Report" in December 1997 in the dead of the night, so to speak. She presents the report at a press conference and tells the astonished public that a large part of it has already been sent to counselling centers and schools. The "sect expert" Anne Rühle explains that this was a "precautionary measure against juristic blockades."

Legal objections by affected groups, which have every right to fear that they will once again be discriminated against in public, are thus considered "blockades" in Berlin, which one tries to prevent by swift action. The fact that one could or should listen to them beforehand, as is customary in a democracy, before saying anything disparaging about them apparently does not come to mind in a state agency, whether in Berlin or elsewhere. (But that is what the medieval Inquisition stipulated: You may not talk to a heretic at all!)

Since this report again contained a whole series of mendacious opinions of the Lutheran sect commissioner Behnk, the Original Christians went to court once again – but this time, too, the justice system in the capital proved to be extremely servile to the church. A quarter of a year after filing an urgent motion, the Administrative Court decided that Universal Life could counter the public warning of the Senate Administration with "diverging statements." The court knows, of course, that this is completely illusory: No Berlin newspaper would print a counterstatement by the Original Christians.

> **Yesterday – Inquisitor:**
> **Persecution all the way to murder**
>
> **Today – Sect Commissioner/Sect Expert:**
> **Persecution all the way to character assassination**

State-Church-Entanglement at Every Turn

To prevent someone from renting a hall to a non-church group, for example, despite all the defamation campaigns by the churches and the state, in the summer of 1999, the Berlin House of Representatives decided that "conflict-laden religious or ideological organizations or psycho-market providers" were no longer allowed to rent public space in the capital. And who is considered "conflict-laden" is determined by the state on the basis of church promptings.

If one allows the term "conflict-laden" to have its effect, one becomes aware of all the insidiousness that hides behind it. The unbiased newspaper reader is given the official impression that these are groups that constantly violate law and order and thereby cause "conflicts." In reality, it is the church and, in its wake, part of the state that violates the rules of the Constitution, thereby causing the conflict in the first place.

"Conflict-laden" could also mean: The more believers leave the mainstream churches and look for an alternative, the more people become aware that there is a discrepancy, an obvious conflict between the Christian claim of the mainstream churches and their un-Christian reality. In the end, this discrepancy contains fraudulent labeling, in that the believers are misled and the name of Jesus, the Christ, is abused for their own power interests – with unforeseeable consequences.

Baden-Württemberg: Who Is the Best "Sect" Hunter?

Where a state government is not quite as tempestuous in vilifying "sects" as the Church would wish, individual politicians are ready to fan the flames of modern Inquisition as best they can.

For example, **Günter Oettinger**, the leader of the CDU parliamentary group in Baden-Württemberg, later Minister-President and even later Commissioner of the European Union. In October 1994, he considered a "detailed investigation" of Universal Life to be "urgently necessary" – without, however, being able to say what he thought the Original Christians were actually guilty of.

The CDU faction then published its own brochure on "Sects as a Danger to Our Democracy," in which it printed defamations from Behnk and the Hessian Broadcasting Corporation.

The SPD won't take a back seat here. **Carla Bregenzer** (SPD) from Frickenhausen, a member of the state parliament, "goes to work" with particular zeal. In 1995, in a state parliament debate on the "danger of sects," she passed on false statements from sect commissioner Behnk. When the Original Christians then invite Mrs. Bregenzer for a personal visit, so that on the premises she can convince herself of the untenability of her statements, they receive no acknowledgement that she received it.

A politician who has swung onto the "sect" horse to make a name for himself will not voluntarily dismount. By investigating the facts, he would ruin his field of work, the discrimination of heretics.
Carla Bregenzer preferred to ignore the facts and continued to spread all kinds of church vilifications ("psychologically and financially dependent," "business concern with a religious cover-up," etc.) about the Original Christians, and in March 1996, she submitted a state parliament inquiry on the topic of Universal Life.

Annette Schavan, the Minister of Education and Cultural Affairs at the time, who had previously been the director of an Episcopal Academic Foundation and, at the end of her career, German ambassador to the Vatican (!), thought nothing of the fact that once again respectable citizens were being made the object of an official investigation

– nor did she consider it necessary to hear those affected. Nevertheless, in May 1996, the result for the Original Christians turned out to be not so bad: **The state government stated there were no indications that "reprisals" against "dropouts" were being carried out in Universal Life. There were no indications that the followers were being "exploited," not even "signs of unconstitutional actions or attitudes" could be found by the civil servants. There were also no objections against the school or clinic.**

However, the ignorance of a minister who does not listen to accused fellow citizens, left its mark on her report. Thus, she adopted unchecked statements from Alfred Spall's sham expert report about the meditation courses in the Homebringing Mission of Jesus Christ, which had been whipped into shape by order of the Bishop of Würzburg (Chapter 3).

Nevertheless: The Original Christians had been publicly rehabilitated for the second time – after Bavaria (Chapter 10) – in an official report. But those who thought the media would take note of this, were mistaken: The press servile to the church withheld the core points, according to which there are no indications of violations of the law – and unerringly picked out the few points where the government had passed on church distortions.

The FDP member of the state Parliament, **Dr. Walter Döring** used this atmosphere to jump on the anti-sect bandwagon to make a name for himself by "emphatically warning against this psycho group, which is also active in Schwäbisch-Hall."

Baden-Württemberg is a good example of how apparently career-addicted politicians try to outdo each other with populist excesses against non-church minorities. **Carla Bregenzer** called for a "foundation for sect victims" and presented a somewhat confused "dropout" who, years after a visit to the clinic, suddenly remembered that she did not like it there so much, after all. And when in March 2003, the mail-order foodstuff company "Lebe Gesund!" put a commercial on TV promoting "vegetarian foods," Bregenzer rushed to ask the public station ARD to stop airing this commercial. "Reason": This would "counteract" the "efforts to throw light" (as Bregenzer understands it) on Universal Life. ...

Meanwhile, **Hans-Werner Carlhoff**, the "sect commissioner of the state government," gives lectures throughout the region, in which he speaks of 50 "conflict-laden groups." In contrast, there is not a single state "church commissioner" who informs the population about sexual crimes committed by priests, for instance, or about the danger of ecclesiogenic neuroses.

In 2013, Baden-Württemberg publishes yet another "sect report," the 9th report of the "Interministerial Working Group for Questions on So-called Sects and Psycho-groups," in which Universal Life is also briefly mentioned. The state is now being governed by Minister-President **Winfried Kretschmann**, who belongs to the Green Party as well as the Central Committee of German Catholics. In this report one can see how much effort this state still puts into comprehensively monitoring all kinds of religious activities of its citizens, no matter how insignificant they may be in terms of numbers, and classifying them under the ecclesiastically shaped pattern of "sect." This includes all activities – except those of the mainstream churches, although the offences occurring there (such as sexual crimes committed by priests) would give considerably more cause for monitoring. And all this is done at the expense of the taxpayers!
Eight out of eleven ministries – almost the entire state government – participate in this report. In addition, non-governmental bodies are also involved. A prominent position is held – how could it be otherwise – by the "Work Group of Christian Churches." All "sect commissioners" of the major

churches in the region are members of their own such "specialist group."

Now it also becomes clear why the Roman Catholic and the Lutheran Churches – apart from their integration in the state – are not mentioned once in the state report. Here, the state makes itself the extended arm of the churches, which have by no means given up their goal of keeping the religious "competition" as small as possible. However, this goal is hidden in the report behind fine-sounding attempts at justification: One must "clarify and prevent," in order to protect the population "from being defrauded and harmed." One can literally feel the regret between the lines when it is conceded: "On the other hand, however, it is also clear today that ultimately, sociality can never be suppressed by belief systems." However, this does not lead to the obvious conclusion that such spying activities against one's own citizens should be stopped, and that the prosecution of violations of the law, if they occur, should be left to competent authorities. No, the costly collection of data continues unabated, and private groups that have no political legitimacy and that are also committed to "sect monitoring" receive state subsidies and thus, a quasi-public status. (References: "Die staatliche und kirchliche Gewalt und die Gerechtigkeit

Gottes," Gabriele-Verlag Das Wort, and Carsten Frerk: "Kirchenrepublik Deutschland.")
Apart from a general cheap propaganda, however, no specific purpose to the actions against the religious activities of its own citizens outside the church is recognizable, because hardly anything is put forward except slogans.

Oddly enough, t*he Universal Life of All Cultures Worldwide* is mentioned only in connection with the *International Religious Freedom Report*. There, Germany was reprimanded by the US government for discriminating against certain religious communities, including Universal Life.

Bavaria:
Minister as Zealous "Sect Persecutor"

Carla Bregenzer's idea of presenting persecuted minorities as perpetrators by setting up "aid funds" for "dropouts" was taken up by the Minister of Consumer Protection **Eberhard Sinner** (CSU) in the neighboring state of Bavaria. Together with District Administrator **Waldemar Zorn** (CSU), in July 2001, he founded a "donation fund" for "destitute UL dropouts." Zorn, of all people, who as mayor of Hettstadt had driven Original Christians out of his village by the score, was now "worried" about followers of Universal Life, who were being "literally mobbed out." And Minister Sinner abused his minister's office, financed by tax money, as a contact point for "sect victims."

Already as a member of the state parliament, Sinner had demonstrated his strange conception of democracy when he massively attacked District Administrator Grein (Main-Spessart) in April 1997: Grein's office had dared to mention in a women's brochure, besides numerous Catholic, Protestant and trade union institutions, an Original Christian kindergarten and the Original Christian social service center *Helping Hands*. The District Administrator had previously sought legal advice and had come to the conclusion that the state could not refuse to include the addresses on grounds of equal treatment. However, he had the affiliation of the Original Christian facilities indicated by a corresponding addition, so that everyone could decide freely. The *Bavarian Broadcasting Corporation* (Report Munich, April 21, 1997) promptly took offence at this and interviewed Behnk, who was once again allowed to warn against the "totalitarian" Original Christians. Sinner accused the District Office of supporting a "sect," whose teachings "have nothing whatsoever to do with the Christian message" and thus "blatantly undermines the efforts of the Church" in the fight against the Original Christians.

The Protestant-Lutheran Sinner could not have better expressed the fact that in his political work, he sees himself not so much as a representative of the people, but rather as an extended arm of the mainstream churches.

Or "with the Christian message," does Sinner mean everything that both mainstream churches have perpetrated in the past centuries until today by abusing the name of Jesus, the Christ: from spreading fear and terror of an allegedly wrathful God who sends His disobedient children into eternal damnation, to the fight against the early Christian communities, up to the Crusades, the persecution of heretics and witches, the participation in wars and sexual crimes against children?
Then the Original Christians really have nothing to do with it.

Nonprofit Status: Orders from "Higher Up" Turn the Truth Upside Down

In this case, the Original Christians were fortunate that in the Main-Spessart district, it was not the CSU, but the Freie Wähler (Free Voters) who held the office of District Administrator – a group in which there was still a high percentage of conservative, but independent politicians. Whereas in the question of a nonprofit status, the Original Christians had to experience how other Bavarian authorities proceeded in the ecclesiastical sense.

Normally, associations that pursue exclusively religious or ideological goals do not have to pay tax on the donations they receive. This was also the case with the Association Universelles Leben e.V. for years. Until in 1990, when Mayor Zorn spread the rumor that Christ-enterprises did not pay "one single mark in commercial tax." Which, of course, was nonsense.

The Munich Ministry of Finance then ordered a detailed audit of both the supporting association, Universal Life, as well as the businesses operated by Original Christians, which, however, in November 1992 led to a completely exonerating result by the Würzburg tax office:

The proceeds and donations received are used exclusively and directly for the statutory purpose. ... There were no indications of misuse of donations in commercial enterprises or of the association being favored by the enterprises... The audit ... did not reveal any findings that would justify revoking the nonprofit status.

However, in stark contrast to all these findings, the Bavarian Ministry of Finance mandated on December 3, 1993:

The Verein Universelles Leben e. V. (Association of Universal Life) cannot be recognized as a nonprofit organization. The assessments of the years 1989 to 1991, which are subject to review, are to be corrected accordingly. The provisional recognition of a nonprofit status for the years after 1992 is to be revoked.

As a justification, the Ministry came up with the idea of attributing to Universal Life the enterprises led by Original Christians in a kind of "overall picture."

With Catholic monasteries, on the other hand, which are economically active in a much more direct way, no authority comes up with the idea of attributing them to the Catholic Church in a kind of "overall picture."

This fiat contradicts the clear results of the relevant investigations and basically constitutes a perversion of justice.

The last sentence of the ministerial writing of December 12, 1993 gives an idea of what is behind it:
The clarification of the issue of the nonprofit legal status of sects by the Supreme Court is of fundamental importance. It is therefore in the interest of the assessment of future cases to enforce the expected legal means.

In a kind of test case, they wanted to financially undermine all non-church minorities of faith. The Original Christians then declared that in the future, they will no longer rely on a nonprofit status, as long as it is granted by a state, which can be made the beadle of the claims to power of the mainstream churches in this way. The Original Christians do not want to accept alms from such a "church state." However, for some years, (trusting in the temporarily granted nonprofit status that had been accounted for in the usual way), the followers of Jesus of Nazareth began a financial process – because the authorities demanded a retroactive "gift tax" for charitable donations received, although these donations had long since been spent, exactly as prescribed by tax law. For the sake of simplicity, the missing facts were replaced by slander and church lies, which had found their way into the files of the authorities on a large scale.

Against this outrage, the community of faith turned to the fiscal court seeking help. But there, they jumped out of the frying pan into the fire. Admittedly, the judges could not approve the basically unconstitutional reasoning of the tax authorities, without exposing themselves to ridicule nationwide. But they got by with a formal artifice: They found out that years earlier a small procedural error had been made in an official record. This had not been noticed by anyone for years and had actually never had a negative effect. But now, in 1998, it sufficed for the judges to make a decision that took into account the expectations of the Church and that expectation was: Withdrawal of the nonprofit status for people who want to live according to the Ten Commandments and the Sermon on the Mount of Jesus of Nazareth.

The same game was repeated in a second trial, which had to be conducted for a further tax period and lasted until 2013 (!): Although the procedural error had now been corrected, the tax administration now found another place in the statutes, which was interpreted in such a way that the nonprofit status had to be denied. For 20 years, nobody had come up with this absurd idea, neither the courts that were involved, nor the countless officials who had the task on ecclesiastical-religious grounds of finding reasons to deny the community its rights.

Nor had this passage in the statutes in any way affected the activities of the community of faith. But it was enough for an interpretation that enabled the officials to make a decision according to church guidelines. Finally, a settlement was agreed upon in order to at least limit the damages. Again, Universal Life is forced to pay considerable sums of money in addition. But the attempt of a ministerial bureaucracy indoctrinated by the Church to stop the movement of the Original Christians in this way fails.

*Rennebach Wants
to Become Federal Inquisitor*

At the federal level, it is, above all, the SPD member of parliament and Lutheran synodalist **Renate Rennebach** who, from 1995 onward, called for "fighting against sects" and wants the position of a "Federal Commissioner for Sects" established for this purpose – apparently with herself as the first office holder. She accuses Universal Life and other faiths in a sweeping manner: "They all violate the dignity of the human being and lead mostly young people astray."
When she is asked to make her assertions more precise or to form her own picture of the Original

Christians, she does not even consider it necessary to reply.

Presumably, she knows quite well that she will not find any evidence of this outrageous slander among the Original Christians in Universal Life – but however, among the church institutions. The baptism of an infant alone is a massive violation of human dignity, as is the threat of an alleged eternal damnation, not to mention the mistreatment and sexual crimes against children and youth committed by priests and pastors.

Only once the Original Christians write to several delegates of the SPD after a "telephone action" on the topic of "sects," in which, next to the SPD representative, the Lutheran "sect expert" Hemminger answers questions from the public, does Rennebach deign to take a position:

You can contribute to correcting your obviously existing impression that we are wrongly or insufficiently informed about the goals and practices of Universal Life by providing us with a meaningful organizational chart of the internal structure of your organization and by giving us information about the companies and holdings related to Universal Life and its leaders. We will then carefully examine these documents and also the question of whether this will result in the need for a conversation.

The entire arrogance of the modern Inquisition speaks from these lines: We do not speak to the "heretic" about his faith – rather, he has to give us comprehensive information! We don't believe him anyway, since the truth is always in our Inquisition files!

And these files are filled, above all, by Rennebach's party associate Wolfgang Behnk. According to a *dpa* (German Press Agency) report, Rennebach claims that Universal Life "has even threatened the sect commissioner of the Protestant-Lutheran Church with religious mass suicide." (Chapter 8)
After a lawyer intervenes, she takes back this wicked defamation – without apologizing, because it had been pronounced and spread.
To push through the establishment of "her" Commission of Inquiry in Parliament, Rennebach frightens the public with "600 sects" in Germany. Only after the results of the inquiry, disappointing for all "sect" hunters, does it become somewhat quieter around Rennebach.

Austria: "You Can Just Pray at Home"

In Austria, the "danger from sects" is also painted on the wall. **Martin Bartenstein**, Minister of Family Affairs, is "ready to take a firm stand against the nuisance of sects" and announces a "brochure on sects," which is then published in November 1996, although Austrian constitutional law does not allow a different treatment of religious communities either, that is, warning against some and not against others.

According to the text of the brochure, although the state may not "be in solidarity with one or more particular churches ..." the Ministry simply copies entire passages from a brochure of the Archdiocese of Vienna concerning Universal Life, and thus, does not even consider it necessary to conduct its own research. A court case against the inclusion of the Original Christians in this report is delayed by the Austrian system of justice.

In the brochure, Bartenstein quite unabashedly claims that the state's obligation to protect freedom of religion refers only to "legally recognized churches and religious communities" with more than 2000 members. Smaller religious communities "are allowed the so-called 'practice of religion at home' ..."

So that's how it is: Under the pretext of membership numbers, anything that does not suit the church is turned into a second-class community of faith which is barely allowed to pray at home.

The brochure is completely absurd when it comes to the criteria of the "dangerousness" of a group. When it says: "Is there little or no criticism allowed in the community?" – who doesn't think of the many doctrinal prohibitions for critical Catholic theologians? Or: "Are members urged to disclose intimate details of their lives?" – who doesn't think of confession?

However, this was just the beginning: A newly created "sect office" was to collect "publicly available data" on non-church minorities, such as "which persons are in leading positions in sects." The mainstream churches themselves are expressly excluded from this spying activity, which is endowed with five million Schillings by the state, in a law passed especially for this purpose.

The United States, which is quite vigilant with regard to freedom of religion, publicly reprimanded Austria for this obvious discrimination and spying of minorities. Such laws are "incompatible with the European Convention on Human Rights and other international conventions."

In Austria, too, local authorities (for example, in Linz) refer to the mention of Universal Life in this brochure, in order to justify, for example, the refusal to rent municipal premises. In Linz, moreover, the Ministry of Family Affairs of the Federal Province of Upper Austria, together with the Episcopal Pastoral Office (!), publishes its own brochure on the subject of "Sects – Nuisance and Ignorance" in June 1998.

The author is the sect commissioner of the diocese of Linz, Andreas Girzikowsky, in person. On the back, there is an advertisement promoting the church newspaper. In a press release, the author warns specifically of Universal Life, which has "Austria and Switzerland on its menu." The Upper Austrian governor **Josef Pühringer** lumps "sects" together with "drug addiction." **Gerhard Schäffer**, President of the Salzburg State School Board, does the same: "Advertising for alcohol, drugs or sects is forbidden in schools."

In the federal state of Salzburg, school principals are incited against "sects, psycho terror and Satanic cult" by church and state "experts," also from Germany. 270 school principals participate in a conference of the state school board – 75 percent of all those invited, as councilor Stöglehner proudly notes. The neighboring state of South Tyrol does not want to be left behind: In September 1998, the state of South Tyrol appoints a sect commissioner...

It is important to remember: Who, actually, determines who is considered a "sect"? Of course, the mainstream churches, and they attach this insult to practically all other communities.

"Nip It in the Bud!"

In Upper Austria, when Governor **Pühringer** publishes another edition of his "Sects" brochure (2002) under the title "In Search of Meaning," Professor Ernö Lazarovits, a former prisoner of the Mauthausen concentration camp and a member of the Hungarian Central Council of Jews, speaks out. In a letter to Pühringer and to Federal President Klestil, he points out that, because of his painful experiences in the concentration camp, he is sensitive to people who meet with hostility because of their religious convictions:

From my experience I can say that the persecution of the Jews began in such a way that we were first made to look bad, which, in turn, provided the pretext for taking the next steps that you are probably also aware of. Today, commemoration ceremonies are held and at each of these events the following invocation is made: Something like this must never happen again! One can only agree with this, but one must especially "nip the beginnings in the bud." It is therefore with great concern that I have to say that the CD-ROM entitled "In Search of Meaning" published by the Catholic Church and the State of Upper Austria, is a treatment of people of other faiths that could be described as collective bad-mouthing, just as the "Star of David" was put around our necks at that time. Then, it was "merely" the Jews, today, it is "merely" the "sects" – where is the difference?

When the Original Christians want to have this remarkable statement of an internationally renown Jewish fellow citizen distributed in Germany through the well-known media agency "News aktuell" (Hamburg) for a corresponding fee, they are refused.

Justice Is Blind in Its Eye to the Church

When the Original Christians were discriminated against by the state at the instigation of the churches, the only way left was usually through the courts, which, as described, however, brought little or no success in the majority of cases. This is not surprising, when one knows that "sect experts" of the churches are allowed to speak for hours about "dangerous sects" at conferences of the Judicial Academy and then spend merry evenings with the judges.

The Original Christians, when they nevertheless took this path, were often called "litigious" by church representatives. Some even got carried away with the hypocritical remark that calling upon the courts contradicts the Sermon on the Mount – which they otherwise do not take seriously themselves, describing it as "utopia." Yet the Bible of the churches itself contains the instruction to bring a conflict "before the community" if it cannot be resolved between the parties involved, even after calling in third parties (Mt. 18:15 ff.) The wrath of the sect commissioners against "heretics" who, as citizens of this world, make use of their civil rights, is therefore probably more likely to be connected with the resulting restrictions on their otherwise unlimited possibilities for slander.

For the Original Christians, in many cases there was no other way around it, but to make use of their right as citizens to appeal to the courts, despite the rather limited chances of success. Each of these court decisions is comparable to a small dam, which, although it does not completely prevent the flood of slander and discrimination, at least partially limits it. A few more examples of this are cited in the following:

Church Incitement in State Garb

At the end of 1994, in a brochure of the Bavarian State Agency for Civic Education, the journalist Holger Lösch publishes an article on Universal Life that is brimming with untruths and maliciousness. And this, in a brochure paid for and published by the state, which is distributed to all Bavarian schools for "clarification"!

In April 1995, the Bavarian Administrative Court, in the second instance of expedited proceedings, rules that eleven places in the brochure must be made unrecognizable. The Original Christians go into the main suit, because the passages that have not been blackened still contain massive slander and are eagerly quoted by "Pastor" Behnk as being "determined by the court" – yet, a hearing of evidence or the examination of witnesses did not take place at all in these expedited proceedings! It is worth the long wait: In September 1998, the Original Christians are upheld in decisive points by the Munich Administrative Court; the remaining copies of the brochure are scrapped and the

Bavarian State Government must send a correction to all Bavarian schools. Therefore, it is clear: Church sect commissioners may indeed spread untruth as opinion within the framework of an almost unrestricted "freedom of opinion" – but the state may not adopt this agitation.

At the hearing in August 1998, embarrassing scenes had occurred for the state's lawyer, who, for example, could not name a single concrete case, in which a supporter of Universal Life had refused medical assistance. "We are actually allowed to publish such a document only if we already have the facts. We are not allowed to go around making pure assumptions," the judge remarked with a frown.

Behnk, however, continued to disseminate the passages of the long-outdated 1995 court order that were favorable to his "work," as though the more far-reaching 1998 ruling did not exist.

Information Stands for Original Christians?

The Original Christians are also successful in the enforcement of civil rights, for example, freedom of speech – even if only after a long struggle. In May 1985, the city of Essen, contrary to the usual practice up to that time, rejects a request of the Original Christians to be allowed to set up an information stand in downtown Essen.
Behind it is the "Sect Info" Essen, whose leader, Heidemarie Cammans, had previously incited local politicians against new faith movements. The Original Christians go to court – however, it takes three years, until October 1988, before they are allowed to set up an information stand in Essen again. Before that, they had theoretically been proven right, but the dates for which they had sued had already expired. Only when they applied for a date one and a half years in advance, were the representatives of Universal Life granted approval by a decision in the second instance five days (!) before this date. The ruling of the Administrative Court of Münster contained the stipulation that road construction authorities may only take into account the requirements of traffic when granting permits for information stands, but are not permitted to make objections regarding content.

There are also difficulties elsewhere. In Berlin, Pastor Thomas Gandow did a thoroughly discriminatory job. Beginning in mid-1986, the responsible district offices in Berlin rejected information stands of the Original Christians and justified this with the "danger" that "especially young people ... under the pretext of religious objectives ... would be mentally and materially harmed."
Before it comes to trial, apparently level-headed lawyers retain the upper hand over the church-indoctrinated officials: From 1987 on, permission is again granted. The inflammatory writing, from which the outrageous slander originated, turns out to be an "internal administrative document." The Senator for Youth and Family refuses to allow the Original Christians to see the pamphlet. A short time later, the former West Berlin smoothly transfers this poisoned climate, this disregard for the rights of non-church minorities, to the new federal capital of Berlin.

After the proceedings against the city of Essen, during the following years, it is usually sufficient to send this judgment to the respective city administration and thus end a looming blockade of information stands.
The intensified agitation of church "experts" prior to the Inquiry Commission of the German

Parliament in the mid-1990s – despite a clear legal position – led to increased rejections, mostly justified with some kind of state "sect reports" or with statements made by the church. In Ludwigshafen, Bremen, Freudenstadt, Baden-Baden, Radolfzell and Obernburg am Main, permits for information stands must again be sought in court, but this time, mostly in short expedited proceedings.

In court, for example, it turned out that the city of Obernburg simply lied to the Original Christians and the court, when it claimed that the location applied for was unsuitable because of traffic impairment. A phone call to the responsible police station showed that other stands had often been set up at the place in question without difficulty. However, the city of Rastatt behaved rather strangely. It approved an information stand at the end of 1994, but charged an utterly excessive "handling fee" of 100 marks. It turned out that the clerk in charge spent considerable time telephoning around to make sure that he had made the right decision regarding the "heretics." He then charged the Original Christians for this.

It is similar to the Middle Ages: The heretic has to also pay for the measures that were taken by the Inquisition!

Some communities also try to stop the distribution of flyers. In Bamberg in 1997, a "fine" of 30

German marks is even imposed, which is withdrawn only through the intervention of a lawyer. The city of Ingolstadt wants to know what's what, and goes as far as the Bavarian Administrative Court, where in 1996, in the second instance, it is clearly ascertained that the distribution of written material, of mainly informative content, is covered by the fundamental right to freedom of opinion.

Even if the cases mentioned were ultimately decided in accordance with this fundamental right, the mere necessity of having to go to court for something that is taken as a matter of course in a democratic state is a scandal, apart from the legal costs incurred, which the general public has to pay – tax money that has been wasted.

Civil Service:
Construed "Conflicts of Conscience"

Social facilities are heavily dependent on the cooperation of people doing community service (since 2011: Federal Voluntary Service). This was also known to the authorities when, in the summer of 1986, they received an application from the Original Christian Social Service Center *Helfende Hände* (Helping Hands) in Würzburg for recognition as an "employment agency for community service." At the beginning of 1987, they flatly rejected this application – with the absurd justification that there was a "commercial facility" in the same building (namely, the service company *Wir Sind für Sie Da* [We Are Here for You]) and that it could therefore not be ruled out that the person doing community service would also be used for commercial work. Furthermore, those doing community service might possibly get into "moral conflicts" because, after all, the association *Helfende Hände* belongs to Universal Life.

The official "brain acrobatics" are considerable: Those doing community service with *Caritas* and Diaconal Work are apparently not exposed to the danger of "conflicts of conscience" in the opinion of the Federal Office for Community Service in Cologne – why then, suddenly with the Original Christians? And "commercial establishments" certainly exist in the vicinity of church social institutions in great numbers, without any authority ever having taken offence.

But no matter how ludicrous the "reasoning": Once again, the Original Christians must go to court. And once again, they have reason to doubt the independence of the German judiciary: In October

1988, the Administrative Court of Cologne decides in the first instance that it was at the discretion of the Federal Office to whom it would award the limited number of possible new civil service positions, due to the limited number of conscientious objectors.

Only an appeal to the Higher Administrative Court of Cologne in June 1991, (five years after the application!) did a positive decision result: The Federal Office is bound by its own practice of giving preference to special nursing homes in allocating new positions (and such a one is run by *Helfende Hände*).

Independent Judges Sought

The examples listed clearly give evidence that a discriminated non-church minority has no alternative to exhausting the legal possibilities – even if the constitutional state, as in the case of the Hettstadt settlers (Chapter 6), sometimes degenerates into a "state of legal recourse," because the legal process can take so long that the demoralized plaintiffs give up.

The legal possibilities must be exhausted – even if the media have often been allowed by the courts to pass on defamations of the church as "expressions of opinion" or "permissible value judgments;" and even if the courts have often pulled the "emergency brake" by simply denying Universal Life the "right to take legal action": If Universal Life is offended, the association Universal Life cannot take action, because it cannot speak for all the followers of Universal Life.

However, the attentive reader will not have failed to notice that the more or less successful cases listed are exclusively proceedings against authorities, state representatives, media or political party organizations influenced by the churches. On the other hand, when Original Christians dare to take church representatives directly to court, they very quickly come up against a strange, but historically explainable, psychological barrier. Here, the judges still draw back – consciously or unconsciously: A pastor, let alone a bishop, cannot be summoned to court or in the end, even convicted! Then the judge will ultimately end up in eternal damnation! It so happens that a mayor may not go all out against the "sects" – but an ostensibly Christian pastor may very well do so; his mendacious opinions are conceded to him by every court as "barely permissible expressions of opinion." And a bishop may cover and support the pastor in this dirty work, although the Church as a "corporation under public law" should be subject to similar standards as the state – not to mention the standards of the Ten Commandments of God and of the Sermon on the Mount.

"Expression of Opinion": May Everyone Say Anything About Anyone?

The German courts, regardless of the issue of "non-church minorities," have over the course of many years maneuvered our state into an extremely critical situation regarding freedom of opinion:

The protection of the honor of an attacked citizen is almost non-existent. A high-ranking Bavarian judge has thus already spoken of a "liquidation of the protection of honor by the Supreme Court."

Since moral standards, such as the eighth commandment, do not play a role for the church sect commissioners and their superiors, anyway – especially in relation to "heretics" – the church representatives and the journalists dependent on them make active use of the almost unlimited possibilities of the legally guaranteed freedom of libel.
If the courts then confirm certain claims about a minority of faith as "admissible value-judgment," they, in turn, go out and peddle it: "According to

the court order the following may be said about them: ..."

Hardly anyone knows that in such cases, the courts in general did not examine the underlying facts, at all. In the uncritical eyes of the public, a permissible expression of opinion becomes an official statement of the court – and the character assassination is complete.

Communities of faith that are discriminated against by the churches therefore find themselves in a constant dilemma: If they do nothing about the mendacious opinions, it will get worse and worse. If they do something, it can again harm them, because all the accused mendacious opinions are repeatedly hashed over in the media, regardless of whether they are permitted or not as "barely permissible expressions of opinion."

Despite this risk, the Original Christians filed injunctions and criminal charges against the defamers – often with little success. Thus, for example, in 1993, criminal charges of incitement of the people against Behnk, Magnis, Bishop Scheele and Regional Bishop Hanselmann were not closely pursued, and the proceedings to enforce charges were all discontinued.

Three judges in Bamberg shamelessly revealed their ecclesiastical convictions. The judges of the

Higher Regional Court of Bamberg did not concern themselves at all with the complaints filed against the church representatives. Instead, in their verdict, they preferred to deal with the beliefs of the Original Christians – although they are not at all entitled to do so by virtue of the required ideological neutrality of the judiciary.

The Bamberg judges, however, set themselves up as religious judges over the Original Christians. They said that above all, the belief in the prophecy of the present time, the belief in reincarnation – all this could also cause "opposition and hostile reactions" among tolerant people (who the judges apparently consider themselves to be). With this, the judges downplayed and justified the consequences of the diatribes that were the subject of the criminal charges. These accusations not only caused "opposition" or "hostile reactions," they resulted in physical attacks, arson, threats, dismissals and much more (Chapter 12). This apparently did not interest the three judges, who themselves were presumably of Catholic or Protestant upbringing, on the contrary: they even applauded the agitators.

What was left for the Original Christians to do? They published an advertisement: "Independent Judges Sought!" However, they had to distribute it as a flyer, because the local press refused to print it. In Bamberg, in front of the court building, two Original Christians were promptly temporarily arrested by the police – although they were merely exercising their right to freedom of expression. ... How "independent" some German judges are is also demonstrated by an incident that occurred in August 1993 in front of the Würzburg District Court building. Two Original Christians were distributing flyers there, pointing out the discrimination by church, state and justice. When a judge passes by and enters the building, he angrily shouts: "The Homebringing Mission, may the devil fetch it, but quickly!"

The Church Lies Before the Court

The personnel linkage and ideological dependence between courts and churches are not always as obvious as in the case of the Hanseatic City of Bremen: There the president of the Bremen Lutheran Church is also the head public prosecutor. In 1995, he should actually have initiated proceedings against himself or his regional church – but did not. The Bremen Regional Church was, namely, under massive suspicion of deception. Its sect commissioner had written a brochure about "destructive cults" and included several vilifications against Universal Life. Thus, he let an obviously fictitious figure called "Jürgen" have his say, who allegedly became a "psychological wreck" because of Universal Life. (As in the Middle Ages: Anonymous accusations are sufficient for a condemnation of the "heretics.") He stated that conventional medicine was replaced by "faith prayers" and "healing meditation," and that the Original Christians had "bought up an entire village."

The Original Christians were informed in advance of the planned text and filed a suit for an injunction against the Bremen Church. But the churchman first published his text in the publishing house *Bonn aktuell* – the passages referred to and more were forbidden before the Regional Court of Hamburg; the book had to be withdrawn. Nevertheless, the Bremen Higher Administrative Court did not consider it necessary to prohibit the church from publishing the passages referred to in its own brochure, which was still planned. Reasoning: One had to wait and see, because the Bremen Church had told the court that it was not yet known which text would be published. This was obviously a lie, because a little later the church brochure was published containing the almost identical slander as in the previous book. The press in Bremen, by the way, reported in detail about the fact that the church was allowed to "express itself critically" about the Original Christians, but did not mention the flimsy reason for this judgment just mentioned, and did not say a single word about the previous ban of numerous passages in Langel's book, either.

Even though the Original Christians could achieve only partial legal successes because of the bias of many judges, their actions at least revealed how low the moral level of the churches is: Not a few of their representatives trample all ethics underfoot, make unrestrained use of their position of power and abuse the freedom of vilification granted to them by the court, turning it into a permanent smear campaign against dissenters. And it became clear where the church draws the line: with money. When the Original Christians sued the Lutheran Church of Bavaria for damages because of the obliteration of jobs due to their sect commissioner Behnk, things became noticeably quieter around the Church Council, at least temporarily.

12. The Effects of the Defamations

The years-long slander campaigns of the cassock wearers and their henchmen in politics and the media had, as stated, considerable effects on the Original Christians, on their families, businesses and facilities. Many of them have already been mentioned – for example, when permission for a private school is denied for as long as possible, when children are verbally abused, when farmers are denied state subsidies, or when Universal Life is not allowed to set up an information stand in a city. This broad field is to be spread out and portrayed in the following, with further examples.

The church experts were primarily concerned with the social and economic ostracism of all those who feel connected to the Original Christian teaching through the prophetic word. The slanderers thus tried to restrict as much as possible the "heretics" in all areas of life. This means,

- firstly, to directly hinder the community of people who turn to the Free Spirit, God in us – without an external institution and without priests;

- secondly, to destroy the livelihood of the Original Christians by damaging the businesses and social facilities that they have built up;

- and thirdly, to harm individual Original Christians by making them feel insecure and intimidated with personal insults and threats, or by taking care that, for example, their home or job is taken away from them.

This description can only give examples, because the actual extent of the cases is inestimable.

12.1. Disturb the Activities of Their Community of Faith!

Don't Give Them any Premises!

In well over a hundred cases, the Original Christians in Universal Life were denied halls for events – mostly without giving any further reasons or with the vague excuse that there had been "calls" and "complaints." It is not difficult to guess who is behind this; and often enough, the "secret" is involuntarily revealed:

- The parish council raises objections (as in 1982 in **St. Anton/Tyrol**), the city pastor issues threats to the innkeeper (as in 1983 in **Altötting**: "You won't get any more pilgrims coming to your inn") or incites his believers against the organizer (as in 1984 in **Garching**, where the owner of a hall was telephoned and threatened that windows would be smashed).

- In **Heidenheim** in 1989, the rental of a public room is rejected – the rejected people were told that the Catholic priest was responsible for it.

- In 1990, a community hall was refused in the community of **Tegernsee** because the district

Youth Welfare Office had contacted a Munich sect commissioner.

- In **Bad Neustadt** an der Saale, the deacons of both denominations write to various innkeepers in 1991, asking them not to rent any rooms to Universal Life.

- In **Baiersbronn** in the Black Forest, in 1995, the Lutheran pastor even preaches against the Original Christians from the pulpit, because they occasionally rent a room in a local café – and the landlady gives in.

- A restaurant proprieter in **Ansbach** does not withstand the pressure either in 1995 – the local pastors make sure that her restaurant, which she occasionally rents out to Original Christians, is boycotted, and a rumor is even spread that she wants to sell the property to Universal Life.

- In 1996 in **Bad Windsheim**, an innkeeper is put under pressure by a Lutheran pastor: The local newspaper threatens with a "nasty article" and the pastor organizes an extra information evening about "sects." The Original Christians prefer to look for another room, so that the innkeeper does not get into significant difficulties. ...

However, sometimes the pastors come too late – which only increases their anger: When in 1993, young Original Christians show a film about the wealth of the Churches in the Mozart High School in **Würzburg**, afterward the deacons Kurt Witzel (Catholic) and Joachim Beer (Protestant-Lutheran) get upset in public. The city's school board even considers it necessary to apologize to the Vicar General of the diocese – for the fact that his authority has adhered to the Constitution!

The Churches consider health resorts as their terrain in a special way, which is why in August 1984, the visitors to a lecture by Universal Life in **Bad Neustadt** an der Saale stand before closed doors. The spa administration refers to the "many calls" that were made. In 1985, the spa administration in **Bad Endorf** speaks openly about the "classification of the Homebringing Mission as a sect."

The ecclesiastically fueled eagerness to reject sometimes leads to involuntary satirical blunders. For example, in 1986, the state spa administration in **Bad Steben** refers to the "successful pastoral care at the spa of both denominations" as the reason for a cancellation of a lecture on the topic "Is There a Life After Death." The spa administration of **Bad Dürrheim** reacts similarly, which in 1988, also wants to bear in mind the "interests of the

Lutheran and Catholic pastoral care at the spa" and sees "no additional need." In **Bad Abbach**, a room the Original Christians had already rented was cancelled – the spa's chaplain had called.

Other public institutions also have difficulties with allocating rooms to the Original Christians.

- In 1987, the faculty of the Education Department of the University of **Erlangen** denied a room "after consultation with representatives of the department of theology" – and thus showed who was in charge here.

- In 2001, the University of **Marburg** refused to rent a room on the grounds that Universal Life is a "sect, which takes a position against the ... churches."

- In 1993, the German Youth Hostel Association cancelled rooms for a meeting of young Original Christians because "considerable doubts arose" regarding whether Universal Life "corresponds to the principles of living together in the German Youth Hostel Association."

- In 1996, even the head mayor of Karlsruhe contacts the youth hostel in **Weinheim** to prevent an event of the Original Christians.

- In 1997, young Original Christians at the **Lam** youth hostel in the Bavarian Forest are told that they cannot be accommodated – they are on a list of "sects" in the Munich branch office.

And if young Original Christians manage to find accommodation in a youth hostel, then it can happen to them, as in 1993, that journalists from the *Hessian Broadcasting Company* set up their cameras right in front of the entrance and literally besiege it for more than a day in order to get as many pictures as possible of allegedly "crazed" young people. The journalists stirred up by church representatives constantly try to penetrate the premises and force the young people to give interviews.

- The city of **Osnabrück** refers to statements made by the Federal Government in 1994 when a hall was cancelled;

- in 1997, the city of **Leverkusen** stated that Universal Life was pursuing "goals that cannot be promoted by an establishment created for a democratic local community."

- In 1999, when canceling, the Novapark Hotel in **Vienna** refers to the Family Minister in Vienna and a "Network Association Against Destructive Cults."

The "reasons" put forward for the refusals are all based on the insinuations and defamations of today's inquisitors and their accomplices in the state and media. The "sectarian stigma," once attached by the Church, often stays in people's heads for a long time and is difficult to remove. Hardly any of the potential lessors knew the Original Christians from their own experience, none formed their own picture – what the official Churches purport is simply dutifully parroted.

In some cases, the Church can exert direct pressure on lessors, because it owns a great number of properties, as is well known.

- In **Heidelberg**, for example, where the local group of Universal Life receives notice of the termination of an already concluded rental contract, because the Protestant-Lutheran Church of Baden has a financial stake in the building.

- In **Paderborn** (1994), it is enough for the lessor and his tax advisor to work together with the Church to terminate a lease after only three months.

- The Original Christians also have to leave their rented rooms In **Wiesbaden** after only a quarter of a year – they are told that the owner of the house is an "asset holder in the sphere of the

Catholic Church." The Original Christians do not even get the broker's commission back.

- Some innkeepers are at least honest enough, as in **Lippstadt** (1984), to state "fear of damage to business" or "public pressure";

- or in **Winterthur**, where in 1994, a hotel used a discriminatory article by Hugo Stamm in the Zurich *Tagesanzeiger* as an opportunity to cancel all reservations. It is "extremely unpleasant for the hotel to be mentioned publicly in connection with you."

- In the Hotel Bayerischer Hof in **Bayreuth** in 1995, there is talk of "damage to reputation."

- But what might the city of **Freilassing** have thought when it refused to rent a hall in 1984, of all things, on the grounds of "neutrality in religious questions!"?

Take Away Their Advertising Options!

Even if renting a hall is successful – in order to inform the population about events, one is dependent on public advertising options. Here, too, the Original Christians feel the effect of the church smear campaigns: The municipal advertising companies in numerous cities (for instance, **Munich, Bremen, Frankfurt, Bamberg**) refuse to accept posters from Universal Life or to rent showcases to the Original Christians, as do the railway advertising agencies in Germany and Austria. When subordinate agencies do so nevertheless, they are very soon "brought to their senses" – like the train station administration of **Neunkirchen** near Wiener Neustadt, which in April 2000 had the posters of the Original Christians that had already been paid for, removed: The regional management of Vienna South had mandated this because Universal Life was included in Minister Bartenstein's "Sect Brochure."

What is left as a means of advertising is the time-consuming distribution of flyers or the setting up of information stands, which, however, as described elsewhere (Chapter 11), often has to be literally fought for in the face of the persistent resistance by the authorities. For good money, one can also place advertisements in the daily press

– one would think. But for Original Christians, this is not so easy, either. More than 200 newspapers and magazines in the German-speaking countries reject advertisements from Original Christians – and if they give any reasons at all, they refer to church sect commissioners, whose defamations they sometimes literally repeat in their letters of rejection. In confidential conversations, representatives of large publishing houses then also refer to the power of the churches, which can also exert economic influence, for example, on advertising customers.

Insults, Threats, Shots

Again and again, it could be felt that church slanders had already found their way into the heads of many people. Well over a hundred threats and insults against Original Christians have been documented, among which "sect pig" is still the mildest of them, and even demands for "gassing" and "putting them up against the wall" are not uncommon.
Frequently, especially after inciting television programs, the aversion against those of other faiths also discharges in a blind fury of destruction: In more than 60 cases, attacks on Original Christian

establishments were committed, including eight destroyed showcases in various cities, graffiti, smashed windows ... The Universal Life building on Haugerring, diagonally opposite the **Würzburg** train station, was particularly often the target of attacks. The free-standing illuminated advertising signs were smashed with stones three times. Information tables set up at the entrance were knocked over or even set on fire. At the beginning of 1989, someone even shot through the windows with a small caliber rifle. Only in the case of the ignited info tables could the perpetrator later be identified – he came from the radical right-wing scene. One can see what "black fruits" the church smear campaigns produce.

12.2. Deprive Them of Their Livelihood!

The businesses and facilities that followers of Jesus of Nazareth built up together very often became the target of church slanderers and their accomplices. People who want to live as Christians, not only in words, but in the deed, and who are therefore striving to follow Jesus, the Christ, the Free Spirit, in their daily lives, create not only an independent economic basis for their livelihood, but they could also show that the Sermon on the Mount of Jesus, the Christ, is not a utopia, even in a work-related or economic activity. This is one of the greatest dangers for the system that distorted His free teaching of peace and of love for God and neighbor into an external religion, with priests as intercessors between God and people – because it does not want to have togetherness and being for and with one another. It wants the principle of "Divide, bind and rule," with rich and poor, with superiors and subordinates, rulers and dependents.

Attacks on Market Stands and Shops

The true prophets of God teach from the one stream; it is – from Abraham to Gabriele – the same Spirit of love for God and neighbor, of freedom, unity and peace, eternally. Just as Jesus of Nazareth said: *Blessed are the meek, for they will inherit the earth*, thus, through Gabriele today, the Spirit of the Christ of God also teaches the love for all creation: for the minerals, plants and animals. The one who gradually opens the love for God and neighbor in himself will respect all life; he will no longer kill and eat animals; he will also love the land and appreciate the fruits that Mother Earth produces.

That is why Original Christians – according to the concept from the Kingdom of God – practice peaceful farming, from cultivation to customer, and offer foodstuffs and products accordingly, in various shops and at the markets.

Peace between human beings, nature and animals – the caste of priests always rejected this as a utopia and did nothing against the cruelty toward our fellow creatures – on the contrary, they encouraged brutality toward creation. Augustine, venerated as a church father, taught, for instance:

We can see from their screams that animals die in agony, but this does not affect man, for the animal lacks a rational soul and is therefore not connected with us through a common nature.
(Translated from: Peter Dinzelbacher, Mensch und Tier in der Geschichte Europas, p. 289)
In the dogmas of the Church, since ancient times, a vegetarian diet has been a "godless teaching of heretics." (See: "Vegetarian – Godless Heretics.")

The Original Christians lead the way with a good example: *for* nature, *for* the animals, *for* life – and already the mainstream churches are again taking action against it. Of course, in Germany, one cannot so easily call for a sales boycott against a minority of faith. The memory of the time when it was said in German cities: "Don't buy from Jews!" is still too vivid. But using slightly different formulations, the cassock wearers of our time quickly find ways to discourage people from buying.

The first one to experience this, was a sales driver who, at the end of September 1986, drove through the Lower Franconian town of **Bergrheinfeld** near Schweinfurt in his sales van, loaded with products from the firm *Gut zum Leben*. He was stopped by the police 500 meters past the Protestant parsonage and had to discontinue his sales trip. Up to then, he had been able to sell vegetables and bread in this village every week with his travel trade license, that is, without additional permission. But three days before, the Catholic priest and the Protestant-Lutheran pastor had jointly "informed" in the official local newspaper that this sales driver was "associated with a sect." They urge their believers: "Check everything, and keep the good!" And just in case anyone among the faithful would not understand the broad hint, the police had been called as a precaution. The sales driver applied for an extra sales permit from the municipality, but this was initially denied "for reasons of traffic management." However, the salesman insisted on an examination of the legal status, and the permit had to be granted, after all.

Matthias Pöhlmann, a theology student and later Lutheran pastor and sect commissioner, earned his first laurels as a modern inquisitor by having a letter to the editor published in the *Fränkischer Tag* in **Bamberg** on December 2, 1989, with the headline: "Organic Food with a Bitter Aftertaste." This refers to the market stand of *Gut zum Leben* at the Bamberg market. So much effort against the "heretics" already during his student days must, of course, be rewarded: Pöhlmann will later get an assistant position at the University of Erlangen with a focus on "sects" – and in the new millennium he will rise to become a full-time employee of the Protestant Central Office for Worldview Issues in Berlin – and in 2014, he will become the "State Church Commissioner for Sects and Questions of Ideology" in Bavaria.

The Pastors:
Damages to Reputation Always in the Lead

In **Coburg**, too, it is the pastor who personally would like to get rid of the market stand. Not mentioning his job title, the Lutheran pastor Michael Thein publishes in the *Neue Presse Coburg* (May 2, 1995) and in the *Coburger Tageblatt* (May 3, 1995) a letter to the editor, which culminates in the demand that *Gut zum Leben* must "also reveal to the uninformed and cursory reader that here, it is the ideology of 'Universal Life.' Then the citizen of age can decide for himself whether he wants to spend his money at this market stand or not." Pastor Thein has learned his trade: You can call for a boycott even in this way. Whether the "citizen of age" noticed that here, Father Thein has basically called for a new form of the Jewish star, this time for "heretics"? One tries – as during the Middle Ages – to maneuver the "heretic" into a hopeless situation: No matter how he goes about it, it is wrong. If he reveals his faith while selling bread, the license for his stand is revoked, because he "proselytizes." If he doesn't reveal it, he's hiding something and he's "dangerous." The only odd thing is that Catholic or Lutheran farmers have never been compelled to hang their baptismal certificates on their market umbrella.

The provost Roswitha Alterhoff in **Bad Hersfeld** strikes a very similar note. "This is fraudulent labeling," she says in the *Hersfelder Zeitung* (January 24, 1996) and adds: "Business probably is better if the customers don't know from whom they are buying." Don't such words remind us of the agitation of the early 1930s, when the National Socialists made sure that everyone knew who was a Jewish businessman and who was not?

In **Simmerath** near Aachen, it is the Aachen sect commissioner Herbert Busch who goes into action –twice a year a market stand from *Gut zum Leben* is set up there. In the *Aachener Volkszeitung* Busch demands that "political and social debate should be sought in schools, adult education, administrations and the press" (what a modern, catchy paraphrase for the old ecclesiastical Inquisition), if one cannot forbid the market stand.

The following day, the local community director declared that they wanted "to check once again whether the Universal Life sect meets the formal commercial requirements to re-enter the Simmerath market." (Mind you: Universal Life does not even operate the stand at all! Just as little, as can be said that the Vatican Church, for example, operates a market stand, when a Catholic believer offers his products at a market. ...)

"As long as the organization operates on the basis of the Constitution and there is no clear legal cause, he can do nothing. ... 'I am a Catholic, but my private attitude may not play a role here.'" This is, therefore, the utmost that the Original Christian market participants can hope for in such a case: A shamefaced rearguard action by the officials, according to the motto: I would like to ban it, but alas, alas, it is not possible. In view of the shrill background music played by the *Aachener Volkszeitung* (July 3, 1993) – with the headline "Must Simmerath Continue Living with the Sect?" – through the stalling tactics of the official, something shimmers almost like a hint of civil courage again.

In **Pforzheim**, at the beginning of 1997, Pastor Hans-Peter Held claimed, quite simply and untruthfully, that on the universal organic farms "the people worked without pay and social security." In the idyllic town of **Tegernsee**, in his parish letter, Pastor Rigam draws attention to a new shop that "one of the most dangerous sects in Germany" has rented. The local newspaper *Miesbacher Merkur* (January 9, 1998) eagerly and dutifully inquired at the district office, the mayor, the criminal investigation department (!) and the director of the Tegernsee grammar school whether there had already been any "points of contact" with the "sect."

The Lutheran parish priest Wolfgang Spengler brings his colleague, the sect commissioner Behnk, from Munich to the holiday resort, where he agitates against the "dangerous, sectarian organization" in front of 50 Tegernseers (*Tegernseer Zeitung*, May 8, 1998). When employees of the company *Gut zum Leben* distribute a handbill in **Tegernsee**, to defend themselves against the slanderous incitement, the *Münchner Merkur* (May 12, 1998) writes: "Universal Life attacks sect pastor" and quotes only one sentence from the handbill – which, however, hit the nail on the head: "A pastor may say anything in Bavaria – even if it is a lie."

Therefore, the shop in Tegernsee has to be closed. When, instead, a shop is opened in the neighboring **Rottach-Egern**, after some time, the firm invites the population to a lecture. However, the press does not report about the lecture itself, but instead, in advance, on the "irritation" it had caused. "It is a shame that our mayor allows a sect to give a lecture in our spa hall," an "outraged Rottacher" is quoted in the local newspaper (March 10, 2000). The woman doesn't want to give her name, "because she fears repressive measures by the sect." This is a trick of church representatives that is just as popular as it is insidious: slander anonymously – and immediately turn the cowardly anonymity into another slander. Instead of referring to the Constitution and the freedom of opinion (which the churches always utilize when it is useful to them), Mayor Konrad Niedermaier explains rather contritely: "None of this is okay for me." Published in advance in the newspaper are allegations by the Berlin Senate Administration about Universal Life: that the goal of the doctrine is to "reprogram the individual into a human being who will stay out of all discussions." Apparently no one notices the contradiction: Such a person would not invite the public to a lecture with a discussion period, at all.

Politicians at Their Dirty Work

In blind obedience, numerous politicians assume the slanderous strategy against the Original Christians as prescribed by the churches, and many a one becomes accordingly active – to further his own career?

In May 1990, Peter Gauweiler (CSU), then State Secretary in the Bavarian Ministry of the Interior, finds it "hair-raising" that *Gut zum Leben* is allowed to maintain a market stand in **Munich** – although, as a member of the state government, he is not even responsible for the affairs of the city of Munich and, moreover, as a representative of the government, is bound by the rule of ideological neutrality.

The deputy CSU faction leader of the Munich city council, Hans Podiuk (who will be made a candidate for mayor in 2002), is even outraged: "The stand license must be revoked. The city should strive for a model case proceedings." The city is smart enough not to do it – because it would have lost the trial. But that doesn't prevent the Munich scene newspaper *Prinz* (5/94) from again agitating against the stand: "Sect Infiltrates Munich's Eco-Scene."

Again and again: "the sect" – an abusive word, which, as already mentioned, is exclusively connected with many negative associations, but which, apparently, everyone is allowed with impunity to attach to anyone. How would it be, for example, if one were to henceforth speak only of the "major sect Catholic" or "major sect Protestant"?

In the following year, it is the Munich Jungsozialisten (Young Socialists) who are "outraged" by the state of affairs: "It is incomprehensible," said their chairman, "that the sect received permission at all." In his letter to his party friend and Mayor Ude ("with socialist greetings"), however, the young socialist reveals a shameful lack of basic legal knowledge for young politicians: He adopts – of course without doing any research of his own – quotes from Inquisitor Behnk (incidentally also an SPD "associate"), which Behnk has had confirmed by the courts as being covered by the right to express opinions. But the young politician writes: "These statements are protected by several decisions … that they were declared legal according to the facts." But whether these statements correspond to the facts – is precisely what the courts have not examined at all. The example shows how character assassination works.

When the CSU also wanted to get rid of the market stand with a renewed city council inquiry, Munich's municipal advisor Georg Welsch makes it clear in November of 1995: The evaluation made by the city years before that the firm *Gut zum Leben* is "an efficient supplier of a really comprehensive range of products from organically certified cultivation" has been "fully confirmed." The company does not engage in any ideological advertising, that "it strictly adheres to the market regulations and meets its payment obligations punctually. ... According to the municipal department, there are no known circumstances that would justify revoking the adjudication."

"Friends of Nature" –
or Servile to the Church?

Meanwhile, however, a sales boycott has long since been propagated on a supra-regional level: In the June 1992 issue of the magazine *Öko-Test*, a long article appears with the headline: "False Prophets in the Organic Shop – Sects Increasingly Secure Economic Power in the Organic Sector." For pages, the author Birgit Schumacher transcribes the disinformation and defamations of church "sect experts." She claims, for example:
After all, the Inner Path is supposed to save the faithful from the end of the world. ... The ark of Universal

Life is being industriously built. Regional and global disasters, whether dying forests or earthquakes, wars, the ozone hole or the greenhouse effect, cause fear. ... Only those who join the community will be saved.

There it is again, the malicious false statement that has nothing to do with the teaching of Universal Life. For what happens or does not happen to a person externally has nothing to do with belonging to a certain group. This is Lutheran or Catholic belief, but not the teaching of the Free Spirit. (The Catholic Church expressly teaches: *And no one can be saved, no matter how much alms one has given, even if shedding one's blood for the name of Christ, unless one remains in the bosom and unity of the Catholic Church.* To be read in Neuner and Dupuis, "The Christian Faith," Margin Note No. 1005).

Schumacher also speaks untruthfully about "giving away savings"; she says that Universal Life belongs to those "communities that build up authoritarian systems with seemingly religious backgrounds that not only take money from people, but also deny them free will and make them incapable of being mature adults."
A malicious lie and again a projection: In his teachings, Martin Luther clearly denies free will to the

human being – for the Original Christians, however, the observance of free will is a central commandment. And what about the free will of a Catholic who, under the threat of an alleged eternal damnation, is forced to follow the church dogma?

With this kind of cheap propaganda, who would think that it is the mainstream churches themselves that demand a regular contribution from each of their members – and on top of that, have it collected by the state?!

The fact that, of all people, reporters working in the ecological sector are trying to make an ecologically, exemplary initiative look bad can – apart from being servile to the churches – perhaps be explained by a reflex of competition or envy. In addition, the desire for meat of some "nature protectors" could also play a role, who possibly fear that a really consistent protection of animals could lead them to abstain from their beloved pork cutlets. ...

On January 3, 1993, the TV program magazine *TV Hören und Sehen* announced a television program on the subject of "Eco-Sects – Dubious Deals with the Environment."

The magazine *FF-aktuell* announces a report on Universal Life for the same program: Consumers should be warned not to shop "in good faith in alternative eco-shops, ... because sometimes there are sect gurus behind them, who are now riding the eco wave." Then a "Markus D." is mentioned, who was "bitterly disappointed" by Universal Life. They took his savings book from him, forbade him sex and demanded "obedience up to surrender of self." That is nonsense, and this "Markus D." does not even exist; investigations remain without result. Thus, Universal Life files a suit for injunction against the magazine that publishes such nonsense – the magazine assures that it will never claim such a thing again, and the proceedings are dropped. But the lies are in the world. Who will undo them?

At least the *Bavarian Broadcasting Corporation* has been warned – contrary to the announcement, Universal Life does not appear in the program in question. But the accompanying booklet *Globus* (2/93), published by the "Bund für Umwelt- und Naturschutz Baden-Württemberg" (Alliance for the Protection of the Environment and Nature), was apparently already in print. Headline: "Weird Prophets on an Eco-trip." "Shrewd wheeler-dealers," it says, "cleverly exploit generalized fears of the future ... Such dubious eco-sects bring other groups from the esoteric and ecological spectrum into disrepute and paralyze politically effective action."

In plain language this means: Only those who are Catholic or Lutheran have a right to campaign for nature conservation and are considered "serious." The author Christa Stewens of the clerically influenced *Bavarian Broadcasting Corporation* interviews in this context Beate Seitz-Weinzierl, Catholic theologian and wife of Hubert Weinzierl, chairman of "Friends of the Earth Germany." She thinks it is "harmful for the environmental movement if the whole ecological repertoire of disasters from dying forests to the hole in the ozone layer and climate change up to genetic engineering has to serve as a doctrine of salvation." But she doesn't say what the Church so far has constructively contributed to a solution in all these areas – and she also cannot do that, either, because ultimately, the Church itself, with its misunderstood interpretation of the words "Subdue the Earth" has significantly contributed to the "repertoire of disasters."

Perhaps it would not harm the environmental movement to think about why the mainstream churches have not given a clear answer to any of the serious environmental challenges:
They have neither spoken out clearly against nuclear power (on the contrary: well-known church representatives even supported it), nor against animal experiments; neither against genetic engi-

neering nor industrial agriculture and factory farming; they have never made a clear commitment to organic farming, for example, let alone advocating for the tortured animal world.

On the other hand, Universal Life takes a clear position on all these questions and acts accordingly, because the commandment of love for God and neighbor also applies to nature and animals.

In October 1997, the women's magazine *Amica* continues the national campaign. The journalist Werner Paczian publishes an inflammatory article with the headline "The Rotten Tricks of the Eco-Sect." The Original Christians learned about Amica's rotten tricks on May 25, 1997, when the photographer Wolfgang Gressmann from Hamburg got up in the middle of one of its Sunday events in Würzburg, pulled out a camera that had been hidden until then and began frantically taking pictures. When he did not stop after repeated requests, he was removed from the room and asked to hand over the pictures that had been taken without the visitors' consent. When Gressmann and a companion, presumably Paczian, then ran away, the police were called. In the presence of the officers, Gressmann handed over two rolls of film to a representative of Universal Life, but they did not contain the pictures taken in the event room. The lawyer for the Original Christians managed to get the Hamburg

Administrative Court to ban the magazine *Amica*, for which the two worked, from using the pictures – but Paczian took revenge with a flood of abuse: "Sect concern," "abomination empire," the quality control of the food is "dubious" (although all food from certified organic farming are subject to strict controls – but under the term "expression of opinion," apparently, anyone is allowed to spread anything about others, whether it's true or not, whether it's damaging to business or not).

Pressure on City Administrations

Such ammunition is then used to exert pressure on municipal administrations, such as that of Hanau. In the *Hanauer Zeitung* of April 6, 1994, one can read that "market customers are repeatedly complaining in town hall" – about the market stand of *Gut zum Leben*, which has been there for five years. It is not difficult to guess which "market customers" these are. The newspaper does not fail to include the latest mendacious opinions from the ecclesiastical side. To grasp the perfidy of such an approach, it is enough to imagine an analogous case: What if a Jew or a foreigner would run a market stand in Hanau or elsewhere – and if certain persons with corresponding anti-Semitic or xenophobic slogans would then constantly "complain" to the city administration? How would the officials, the politicians, the entrepreneurs react? what would the newspapers write?

Why the double standard? In 1997, when a representative of the Junge Union of Hanau asked the city to "check out" the market stand, Mayor Margret Härtel answered almost submissively, "that she will do everything in her power to revoke the stand's license if there is any evidence of a connection between the market stand and the sect. The mayor further emphasizes that she will do everything to prevent a sect from being established in Hanau." (*Hanauer Anzeiger*, October 18, 1997)

What has become of the obligation of neutrality required by the state? And since when is it the task of city leaders sworn to the Constitution to drive minorities of faith out of their cities? The fact that Hanau was once a city in which a persecuted religious minority, the Huguenots, found acceptance in 1597 seems to have left no trace in its historical memory.

Encouraged by this, and by the example of their party friends from Neu-Isenburg, the Junge Union (CDU youth organization) repeats its "warning" in April 1998 and adds: "A boycott would hit the sect in its most sensitive spot."

Church Controlled Media

In February 1994, a coalition of church representatives and church-controlled media in the **Frankfurt** area zeroed in on the market stands of *Gut zum Leben*. The *Hessischer Rundfunk* (Hessian Broadcasting Corporation) starts it off. In its program "In Hessen unterwegs" (February 1, 1994), there is talk of a customer who felt "great anger" because he had "probably directly co-financed a sect" – in Frankfurt's Kleinmarkthalle (Little Market Hall). Universal Life is accused of a "hard-hitting persecution of dissenters." In the Würzburg area, they are "buying up whole villages and infiltrating them." This lie is obviously being used to justify the expulsion of Original Christians from the village of Hettstadt near Würzburg.

On February 25, *Radio FFH* takes over the relay slander. A journalist interviews customers in the Kleinmarkthalle, whom she had previously "enlightened" about the alleged danger of the sales stand. The answers are accordingly, from which can easily be deduced what mendacious opinion the journalist spread in each case: "If that actually is a sect, I simply cannot support that" – "I don't want to support anyone who discriminates against other people" – "Then I don't want to go there anymore, because you have to count on the fact that at some point, they will want to know where I live."

When *Gut zum Leben* opened a new shop in Frankfurt's old town in February 1994, the Protestant sect commissioner, Kurt-Helmuth Eimuth, spread a "warning against organic sects" through the *Evangelische Pressedienst* (Protestant Press Service). "Consumers should know whom they are promoting by buying such products," says Eimuth. The "religious delusion" of these people has, in his estimation, "become worse and worse in recent years." In the *Frankfurter Neue Presse* (February 24, 1994), Eimuth adds to his warning about the new store, the well-known standard mendacious opinion that Universal Life prophesies an "end of the world," which "only the saved" would survive.

So that even the last person will catch on to what a well-behaved state-church citizen has to buy or not to buy, the public television program "Trend" brings up the "obscure sect" Universal Life and enumerates its stands.
The church experts use the word "sect" as an insult – and hardly anyone takes the trouble to see for themselves what the Original Christians are really about.

The large-scale smear campaign in the Frankfurt area shows the effect desired by the churches at least partly: In March 1994, some regular customers tell the salespersons of the *Gut zum Leben* stand in the Kleinmarkthalle that they no longer want to shop there "because of the television broadcasts." In nearby **Darmstadt**, on March 5, a woman shouts in front of the *Gut zum Leben* market stand there: "You should be strung up!" – and she mentions the TV show. As late as May 1996, a customer at the market stand is quoted in the *Frankfurter Neue Presse*: "Yes, this is a kind of community that calls itself religious, but which scares whole villages near Würzburg." This is how demagoguery works, because the inhabitants of these villages are not terrified by the Original Christians, but, if at all, by the slander of church representatives.

In November of 1995, the newspaper of the Frankfurt University of Applied Sciences *(Nordwestwind)* stirs up hatred against the *Gut zum Leben* stand in Frankfurt's Northwest Center. In their parish letter, the Praunheim Resurrection Messenger, the Lutheran pastors Andreas Goetze and Bernd Durst call on the faithful "not to buy any fruits of religious madness." The pastor Ines Fetzer from Maintal-Dörnigheim near Frankfurt imitates them:

In the *Maintal-Tagesanzeiger* (May 24, 1996) she spreads the rumor that there are "doubts that the products really come from organic farming and that in the past, investigations had shown that the fruit sold was by no means organically grown."

That is an untruth that damages business.

Call for Boycott in Neu-Isenburg

On October 28, 1997, the *Frankfurter Neue Presse* then attacks the shop of *Gut zum Leben* in the shopping center of **Neu-Isenburg** near Frankfurt, unmistakably using Werner Paczian's defamations. Under the headline "IG City Fights Against Totalitarian Sect's Trade," the newspaper quotes a spokesman for the "Interessengemeinschaft City," (Interest Group City) which rents out the shop and has long been trying to "ban the sect from the weekly market." "We'd be happy to have it gone again," says a spokesman. The Junge Union of Neu-Isenburg is obviously trying to continue the historical tradition of the Counts of Ysenburg, who in the 17th century were among the worst witch-burners in the Protestant region, especially in their residence town of Büdingen. It wants to use the situation to distinguish itself and "calls ...

on the citizens to boycott the *'Gut zum Leben'* merchants," according to the *Frankfurter Neue Presse* (October 30, 1997). It says that Universal Life is striving for a "totalitarian state" and has the goal of "abolishing the democratic legal order."

An outrageous accusation, with no foundation whatsoever. Original Christians follow Jesus of Nazareth, who said: *My kingdom is not of this world.*
Those who in reality constantly trample on the spirit of the Constitution are the slanderers in cassocks and their helpers.

The Junge Union, an offspring organization of an allegedly Christian party, calls on the citizens not to spend "a single cent" in the shops. This call for a boycott is repeated in the Neu-Isenburger *Anzeigenblatt*, in the *Dreieich-Spiegel* and the *Offenbach-Post*. A few days later, the Neu-Isenburg Greens party also declare their "solidarity" with the Junge Union in the fight against "allegedly organic agricultural products." "Information from the Hessian Parliament has confirmed that this sect is totalitarian, that it exploits its members and persecutes those who want to drop out." **We see here how church mendacious opinions are first taken over by politics and then again played back to the public as "confirmation."**

Through a lawyer, the company *Gut zum Leben* asks the Junge Union to withdraw the boycott appeal. "You are vilifying people with this, who are not guilty of any wrongdoing... In an age of mass unemployment, it is an unprecedented ruthlessness to drive companies to ruin with such slogans," writes the lawyer. On January 8, 1998, the Darmstadt Regional Court, however, merely forbids the Junge Union to claim that "they work for a starvation wage" in the shops; anything else would be "critical expressions of opinion" and therefore, permissible.

The main action was also dismissed on October 15, 1998 on the same grounds.

It was in January 2000 (thus, more than two years after the slander!) that the Frankfurt Higher Regional Court **forbids** the young politicians from making claims that anyone who buys from *Gut zum Leben* "must know that in doing so, they are financially supporting an organization which strives for a totalitarian state" and that "the sales outlets of the plaintiff are an economic activity that has the clear aim to abolish the democratic legal system." And the judges – a rare, all the more gratifying exception – make the zealous young heretic hunters take the following to heart:

It would help the defendant [the Junge Union] to understand the problem if it were to open itself to the realization that a call for boycott against a company, for example, that operates in a qualitatively excellent and legal manner cannot be justified simply because it employs only Shiite Muslims, and because the fundamentalist clergy of this variety of the Muslim faith is alien and even hostile to the local understanding of democracy, or that one may not boycott a self-sufficient economic enterprise of the Catholic Church, for instance, because its "head shepherd" claims infallibility in decisions concerning religious-dogmatic questions.

Apart from the fact that the understanding of democracy of the Original Christians has nothing to do with the views of fundamentalist Islam or the Catholic Church: **It is characteristic of our state that such tutoring in civic education must take place only after a more than two-year-long legal battle in front of a court of law, because parents, the school and the older "Christian" party friends (themselves involved in embarrassing scandals) have failed on this point. They do not oppose the indoctrination by the pastors; on the contrary, they often take it over without examining it.**

One can see from their reaction after the judgment that neither insight nor an about-face has taken place in the young politicians. According to a report in the *Frankfurter Neue Presse* (February 11, 2000) they want to "stick to their main points of criticism." This report is also remarkable because it clearly shows how differently one can report on a judgment. While the *Frankfurter Rundschau* (February 11, 2000) writes that the Junge Union was forbidden to call for a boycott of *Gut zum Leben*, the *Neue Presse* brings the whole thing under the headline "Junge Union May Continue to Criticize Sect." Here, the few points that were not prohibited are listed first of all, because the court considers them as just barely permissible expressions of opinion. The forbidden statements are then prefaced with the cliché "Merely the formulation ... the JU must refrain from them." And in the end, it is even claimed – contrary to the truth – that the boycott appeal of the Junge Union "was not at all the subject of the hearing."

A few days later (February 16, 2000) the *Frankfurter Neue Presse* has to admit that it simply copied this embarrassing false report from a press release issued by the Junge Union. ...
On September 26, 2000, in its choice of words, the *Frankfurter Neue Presse* expresses its servility to the Church in a further article – namely, with the headline "Sect Spreads Out in the Market Hall."

It's about the Frankfurt Kleinmarkthalle and says that the "sisters and brothers of the faith" already have three market stands "firmly in their hands." A Green party city councilor also reveals that he has no idea what he is talking about when he states: "They probably wouldn't get much money for their work at the market stands; they'd have more possibilities under the guise of being non-profit." If the city council had inquired, it would have learned that the salespersons are not only well paid, but that as a commercial enterprise, the company *Gut zum Leben* has never had a non-profit status.

Despite their legal success against the Junge Union, the days of the firm *Gut zum Leben* in the Neu-Isenburg shopping center are numbered. At the beginning of 2002, the company was informed that in the course of a remodeling project, all shops would have to temporarily leave the building one after the other, and then move back into the remodeled center. All of them – except one: *Gut zum Leben*. Because of the "sect image," the management of the ECE-Group in Hamburg does not want to let the company back in. Another nationwide operator of shopping centers, the company ICM, also bars the Original Christians from their buildings. In Aschaffenburg, for example, *Gut zum Leben* is not allowed in the City-Gallery. The power of the Church, the applicants are told, is "very strong" here – a church that calls itself Christian, but has no scruples about endangering the jobs of honest working fellow citizens.

Heretic Hunters –
Right Across Political Party Lines

The poison spread by the churches against the Original Christians is effective – hardly any party is immune to it. In December 1994, the **Darmstadt** city council faction of the Green Party demands that the license for the market stand of the firm *Gut zum Leben* be cancelled. The Greens "feel uneasy" that "these sectarians might now want to spread out in Darmstadt as well."

In **Karlsruhe**, too, it is the Greens who, in March 1999, direct a request to the mayor's office regarding a *Gtu zum Leben* market stand. The answer is exeedingly outlandish: The "Office for Citizen Services and Security" considers Universal Life to be "an organization with totalitarian structures." There, the word religion "is used merely as a guise to in actual fact gain money and power" (*Badische Neueste Nachrichten*, April 21, 1999). A particularly fanatical "sect" hunter occupies this office. When the firm *Gut zum Leben* wants to become active at the Karlsruhe Christmas market, this official explains that they do not want such a "sect" at the Karlsruhe train station, a sect in which "bad machinations" are going on (of course, he cannot name any specific ones). At the beginning of 1997, the police officer had publicly declared during a lecture in Karlsruhe that he would like best to "close their market stand."

In **Rhineland-Palatinate**, even the SPD/FDP-governed state (FDP: Free Democratic Party) takes on the role of the informer. Minister of Culture Rose Götte (SPD) warns of the market stands of *Gut zum Leben* throughout the state, because, according to the minister in the *Rhineland-Palatinate* (October 11, 1996), "it cannot be ruled out that 'Universal Life' might try to recruit new members via the market stands." It's just odd that nobody would think of warning about a monastery whose monks, like those of the Benedictine Abbey Plankstetten in Nuremberg, run a market stand wearing black robes and, incidentally, inform about their events in the monastery. ...

The Truth Is Not Interesting Anyway

The Lutheran minister's daughter and SPD municipal politician Ele Schöfthaler attacks the market stand in **Schwabach** near Nuremberg on June 4, 1997, with a letter to the editor in the *Schwabacher Tagblatt*. She claims that anyone who "has fallen into the clutches of the sect" must "renounce their own children and partner." (To put it clearly: this is nonsense.) She calls on the Schwabach administration to be "just as courageous" as the one in Ansbach, where they have expelled the stand.

The administration then actually had courage – and publicly contradicted Mrs. Schöfthaler's statements. In a letter to the editor dated June 12, 1997, the city's press office replied that they had informed Ms. Schöfthaler that the Schwabach market – in contrast to the Ansbach market – was regulated under public law and that therefore, no "examination of the stand operator's ideological views could be demanded." It continued to say that it was "incomprehensible" why the writer of the letter to the editor "against better judgment, nevertheless implies to the readership with her explanations, that the City of Schwabach merely lacks the necessary courage to ban the sales stand."

But the cheap propaganda continues. It now becomes clear that the attack on the market stand was only the beginning of a larger smear campaign. In September 1997, Ele Schöfthaler postulates further claims about Universal Life in a public lecture at a Lutheran parish house, stating that the children are forbidden to play with children of other faiths (which is not true – but there are credible testimonies of cases where it is the other way around); that workers have to work in Original Christian enterprises "for next to nothing;" that there are "family tragedies;" that outsiders are regarded as "sub-humans" and other mendacious opinions.

In the course of a temporary injunction, the Nuremberg Higher Regional Court forbids her to make any of these statements, mainly because, as it turns out, most of them are not based on direct observations, but on general suspicions of third parties that have been passed on as "facts." In the main proceedings, however, with a different set of judges, the court suddenly takes a different legal view and says that Universal Life has no legal standing at all (with the result that most of the disputed allegations are in limbo) – and that "for next to nothing" is a "relatively insubstantial statement," that is, not defamatory (!). Only the assertion that a teacher of the Original Christian school forbids children to talk to other people remains prohibited. The reaction of the press is significant: "Sect stops opponent" is said after the prohibition – then, "freedom of opinion wins," after the main proceedings.

The fact that opinions (covered by jurisdiction) can also contain deliberate untruths and slander, obviously is of no interest to journalists or church representatives – just as little as the fact that a minority of faith is deprived of the exercise of its right to the protection of honor by a legal procedural trick (alleged lack of legal standing). In the course of the proceedings, women from all kinds of church groups declare their "solidarity" with Schöfthaler, without checking for a second whether the allegations are at all true.

Always the Same Old Tune

However, most journalists are not interested in this either, when it comes to exploiting the "sensation" of a "sect market stand" allegedly shrouded in mystery, for the local pages.

One newspaper copies from the other – and the patterns are similar. An introductory sentence, for example: "The shop in **Heilbronn** is bright and friendly, displays of samples invite you to try the products ..." is inevitably followed by: "But only a few customers know that with their purchases ... they support a totalitarian sect" – thus, the *Rhein-Neckar-Zeitung* (August 8, 2001). The articles are almost interchangeable.

On April 13, 1993, the **Pforzheimer** *Zeitung* writes about "Organic Products in the Twilight of a Sect"; on May 14, 1993 the **Nürnberger** *Nachrichten* writes about "Bread with a Message." Almost every market stand of the Original Christians is discriminated against at some point in the local press as a "sect stand," whether in **Sindelfingen, Böblingen, Reutlingen, Tübingen, Marktredwitz, Konstanz, Gelnhausen** – to name just a few examples. In the last place listed, a letter to the editor at least pointed out that Gelnhausen was the first community to announce itself "free of Jews" in 1938 – apparently, with the tenor that the prospect of "Gelnhausen – free of sects" alarms him.

In **Ingolstadt**, they come up with something very special: On January 20, 1994, the local television station *IN-TV* sends a camera team to the marketplace, which ostentatiously sets up their equipment in front of the *Gut zum Leben* market stand. They film the customers and ask them in front of a running camera whether they knew that there is a "sect" behind this stand. The method immediately brings the desired success: "That's a good point," says one customer into the microphone, "Now, I'm afraid I can't buy any more vegetable patties." Whether the "point" consists of the accusation against the "sect" or of being filmed close-up for the local evening news is left open.

So it still exists, the pillory of the Middle Ages – today, for example, you are shown on local television.

Also at the end of June 2006, a television team sets up in front of a market stand in **Munich**, where bread and vegetables from peaceable farming are being sold. This time, it is the team from the program "Quer" on *Bavarian Television*. The customers who have just shopped are asked in front of the camera: "Do you know that there is a sect behind this?" These images are then broadcast on the show. As can be seen, some customers react evasively or try to justify themselves (as if they had to, when buying healthy food at the market!) One customer, however, says: "No, I didn't know that. Then I won't buy here any more."

"Bravo," is the unspoken tenor of the program: "That's the right, the Catholic, reaction!" At the same time, it is conveyed to the viewers that if you go shopping there, you may also one day be confronted by the *Bavarian Broadcasting Company* in front of a running camera. Do you want to risk that?

And in **Bad Neustadt** an der Saale, a journalist, this time from the *Main-Post*, ostentatiously stands before the *Gut zum Leben* market stand on December 2, 1994, and asks customers whether they know that they are shopping "at Universal Life" here.

On June 12, 1992, one can read in the **Wiesbadener** *Kurier*: "Access to the Soul via Organic Vegetables and Whole Grain Bread? At the Wiesbaden weekly market, a Universal Life stand does business with natural foods." Significantly, it is such articles that refer to the background of faith of the stand operators in the first place. Otherwise, the customer at the stand would not even know about it at all, which means that he is in no way proselytized – which is also repeatedly confirmed in letters to the editor.

In **Offenbach**, the *Offenbacher Zeitung* (December 3, 1994) acts as an informer and calls the attention of the director of a department store to the fact that a "totalitarian sect," *Gut zum Leben*, is selling its goods right in front of his store. "We had no idea about the sect affair," the director dictates into the journalist's notepad. In August 2000, the newspaper reader learns that there had been a "political inquiry" in the city council in 1996, and that the head of the city office had inquired with the "Sect Commissioner of the Diocese of Würzburg." Count Magnis replied that he "could not imagine prohibiting commercial activities for ideological reasons." Here the circle closes in a way. Twelve years after he had set off an avalanche – that is still rolling – by attacking the market stand of *Gut zum Leben* in Würzburg (Chapter 4), the Catholic Count was finally, at least informed about the legal situation. A word of apology about the damage to business and the incalculable damage to honest citizens, which emerged and continues to emerge over the years, never came.

When an organic shop of *Lebe Gesund!* and a branch of the secondhand furniture store *Das*

Karussell open in **Frankenthal** in the spring of 2002, the *Rhine-Palatinate* (March 6, 2002) pulls out all stops. It takes from the Berlin Senate and the regional government of Rhineland-Palatinate and the Catholic sect commissioner Christoph Bussen, everything it can find in the way of reputation-damaging statements. Bussen and his Protestant-Lutheran colleague Ziegert hold lectures in the small town – the sales in the shops decrease. The FDP member of the state Parliament, Peter Schmitz, even tries to make a political gain out of this discrimination, by submitting a question to the Parliament in April 2002: "Is it true that the state government of Rhineland-Palatinate has warned against Universal Life, and why?" Mind you: He is not asking what one can concretely accuse the Original Christians of, that is, what they are verifiably doing wrong. In her answer (April 11, 2002), the Minister of Social Affairs, Malu Dreyer (SPD), who later became Minister-President, states that "extensive legal proceedings" had "confirmed" the ministry in its evaluation.

But the only specific facts that can be distilled from the nebulous answer are that the Original Christians occasionally distribute flyers. And that is not forbidden. Does that justify a state warning?

When one reads the examples of the smear campaigns presented here, then it has the effect of a brainwashing staged by the churches, which is carried out in the heads of the people through the media: the insulting word "sect," the constantly recurring discrimination, mockery, lies, suggestions, enemy images, distortions. ... Nevertheless, the question suggests itself: Why has it hardly occurred to anyone that there is not a single proven accusation against the Original Christians? They do nothing wrong. In their businesses, in their shops and at the market stands, they offer excellent products; they respect the laws of the state; they do not proselytize. They strive to live in peace and to put the Ten Commandments of God and the Sermon on the Mount into practice in their lives.

Some may think: "Then why do the churches go against them in such a way?" The answer can be found in the history books – all communities that were not church-affiliated but remained faithful to Jesus, the Christ, the Free Spirit, and to the early Christian principles were persecuted by the mainstream churches.

The *Südkurier* (Dec. 14, 2001) also took part in the hunt – and is proud that, "after the SÜDKURIER presented itself at the farmers' market," the products of *Gut zum Leben* "disappeared" from the shelves of the **Radolfzell** farmers' market.

Here, the "sect" hysteria involuntarily takes on satirical overtones: "With horror," says the *Südkurier*, "... it was discovered on Tuesday that the products of the sect are also being marketed and sold here." "They are actually everywhere and very friendly," says one buyer. You can see from this example, how deeply medieval patterns of thought ("Doing business with heretics can cost us all our heads! And don't trust your feelings!") can still be in the collective subconscious. Four days later (December 18, 2001) the *Südkurier* also has its sights set on the market stand in neighboring **Singen**.

On November 26, 1992, the *Mannheimer Morgen* also incites against the market stand on the **Mannheim** market square with quotes from the sect commissioners Bussen (Speyer) and Behnk (Munich) ("Believers Rise to the Bait of Whole Grain Bread"). The Greens repeat the defamations in their house newspaper *Grüne Liane* (February 1993). When, in addition, a new shop is opened, it is Helga Lerchenmüller of the Aktion Bildungs-In-

---

Yesterday – Inquisitor:
Persecution all the way to murder
Today – Sect Commissioner/Sect Expert:
Persecution all the way to character assassination

formation (ABI Education Information Action) from Stuttgart, who agitates against *Gut zum Leben* in the *Mannheimer Morgen* (March 10, 1994).

The ABI, which receives subsidies from taxpayers' money for its cheap campaign against minorities of faith, was also present in **Stuttgart** in September 1994 when the *Stuttgarter Zeitung* (September 12, 1994) attacks the market stand of *Gut zum Leben* in the local market hall ("People Catch," "Wolf in Sheepskin"). According to Helga Lerchenmüller, whoever works there is "lost to his family" – although the Original Christians, in particular, with the help of the Sermon on the Mount of Jesus of Nazareth, support peacefulness in families and marriages. In the *Stuttgarter Nachrichten* (September 15, 1994), the mayor of economy, Blessing, announces that he wants to make a strong case for "not allowing the sect to remain in the market hall." The Stuttgart Scene newspaper *Lift* also runs down the Original Christians and their market stand in March 1995 and May 1996: As is well known, a constant drop of damage to reputation wears away the stone. On this occasion, the head of the market office, Lothar Breitkreuz, quite unabashedly expresses his "regret" that the *Gut zum Leben* employees sell their goods properly and therefore provide no reason to "intervene."

ABI also spoke out again in 2001, when it was time "to stand by" the city of Stuttgart against a "dangerous" market stand of the firm *Lebe Gesund!* operated by Original Christians. On July, 14, 2001, the "International Committee of the Stuttgart City Council" had received a prize from the Theodor Heuß Foundation in a competition for "New Alliances for Democracy" – Head Mayor Wolfgang Schuster praised the "mutual understanding and tolerance" in the city.

Shortly after, however, the city gave notice to the *Lebe Gesund!* stand in the market hall, under the pretext that they had made "propaganda" for the "sect" there. That's how you get people agitated: In reality, an information leaflet available at the stand merely contained an advertisement for the Original Christian *Publishing House Das Wort.* The parties represented in Stuttgart's city council and a part of the Stuttgart media literally fought for the "honor" of finally being allowed to finish off the "heretics" economically. In a motion, city councilor Andreas Reißig of the SPD demanded that the stand be thrown out of the market hall and accused CDU mayor Beck of having "totally failed in the fight against sects" (*Stuttgarter Zeitung*, June 23, 2001). The journalist Michael Ohnewald of the *Stuttgarter Zeitung* describes the CDU man as "dozy" – whereupon the latter expresses his negative attitude toward minorities of faith in the same newspaper by saying that he is surprised "anyway, about how many people buy there, although it's been known for years who is behind this shop" (*Stuttgarter Zeitung*, June 26, 2001) – a "boycott-like appeal," as a lawyer notes (*Stuttgarter Zeitung*, June 28, 2001). Werner Wölfle of the Greens also demands a ban on the market stand.

The most eager to act, however, is the CDU faction leader Michael Föll. On July 19, 2001, he writes in the *Amtsblatt Stuttgart* (which should actually be an ideologically neutral forum!) that it is about a "despicable organization" which should be "outlawed" – and he refers to the sect commissioners of the churches in this opinion. Föll is then charged with rabble-rousing by a lawyer of the company *Lebe Gesund!*

Eberhard Kleinmann of the ABI now goes to the press as an "observer" of Universal Life, speaking (in a far too exaggerated manner) of "more than 100 commercial enterprises" that are close to the "fundamentalist end-time cult" Universal Life, and again spreads the false statement that one is "paid far below the union wage" – which he is promptly forbidden by the court to claim.

Strange: In all the years, none of the modern inquisitors, who spoke of the number and alleged "economic power" of the businesses run by the followers of Jesus of Nazareth, has ever taken offence at the economic empire of the mainstream churches, which especially in Germany are known for their lucrative investments – on the real estate market, on the land market, in various company holdings and with their own stock funds. They are the largest non-governmental landowners in Germany. In addition, they are subsidized by the German state from the general tax coffers with billions. They have the salaries of bishops, religious instruction in government schools, the training of their theologians, and, of course, of the sect commissioners, paid for by the state – in other words, by the tax money of all citizens. (Carsten Frerk: Finanzen und Vermögen der Kirchen)

But in Stuttgart, they are determined to finally get rid of the organic market stand, which is popular with customers, but has been banned by the churches. In order to conceal the religious-inquisitorial background of the expulsion, the first notice – "Reason": alleged religious advertising – is replaced by a second notice which no longer contains any reason at all. The city claims that the market hall is not a public institution, which is why it is allowed to terminate the contract without giving reasons.

The firm *Lebe Gesund!* defends itself in court against the expulsion, but gets no justice in the first two instances, as the courts let this easily seen-through maneuver go through. The fact that the termination was obviously based on reasons of faith does not interest the judges. The Federal Supreme Court also refuses to grant the firm provisional legal protection at least until the final court decision – the stand must be cleared out by the end of August 2002. Instead, the firm *Lebe Gesund!* moves into a shop in the city center.

When in addition, *Lebe Gesund!* temporarily takes over a stand in Stuttgart's main train station, the *Stuttgarter Zeitung* publishes an article at the end of May 2007, which the Federal Railroad promptly displays on the information boards of the platforms – removing them again only after protests. You have to imagine that: A landlord publicly discriminates against his own tenant, who has done nothing wrong. This is how far the power of the churches reaches. ...

And it becomes particularly clear when – seldom enough – a positive article about a market stand is published. At the beginning of July 2013, the *Nürnberger Nachrichten* reported on a special market at the market square of the city of **Nuremberg**.

Organically-grown food was sold there. On one photo, a market stand of the company *Lebe Gesund!* was shown. The name of the company was not even mentioned in the positive article, only the stand was shown. But this was apparently enough for church lobbyists to exert pressure: A few days later the same newspaper refused, "for fundamental considerations," an advertisement in which the company *Lebe Gesund!* in the Nuremberg area sought a saleswoman. Such advertisements had previously been accepted without complaint over a long period of time.

Something Always Sticks

In view of the numerous attacks on the market stands and shops of the Original Christians, it is almost a miracle that so many of them can still offer their healthy products day after day. No one will ever know how many customers have been permanently deterred from buying through the constant slanderous work, as well as what financial damage was caused by this.
And what about the customers? What happened when one of the modern inquisitors placed another malicious article in the newspaper? The next day, many a shop was sprayed with obscene

slogans. On such days, and for many days after, you could also see people walking past the stand, pointing their fingers at it and saying to their conversation partners: "Look, that is the sect stand. They should be banned; they are dangerous." Or they addressed other passers-by directly: "How can you shop at this sect?"

Who can empathize with how the people affected feel, for example, the men and women who work in the shops? They have to live day after day with the fact that they are being wronged, that rejection, sometimes even downright hatred is thrown at them, that they have to fear for their jobs – because the large church concerns have stamped them with "sect" and the people and politicians are subject to the church brainwashing.

At times, the salespeople felt like they were in a zoo; they were eyed disparagingly and loudly insulted: "You don't belong here! Get lost!" Some customers continued to shop, but asked for plain unprinted bags, because otherwise, they wouldn't dare go back to their office.

Lutheran religion teachers in several cities sent entire school classes to the market stand. The young people then stood around somewhat embarrassed and eyed everything. It turned out that they were supposed to write an essay about the sect afterward. According to the curricula for Protestant and Catholic religious instruction at government schools, which is paid for out of general tax revenues, the religion teachers must cover this subject with their students and warn them of the sects that the churches consider dangerous. And for this purpose, the pastors' prefabricated disparagements about sects are then implanted in the children – the enemy image is built up.

Such effrontery leaves one speechless: Here, the priests stand in front of young people and point their finger at the alleged "sect" – while in their own ranks, the thousandfold sexual abuse of children was hushed up and the sexual criminals in priests' cassocks were merely transferred, whereby they could then continue unhindered to abuse other children in their care.

*Those who Resist
Shall Be Intimidated*

In March 2006, the headline "Dubious Sect Runs Organic Stand" was attached in large letters to all newspaper stands of the *Bild-Zeitung* in **Munich**. Several of these stands are also set up around the market stand of *Gut zum Leben*. The originator of this action was once again the Lutheran sect commissioner Wolfgang Behnk.

This example shows once again that today, pyres are superfluous. Instead, the flames of slander can now flicker from newspaper stands or from a talk show or a television magazine, and effortlessly reach an audience of millions.

The followers of Jesus of Nazareth defended themselves against this agitation with a flyer. In it, the Lutheran Church was described as an "Inquisition sect," which works against those who leave the churches "with character assassination, invectives and slander that is damaging to business." In addition, it said that the Lutheran Church had not yet dissociated itself from its anti-Semitic past.
Several weeks later, the police were sent to the apartment of the signatory of the flyer at 7 a.m. to conduct a "house search." The Lutheran Church

had reported him for "libel." Behnk's superior, Regional Bishop Dr. Johannes Friedrich, had, in fact, been expressly named on the flyer as responsible for the activities of his "expert." And the hierarchs who usually let others do the "dirty work" do not like that.

A criminal trial was conducted before the Würzburg Regional Court, which ended with "only" a "warning" – presumably, because the community of faith defended itself with peaceful demonstrations and because international film teams drew attention to the growing discrimination against minorities in Germany.

On the other hand, a church representative has – despite numerous criminal charges filed in this regard – never been put on trial for offensive statements against Universal Life or the prophetess of God or for vilifying the Original Christian ideological beliefs. Prosecutors back off from this to this day; church indoctrination sits very deep in most of them.

The Insanity Continues

Thus, the smear campaigns continue. Particularly bizarre is the behavior of the Lutheran pastor and CSU city councilor Peter Bielmeier, who, in the spring of 2004, in all earnestness demanded that the city of **Nuremberg** ban a market stand at the main marketplace operated by followers of Jesus of Nazareth. The Lutheran even went so far as to give the ludicrous "reason" that Nuremberg, as a "City of Human Rights" could "not permit itself" such a market stand. What is particularly shocking here is: He does not even notice that it is his own motion, which recalls dark times in German history and is a direct indication of how endangered human rights in Germany apparently still are.

The motion of the CSU faction becomes utterly ridiculous when one knows that a stand of the Catholic monastery Plankstetten is located at the same market. A comparison of the two stands is worthwhile: By no means are only followers of Universal Life working with the Original Christians, but members of the most diverse nations and religious orientations. In a monastery, however, there can only be Catholics. Employees of the "heretics" receive the full salary within the framework of the collective agreement and are fully covered by social insurance – in contrast to the inhabitants of monasteries, who, as a rule, receive only pocket money and are marginally insured at a flat rate. At the monks' stand, church services and retreat days in the monastery are often advertised – which nobody holds against them, but which the "Christian" politicians of the CSU attributed to the "heretical" stand, although such things do not occur there.

Thus, the "examination procedure" initiated by the CSU came to nothing– since a legal possibility to revoke the license of a decent market dealer because of his prayer book fortunately does not exist in our country up to now.

But the insanity continues. In April 2009, the Protestant pastor Stefan Schrick tries to make a name for himself in **Bad Homburg**, especially as he is about to be evaluated by the presbytery of his parish. He looks on the Internet, finds the usual mendacious opinions, adds a few things – and the *Taunus Zeitung* promptly prints it. Its journalist, without revealing herself as such, had previously shown up at the local market stand, whose operator is associated with Universal Life. However, the journalist includes almost nothing from the young market vendor's statements – which would have refuted the pastor's accusations.

Yet "heretic" hunting must also be learned. The newspaper promptly incurs a counterstatement and a cease and desist order, because in his overzealousness, the pastor not only uttered the usual disparagements – disguised as barely permissible expressions of opinion – but also verifiably incorrect factual assertions, for example: *Universal Life* is being monitored by the Office for the Protection of the Constitution, or: *Universal Life* is the operator of the market stand.

The cases listed here, despite the large number, are merely a selection from all the barely veiled public calls for boycott that have been documented. In addition, there are countless cases in which discrimination can only be assumed. For example, at the end of 2016, when the German Federal Railroad terminates the contract with the firm *Lebe Gesund!* for a shop in **Mannheim's** main train station, without further explanation. In the middle of 2017, the space is still empty. ...

What can be the reason, when a commercial enterprise "voluntarily" forgoes revenue? At the end of 2012, the *Distelhäuser Brewery* in **Tauberbischofsheim** tells the company *Lebe Gesund!* that from now on, it will no longer deliver beer. A reason was not given, but it is clear: There is fear that the church authorities will associate them with "heretics."

In any case, the effects of the character assassination against the shops and market stands cannot be overlooked: Many a customer understands the broad hint from the Church, lets himself be intimidated and with a heavy heart, stays away from the stand with the tasty and wholesome vegetarian food. Again and again, new employees of the shops and market stands resign after a few days, once they are approached about the "sect" or read slander on the Internet – and this, in a time of growing unemployment.

But despite everything, it can be said today that the attempt to thus deprive the followers of Jesus of Nazareth of their economic existence has failed. Peaceable farming and the distribution of its products – from cultivation to customer from a single source – is convincing more and more people.

Disassociate Yourselves from the "Heretics"!

All the more furious are the attacks against the newly emerging Original Christianity in all its facets. And there, where a boycott is openly or underhandedly called for, in its hysteria, the deliberately instigated ostracism repeatedly leads to strange results – it strikes, for example, the "wrong ones," that is, the non-heretics.

Just as during the Middle Ages, in such cases, artisans or shopkeepers asserted they were not "heretics"; just as in Germany in the early thirties, doctors, lawyers or shopkeepers gave assurances in newspaper advertisements that, for example, "Dr. Sommer is not a Jew" (Nuremberg, 1933); so, too, in Lower Franconia at the end of the 20th century, businesses and entrepreneurs repeatedly dissociated themselves from the Original Christians.

For example, a bakery puts up posters at its branches in and around **Würzburg**: "We are not part of the Homebringing Mission. Rumors to the contrary are without any foundation or truth whatsoever." In a café in **Wertheim**, the same company even lets customers know: "We are practicing Catholics! – The Management." Restaurants in **Würzburg** also dissociate themselves with newspaper advertisements: "For all those who know first hand – we know better! We do not belong to Universal Life – and that's the way it will stay." The reason for the rumors was, apparently, that some followers of Jesus of Nazareth had often dined in this restaurant (which, of course, they no longer did after this dissociation and about which they informed the public at the same spot per advertisement). Two doctors who had their practice in the building next to the House of Universal Life in Würzburg had a sign put up: "Due to the local situation, we would like to point out that there is no connection between us and Universal Life."

In 1994 the dissociations became so prevalent that the *Fränkisches Volksblatt* reported on it (September 10, 1994):
They appear again and again: advertisements, flyers and posters with which Würzburg businessmen want to create "clarity." "Clarity" that they do not belong to Universal Life – despite all rumors. It is no longer just shops from the more alternative or organic scene that are affected. In the meantime, a renown Würzburg hotel is struggling against it, just as much as a bookstore, a bakery or a sports center.

The article is apparently intended to arouse sympathy for the companies concerned. However, the Catholic *Volksblatt* does not consider the fact that these dissociations are the result of years of a church smear campaign against respectable fellow citizens.

The fact that the ostracism and discrimination of a minority constitutes a danger to a democratic state is not something that occurs to either the dissociating business people or the media. Everyone is apparently in agreement that the Original Christians should neither work nor earn anything – Catholics or Protestants, of course, should not be affected.

But there are even escalations. For example, an advertisement from a farming family in Kreuzwertheim, apparently to avoid losses in their sales directly from the farm announced in the parish newspaper in 1996:

To the attention of my esteemed customers! There have been several inquiries regarding whether we buy produce from Universal Life. I must firmly oppose this rumor; it is not true.

The trigger for such an announcement is the medieval thinking that the churches have hammered into their believers over centuries: Not only do I not buy from someone who is a "heretic" – I also avoid anyone who associates with the "heretic" in any way, for example, who buys something from him! A (devout Catholic) heating oil supplier from the vicinity of Marktheidenfeld experiences a similar situation. Various customers turn away from him because he "also delivers oil to the Universals." It's like the Middle Ages: Anyone who does business with the "heretics" is afraid that he will inevitably end up in the mills of the Inquisition – only that the latter has "modernized" itself today.

Pastor Collects Defamations –
and Spreads them in the Internet

Church "sect experts" also use digital media for their disreputable craft – such as Pastor Michael Fragner from Uengershausen, who eagerly collects and circulates all the disinformation data of his "colleagues." When a company run by followers of the Nazarene plans to refinance some properties in 2005, a financing package already negotiated with several banks falls through at the last minute: The bank managers had clicked on Fragner's hodgepodge on the Internet. The company sued for damages.

Although the courts appealed to did forbid the further dissemination of the false statements that were objected to, the judges let the victim sit on

the damage caused. They found nothing wrong with the fact that "connections" of companies to communities of faith were indicated – namely, because meanwhile, many people categorically rejected contacts to communities of faith of any kind and their activities," thus, the *Main-Post* journalist Tilman Toepfer quotes from a judgment. The headline: "Regional Church Permitted to Enlighten about UL Activities" (December 11, 2006).
"Enlighten" – this is also how one can call cheap propaganda against people of different faiths. *Who* has seen to it for years that many people are "meanwhile" stirred up and incited is left out. That could open the eyes of the readers.

At the same time, the accomplices of the slanderers pounce on every detail to make things as difficult as possible for the "heretics."
Just one of many examples: In the summer of 1993, a pharmacy in **Esselbach**, a remote Spessart village, run by followers of Jesus of Nazareth, installs a prescription box into which the villagers can drop their prescriptions, in order to quickly receive the appropriate medication. But the box is damaged several times. Previously, a pharmacy from a neighboring village had supplied the remote village with medications, but now the nearby new pharmacy in Esselbach has also agreed to

do so in response to a request from the "Apothekerkammer" (Professional Association of Dispensing Chemists). The chamber provides for a one and a half year cycle, in which the pharmacies alternate. A completely normal procedure? Not if Christ-friends are involved.

The pharmacist from the neighboring village undermines the rotation by printing flyers on which he states his willingness to continue to supply medicines and by leaving his box – with the inscription of a different name – hanging in the remote village. The *Main-Echo* (June 26, 1993) reports about "uncertainty" among the citizens (who made them feel uncertain?) and about the "fear ... that Universal Life, by delivering the medications, could get to know the domestic circumstances of the inhabitants well, and try to offer the services of Universal Life (nursing services *'Helping Hands'*)" – a scandalous insinuation!

Thomas Müller, an Inquisition assistant, writes a letter to the editor in which he complains about the pharmacy association, which is indifferent to the faith of the new pharmacist (which, for once, complies with the Constitution!) and concludes: The village "must help itself!"

It was the same during the Middle Ages: Anyone who wanted to eliminate a competitor simply denounced him or her as a "heretic" or a "witch" – and the "case" was "settled." Since after the church propaganda in the village, the pharmacy's prescription box was hardly used anymore, the Original Christian pharmacy did without it.

Or another example: Farmers who practice peaceable farming are repeatedly hindered in leasing land. In November 1990, the mayor of **Esselbach** promised the farm in the Kredenbach district the lease of some fields owned by the village. Then, however, the local Catholic priest was invited to the local village council, where he was allowed to "lecture" on Universal Life. Result: The leasing of the fields is rejected.

In 2013, the state-run Würzburg-Schweinfurt University of Applied Sciences began to produce a "**Würzburg** Atlas of Homes For the Elderly," which should list all the city's nursing homes. This includes two facilities run by followers of the Nazarene: the "House for the Inner Home" and the "House of the Common Good."

However, in July 2013, the student carrying out this project surprisingly informed the head of these facilities that she could not include these facilities in the list. Reason: *Since our project is mainly financed by the Free State of Bavaria, we cannot con-*

sider your facilities due to the organizational and ideological background of your provider.

It should be noted that all the homes are regularly inspected and there have been no complaints whatsoever. The sentence just quoted suggests that the "veto" against publication again comes from the government or the authorities of the state of Bavaria. The "ideological background" is nothing other than the home management's conviction of faith, which differs from that of the mainstream churches.

But why is the "organizational and ideological background" of the mainstream churches not scrutinized more closely? For example, that of the Vatican Church with its claim that everyone must submit to its head, the pope, in order to attain salvation, or otherwise be eternally damned? Or that of the Lutheran Church with its misanthropic founder?

12.3. Isolate and Discriminate Every Single One of Them!

But it is not only businesses whose employees aspire to live and work according to the Sermon on the Mount that are targeted by the modern Inquisition. Individual "heretics" can also be dangerous to the Inquisition. It is precisely the affiliation with an Original Christian community of faith that can give individuals the strength to stick to their convictions even without social recognition. And every "heretic" who lives and works among "orthodox believers" can soften the carefully constructed concept of the enemy that all "sectarians" are fanatical, opinionated, disagreeable and much more. Therefore, individual followers of the Nazarene are also hindered in their normal daily life.

Occupational Ban for Reasons of Faith

The cassock wearers react particularly ruthlessly if a "heretic" has to do with children or young people on an occupational basis. It does not matter whether the persons concerned bring their faith into play at work or not, whether they work in a church or state establishment – the fact that with a non-church faith, they work in a social occupation is sufficient for taking appropriate measures.

The first to feel this is the kindergarten teacher Angelika B., who works in a municipal kindergarten in the Hohenlohe town of **Untermünkheim**. When she left the Protestant-Lutheran Church in March 1984, Pastor Martin Völlm wrote to the community of Untermünkheim, which runs the kindergarten, on behalf of the Protestant Church Council:

Even though, the entire Church Council has no doubt about the professional qualification of Ms. A. B., because of her spiritual-religious attitude, it is of grave concern that in the kindergarten she will no longer be able to convey the Christian faith in the biblical sense. Despite her promise to keep silent in the kindergarten in Untermünkheim about the "special teachings" from Würzburg, there is still a conflict between the ideology of Ms. B. and the parents, as well as the parents and children cared for and influenced by Ms. A. B. In the view of the entire parish council, her work no longer corresponds to the guidelines of the Working Group for Protestant Kindergartens, which the contracting parties to the agreement between the civic town of Untermünkheim and the Protestant parishes ... have jointly recognized.

Therefore, the entire Church Council proposes to the town hall administration and the civic town council of Untermünkheim to once again invite Ms. B. to a further conversation and suggest that she resign her position as head of the kindergarten on her own initiative, in order to avoid long term conflicts in the area of faith. The Church Council requests that it be represented at this meeting.

It is as simple as that: The Church, which lets itself be subsidized in all issues by the state, wants to determine the faith of the employees, not only of the Church, but also of the state facilities. It does this with the "reason" that it wants to avoid "conflicts" – which, however, would not even exist without it, and which it provokes in the first place, itself. As Karlheinz Deschner said in his "Aphorisms": *Church – a practice that makes people ill in order to be able to heal; that helps in hardships that one would not even have without it; that "bosses around" those who still believe, by those who no longer do.*
However, Angelika B. is not so easily intimidated. She refuses to give notice herself, because she has nothing to reproach herself for; she has not influenced a child in the meaning of her faith. Now the town has a problem: To comply with the urging of the Church, it has to commit a breach of the Constitution. It then does commit this breach – but un-

dercover: From now on, Angelica is no longer the director of the kindergarten. Instead, the mayor takes over the arrangement of the newly added children into the individual groups. Angelika's group is reduced to the minimum possible within the guidelines. And in the town, at beer festivals and other occasions, rumors are now being spread against the woman, who is recognized as capable and irreproachable. She is summoned repeatedly and in the presence of the pastor and mayor is veritably interrogated about her faith. When she cleverly avoids the affair, the dignitaries complain: "But you do make things hard for us!" Even trick questions asked by eager parents in the kindergarten in passing do not bring the desired result.

After more than a year, the mayor managed to get four parents to withdraw their children from Angelika's group – *only* four, one would have to say, in view of a campaign lasting several months. To secure herself a provisional protection, the chairwoman of the parents' council convenes another parents' evening – but only for parents of the two groups that Angelika does *not* lead. As the leader of the kindergarten, she is not invited, however, the Protestant-Lutheran pastor is. It is easy to manipulate the parents there in such a way that they unanimously declare that they do not want to allow their children to switch to Angelica's group. Then in autumn 1985, Angelica was dismissed with the "reason" that her group had become too small. A year and a half of running the gauntlet comes to an end – the town, however, had to agree to a compensation payment before the Heilbronn Labor Court. What had been done to this woman did not remain hidden in the town. For example, shortly before her dismissal, a family deliberately registered their child in Angelika's group with the reason: "As Christians we cannot behave as was done to this woman." (The mayor, however, does not allow this re-registration.) Another woman moved away from the village a little later, because: "I won't continue to live there!"

What would Angelica B. have done in this situation, if she had not had friends in her community of faith? Because of her faith, she was de facto banned from working in her hometown, and so she moved to Würzburg to work in an Original Christian kindergarten.

Witch Hunt in Lindelbach

Ten years later this case is repeated: This time, it is the kindergarten teacher Christine L., who works in a public kindergarten in Lindelbach, a district of **Wertheim**. They are also very satisfied with her – until the beginning of 1994, when it becomes known in the village that Christine is close to Universal Life.

The Lutheran pastor Hausmann then invited the Lutheran deacon Rüdiger Beile to an "information evening," where the latter disparaged Universal Life with defamations from Pastor Haack.

Of course, the kindergarten teacher is not invited; after all, that might disturb the flow of slander.

A few days later, Christine is summoned to a parents' evening where she is confronted with accusations: She told the children not to pick flowers anymore. (Not to pick at random, she had told the children, and if they did, then put them in a vase). She had scolded the man who wanted to mow the lawn in front of the kindergarten. (She had said: Let the grass grow a little more, so that the lawn does not burn again in the hot sun.) In addition, one child didn't want to eat sausage anymore.

One is reminded of a "witch hearing" or an Inquisition tribunal, where an accusation is to be put together from muddled trivialities. At the end, a

vote is taken on which of the parents present still want to send their children to this kindergarten teacher. 20 out of 26 parents said no. In a letter to the church elders (it is, mind you, a village kindergarten, not a church kindergarten!) and the village administrator, pastor Hausmann writes that one must "check ... whether the teacher is willing to turn away from Universal Life." (It is unbelievable: One used to say "abjure" or "recant!") He added that the "concern of the parents" has "priority" – a "concern," which the pastor himself had created with his cheap propaganda in the first place!
Conversely, as has now become clear, don't parents need to be concerned when they place their children in church facilities?

Now the question was: How would the city of Wertheim react? Would it stand up for the employee, whom it has a duty to care for as an employer? Again the question is asked: How would a city have behaved if a kindergarten teacher with dark skin, for example, had been rejected per vote by the parents? Wouldn't it have tried everything to stem the burgeoning racism, to call for moderation, to stop the campaign's originator?

But in a country that is proud of its democracy, members of non-church minorities are not second-class, but third-class citizens. Under the leadership of Mayor Gläser (CDU) (Chapter 6), Wertheim does none of the above. The city dismisses the kindergarten teacher – illegally, as the Crailsheim Labor Court determines. Wertheim, therefore, has to pay a high severance pay – but the kindergarten teacher still has to find another job. An attempt to become self-employed fails due to the public stigmatization as "sect member." She finally finds work with the Original Christians, but cannot work there in her chosen profession, since the positions in the educational sector are already filled.

Obstruct their Vocational Training!

It is also significant that the cases in which young Original Christians were denied apprenticeship opportunities were almost all in the area of social professions.

In 1987, a young pediatric nurse was dismissed at the end of her probationary period in Würzburg. She would have been employed further if she had dissociated herself from Universal Life within a week.

In 1997, another Original Christian woman is refused an internship in a Protestant-Lutheran nursing home in Wertheim, because she does not be-

long to either of the mainstream churches. The company *Gut zum Leben* was listed in her résumé. Be it a training course for home directors or an internship as a journalist at the *Tauber-Zeitung* in Bad Mergentheim – the "wrong" faith bars the doors.
And where the doors can't be barred for legal reasons, there is sometimes a last-minute pinprick: In 1993, shortly before being sworn in, a candidate for a teaching post is asked if she isn't "under psychological pressure" because she also belongs "to this sect."

A teacher in Baden-Württemberg is not allowed to teach ethics because he is an Original Christian. A young graduate of the school *Learn with Me* wanted to do a voluntary social year starting in summer 2013. The Red Cross referred him to the Juliusspital – a Catholic hospital. There, however, they found out from the records where he had gone to school – and refused him voluntary employment, although the young man only needed to be paid pocket money. He was told that in the hospital's statutes it states: Sect members may not be employed. The irony of it is that the young man and his parents are Catholic, since the private school is open to students of all faiths. After the parents informed the hospital of this, the hospital was suddenly ready to again accept the student.

We Do Not Employ Such People

Time and again, trained specialists are denied jobs because they are close to Universal Life. For example, Christian S., who in 1988 was looking for work as a psychologist at the Technical Inspection Agency of Lower Franconia. They required a promise from him that he would not appear in public as an Original Christian. Or Iris K., who was refused a job at a social service center in Lohr in 1993 on the grounds that she followed the Inner Path in Universal Life. Iris K. is Jewish. Or a mother who in 1996 in Marktheidenfeld wants to work again in her occupation as an office clerk. When it is learned during the job interview that her children go to the school of the Original Christians, the interview is abruptly brought to an end.

Even those who have a job are not safe from being dismissed for reasons of faith – although another reason is usually given as a pretext.
Artisans associated to Universal Life (mind you: not working in companies of the Original Christians) lose customers when their faith affiliation becomes known. In the area of Würzburg, the search for an apartment can also end very quickly after the question: "Are you close to Universal Life?"

An Original Christian in Waldbüttelbrunn was even rejected as a gymnastics teacher by the senior group of a sports club. They said they would all rather leave. At least the club reacted unperturbed and gave her another group.

Church Incitement as a Weapon in the "War of the Roses"

The situation is less relaxed when private disputes are carried out among relatives. Here, too, church slander is sometimes used as an "argument."
In April 1990, a 31-year-old woman from the Bavarian Forest is abruptly kicked out by her husband after attending a seminar in Würzburg.

In 1994, a man from Austria states as a reason for his divorce petition, among other things, that his wife was urged for over ten years by Universal Life to avoid physical contact. In reality, the wife knew the Original Christians only briefly and for a much shorter time period – and, anyway, no forbiddances are imposed there.
In July 1993, a father from Darmstadt threatens to disown his daughter and disinherit her because she is participating in a meditation course with Universal Life.

A mother from Villach informs her son in October 1993 that she wants to disinherit him. Shortly before, "Pastor" Behnk had been in Villach and had claimed that the followers of Universal Life had lost their "right to dispose of their property."
Such "arguments" are also used in disputes over the custody of children.
In Munich, in 1996, a mother wants sole custody of a child because her partner is "still a practicing member of this sect," while she has "seen through the dangerous, manipulative practices and techniques of this association."
Conversely, in Berlin in 1993, a father wants to revoke his wife's custody of their child (they live separately), because she is with a "dangerous sect." Previously, he had verbally abused his former partner saying: "Suicide would be the ideal solution for you in this case!" (Also a result of the malicious mass suicide thesis of Pastor Behnk: Chapter 8.) At a first hearing, the judge allows herself to be influenced by this and expresses "doubts" as to whether the mother could raise the child to be a "critically thinking person." (Strange: Parents influenced by the Church are not asked such questions in divorce proceedings – although in their doctrines, churches threaten the faithful with eternal damnation if they do not believe the church tenets are true). The child occasionally visits the father;

only after a hearing on the main issue in 1995, is the mother granted sole custody, among other things because "the court ... is not entitled to take the religious conviction of one of the parents as a criterion." "The religious attitude and conviction of a person, as here the mother's, is protected by the fundamental right of freedom of religion according to Article 4 paragraph 1.2 of the German Constitution." Regarding assertions about Universal Life, the court merely states: "Also with the 'mainstream' religious communities" – note the quotation marks – "depending on the point of view, some vehement criticism is frequently practiced." But the question remains: Why does one have to go through two years of litigation in this country to have such self-evident facts established?

The Atmosphere of Ostracism and Its Inflamers

But those who have been inciting people for years, who have thoroughly and lastingly poisoned the atmosphere in the whole country, always wash their hands in innocence – as if it was not they themselves who lied and slandered for so long, until incited and indoctrinated people follow their hate slogans with physical acts.

How does it feel when children no longer dare to go out in the streets because they fear being called "sect pigs" or because neighbors have forbidden their children to play with them? When it is difficult to get an apartment because the landlord immediately asks you about your faith? When after ten years, your market stand and thus, your job are terminated for flimsy reasons, and you don't know what's next? When you lose your job as an artisan? When you constantly have to read defamations in the media? When family members, upset by visits from the sect commissioner, want nothing more to do with you? When, as a grandmother, you are forbidden contact with your grandchildren? When family members cut off contact with you for years, just because the sect commissioner has been spreading mendacious stories about you? When, in the event of a divorce, the husband demands custody of the children simply because the mother is with a "sect"? How does that make you feel? That is Inquisition today. It's all about isolation, stigmatization and eradication. Pastor Haack himself once said it to the Original Christians: *In the Middle Ages, we would have treated you very differently.*

And what is it like for the prophetess of God, Gabriele, who, out of love for God, took upon herself to bring the word of truth from the Kingdom of God, the teaching of the Free Spirit – God in us – to the people of today? How does it feel to know that the Spirit of the Christ of God, in His word of revelation, gives an understanding of the love of our eternal Father to us human beings, gives us help after help for all spheres of life and shows us the way into our eternal homeland – and then to have to experience that one is slandered and pilloried for the sake of His word. And that the word of the Eternal is ridiculed and people are often prevented from learning about His wonderful teaching of love for God and neighbor, of freedom, unity and peace?

Only a person who truly lives in God and serves Him alone finds the strength to endure this – over several decades.

Indeed, we are living in the twenty-first century – but in its specific effects, the church incitement is still very current. The poisonous ammunition, fired over years, continues to be effective.

13. Despite Hostilities and Chicanery: The Kingdom of Peace Is Emerging

A Kingdom of Peace on this Earth – this is an ancient longing of humankind: On Earth it shall be as in heaven!

In the Bibles of the churches, too, the coming messianic kingdom is mentioned several times. In the great prophet of God, Isaiah, for example, under the heading "The Messiah and His Kingdom of Peace," it says what God, the Eternal, announced through Isaiah:

The wolf shall dwell with the lamb, and the leopard shall lie down with the young goat, and the calf and the lion ... and a little child shall lead them. The cow and the bear shall graze; their young shall lie down together; and the lion shall eat straw like the ox. The nursing child shall play over the hole of the cobra, and the weaned child shall put his hand on the adder's den. They shall not hurt or destroy in all my holy mountain; for the earth shall be full of the knowledge of the LORD as the waters cover the sea. And the Eternal spoke, likewise through His prophet Isaiah: *For behold, I create new heavens and a new earth; and the former things shall not be remembered or come into mind. But be glad and rejoice for ever in that which I create ...*

Such announcements are also found in Jeremiah (Chapter 32), Daniel (Chapter 7) or Ezekiel: *I will send down showers in their season, they shall be showers of blessing. ... And I will provide for them splendid vegetation ... (Ez. 34)*
This kingdom is also described in the Revelation of John, and there, the "New Jerusalem, the city on the mountain" is mentioned extensively.
The Kingdom of Peace shall emerge on the Earth – through people who do His Will, by fulfilling His eternal law of love for God and neighbor.

This time has come. On November 6, 1987, in Würzburg, the Cherub of divine Wisdom revealed through Gabriele, the prophetess and emissary of God, the following, among other things:
The trumpet of divine Wisdom resounds over the ether ... The great time is near ...
You human beings are facing a mighty turn of time. The Lord comes in the Spirit. Already now, He is preparing the Kingdom of Peace, His Kingdom ... my friends, awaken! ... Satan will be bound – indeed, he binds himself through his negative workings. ... Recognize: The darkness feels very well that its power is coming to an end. The forces of darkness are rebelling and endeavoring – as in all time – to annihilate the true followers of the Lord. A stealthy persecution of Christians is underway. ...

Truly, My human brothers and sisters, the Earth is vibrating – and the more the magnetic poles come into vibration, the more there will be changes on this Earth. ...

In the Spirit, the Kingdom of Peace already stands on this Earth – and through you it shall be transformed into the material form. ...

Oh see, many say: "The Kingdom of God is a spiritual kingdom." That is correct. First, people must open up the inner kingdom, and radiate this inner kingdom through love, through peace. But what forms and takes shape within will also be visible externally.

The "Demythologization" of the Kingdom of Peace

It is the fulfillment of the vision for which Christianity has been praying for centuries in the Lord's Prayer with the words, *Your kingdom come, Your will be done, on Earth as it is in heaven* – and this is what churches are working against!

The reaction of the church representative Haack to this revelation from the Kingdom of God shows that the cassock wearers of the church institutions have nothing at all to do with the primordial basis of true Christianity – nor do they know the content of their own Bibles, or they take it just as little seriously as the commandments of God and the teachings of the Sermon on the Mount of Jesus of Nazareth, which can be read in it to this day, as well as the announcement of the Kingdom of Peace by the prophets of God.

On December 31, 1987 could be read in the *Main-Echo*:

In an initial statement on the beginning of a new era proclaimed in Würzburg, the Protestant sect pastor Friedrich-Wilhelm Haack (Munich) declared that the belief in an imminent ... reign of Christ and his faithful before the Last Judgment is nothing new. Already during the first century after Christ, there were fierce arguments about it.

Haack also pointed out that the description of this period of time in the book of Revelation of the New Testament is extremely reserved. So there are no hints of a "Golden Age" as it has been invoked again and again, by the most varied religious groups throughout the centuries up to the present day.

Haack deliberately states an untruth here – as a theologian, he of course knows that the announcement of the Kingdom of Peace in the Bible of the churches is by no means as "reserved" as he claims.

But the promise of a kingdom, in which there is peace between human being and animal, where evil has no more room, has perhaps long since fallen victim to a "demythologization" with most theologians – and obviously with Haack as well. For the Protestant theologian Rudolf Bultmann (1884-1976), who coined this word, such visions – and, of course, also the idea of a preceding "onrushing end time under cosmic disasters" – have long since been "dealt with." They are considered time-conditioned admixtures that must be gotten rid of. All that is then left is a bloodless rationalism. Moreover, for the churches, which have repeatedly sown discord over centuries, the idea of a "Kingdom of Peace" is obviously not at all attractive. Under the scandalous abuse of the name of Jesus, the Christ, the Prince of Peace, they justified, permitted and promoted wars – and this, right into our present time. The pope, the "Holy Father" of the Church of Rome, still bears the title of "ruler of the world." Where is there room for the Kingdom of Peace of Jesus, the Christ? (See: The Rehabilitation of the Christ of God.)

In May 1987, a few months before the publication of the divine revelation mentioned above, Pastor Haack had even claimed at a lecture in Marktheidenfeld (Chapter 7) that there was no announcement of the Kingdom of Peace in the Bible at all, and that only the devil speaks of an earthly kingdom of Jesus in it. So anyone who strives not to postpone the application of the laws of God to a far-off hereafter, but to start with them here and now, must be, from Haack's point of view, the devil. But if the cassock wearers, Haack and his colleagues, do not want to strive for the laws of God, then they are saying that Jesus of Nazareth was a liar, because He said: "Follow Me!" And the question literally comes to mind: So then, who are they following?

The Defamation Machine Rolls On

The mere announcement of a more peaceful society apparently puts the cassock wearers on alert. They get their energy from their overwhelming wealth, from the power they wield, from the dependency of their members, from the quarrels, from conflicts that they themselves conjure up with their enemy images, from the fear of an alleged eternal damnation that they spread. They immediately turned this announcement into a new abusive word, that of the already mentioned "end time disciple" (chapter 10), and added it to their repertoire of character assassination.

In March 1988, the Würzburg deans of both denominations – Dean Martin Elze (Lutheran) and City Dean Helmut Bauer (Catholic, later promoted to Auxiliary Bishop) – took up the topic of the "Kingdom of Peace" in a second "clarifying word" (the first one was published in 1985: Chapter 5). "This term," according to the deans, "is used in the last book of the Holy Scriptures in a completely different context and is part of the pictorial language of this book." And pictures, one could add, need not be taken seriously – they can be safely "demythologized" and then conveniently disposed of.

We Christians, the deans continue, *have always lived in the end times. The fact that the end times only begin today contradicts the Holy Scriptures. ... The business of fear, which has often been used in church history with "apocalyptic dates" – in Universal Life there is no such thing at all! – "is rejected by us Christians."*

The "business of fear" – here, the churches are the experts. With the fear of eternal damnation, many "sheep" can still be kept in line – and one can cash in on them. The so-called "eternal damnation" is still a fixed component of the doctrine of both major churches. Even today, the Catholic dogma mentioned earlier is still valid, that *no one remaining outside the Catholic Church, not only pagans, but also Jews, heretics or schismatics, can become partakers of eternal life, but they will go to the eternal fire prepared for the devils and his angels, unless before the end of their life they are joined to it (the Church).*

So the mainstream churches do not want to know anything about a Kingdom of Peace – from their point of view, this is also logical, because there, it will no longer be the mainstream churches with their mediators between God and the people who rule. The center will be solely Jesus, the Christ, the Free Spirit, and in His Spirit of love and unity, people will live in peace with one another and with nature and the animals.

The Nucleus of the Kingdom of Peace in the Sights of a Church Defamer

In the Spirit, the Kingdom of Peace already stands on this Earth – and through you it shall be transformed into the material form. ...

That was announced by the Cherub of divine Wisdom in November 1987. But just as a mighty tree emerges from a small seed, everything truly great begins in a small, almost inconspicuous way. Thus, it has a background. And it is certainly not by chance that already the first small seed of the Kingdom of Peace on this Earth was fiercely attacked by church representatives almost from the beginning.

In August 1991, the news spread in the villages near Würzburg that followers of Universal Life had acquired an estate with 130 hectares of land. The previous owner, a seed producer, had moved on to build a new existence in the new German states.

When asked by a *Main-Post* journalist whether she could confirm the sale to the Original Christians, the previous owner's wife replied: "Would it be worth publishing if a Catholic or Protestant were to buy the farm?"

The followers of Jesus of Nazareth began to clear up the farm and to plant the first fields where they grew grain – without artificial fertilizer, without agricultural poisons, without manure and slurry, that is, in peaceable farming, as a concept from the Kingdom of God that had been given through Gabriele. But they could not work in peace and quiet for long. On April 21, 1993, Pastor Behnk publicly spread the mendacious opinion of an allegedly impending "mass suicide," like the Davidians in Waco, in the US that was imminent on this very estate (Chapter 8).

These diatribes led, as described, to a veritable "pilgrimage" of sensation-seeking journalists. These people obviously did not care that the low-flying helicopters used to take aerial photographs terrified the animals living on the farm almost to death. One of the journalists who entered the premises with a camera team and without advance notice was Detlef Cosmann. His report was broadcast as early as April 25, 1993, that is, only four days after Behnk's targeted character assassination attack in the TV program "ZAK" of *Westdeutscher Rundfunk*. Cosmann claimed, among other things, that the farm was "secured with elaborate electronics, a double fence with a security wing for border guards and watch dogs."

Professional slanderers know exactly which keywords they can use to elicit fear and loathing in the viewers. In this case, an attempt is apparently being made to deliberately create an association with the divided German border – the fall of the German border wall was just a few years back, at that time. Just how malicious and absurd this allusion is, becomes clear when one knows what the actual situation was like on the grounds of the farm, where to this day, honest farmers carry out their peaceful work: In reality, the alleged "double fence" was nothing but a new pasture fence, behind which some posts of the old fence had not yet been removed. And even though the Würzburg Regional Court forbade the station from making this false claim on June 23, 1993 – the fence shown in the film, optically distorted from below in grotesque enlargement, has long since been imprinted in the minds of the viewers.

A few days later on 9 May 1993, television viewers experienced an intensification of this agitation in the program "Die Reporter" on *Pro 7*, where the course was already set during the introduction:

The mass death, the burning pictures from Waco startled everyone. In America alone there are over 3000 fanatical sects. But anyone who thinks that such an inferno is not possible with us is mistaken. The proclaimers of the Moon sect, Universal Life, the Scientologists or the Philadelphia community – they live among us. And as different as the teachings of salvation of these soul-sellers may be, they have one thing in common: religious fanaticism. Their followers give the prophets their money, their labor, their health and, not seldom, also their lives. They follow them blindly into the kingdom of evil.

Again, a monstrous cheap propaganda – a mixture of frightening images and insinuations, with which fear and loathing are generated in the viewer in an almost diabolic way: Money, work capacity, health – everything that constitutes a person's existence seems threatened.
And who was behind it, pulling the strings? It was – and still is – church representatives like Behnk, who have always demonized everything that is not church-related – but above all, who again and again tried to drag the pure teaching of the Spirit of the Christ of God through the dirt.

For the Original Christians, the only way left open was to take legal action against this satanic deluge of calumnies – but without success. On August 10, 1993, the Regional Court of Würzburg decided that the assertion by the *Pro 7* station that the "followers ... give the prophets their money, their labor, their health and not seldom also their life," could not be banned, because it was "not offensive to honor. Within the Catholic Church, it is also the rule that on joining an order, the assets are transferred to the respective community. This assertion is ultimately, merely a symbolic depiction of the members' devotion to the respective community of faith."

This ruling is scandalous. The reader may judge for himself whether he also comes to this conclusion after reading the above-mentioned introduction. Incidentally, the difference lies precisely in the fact that after the Waco catastrophe, no television station in Germany came up with the idea of suggesting impending mass suicides in Catholic monasteries.

The absurd ruling by the Regional Court becomes even more incomprehensible when one considers that in the film report by *Pro 7*, immediately after these introductory words, pictures of mountains of corpses were shown, accompanied by following words:

August 8, 1969: Charles Manson and the followers of his demonic sect brutally kill eight men and women in California. Most famous victim: the heavily pregnant actress Sharon Tate. November 18, 1978: Jim Jones, leader of the popular Temple sect, persuades thousands of his followers to poison themselves with cyanide in the South American jungle in Guyana. Most recent case, April 19, 1993: 86 Dav-

idians die in the flaming hell of Waco, led by the self-proclaimed Messiah, David Koresh.

What makes television journalists associate respectable citizens who follow Jesus of Nazareth, and have begun to put His Sermon on the Mount and the Ten Commandments of God into practice in their daily lives, with cruel crimes and mass suicide?

After the horrible words (and pictures!) at the beginning of the film report, can the viewer still perceive that what is then presented to him can have absolutely nothing to do with all the horrors of the introduction? He was, after all, attuned to extremely negative things – and that's exactly how slander and manipulation work in the church-controlled mass media.

A Journalist as Church Spokesman

TV reports such as the one just described – and there have constantly been similar ones – did not remain without effect on the people, especially in the villages in the immediate vicinity of the farm. And the reactions directly after Behnk's mendacious opinions of Waco were particularly violent.

When at the end of May 1993, four weeks after Behnk's diatribe, the annual border walk of the village of Hettstadt leads to the vicinity of the farm, a call comes shortly before: "Tomorrow we'll come from Hettstadt with cannons!" A little later the next phone call: "We'll be there at noon, you can call in the fire department!"
The "cannons" of the church-manipulated mass media had spoken a few days earlier – and the fires of slander were far from extinguished, for the "fire department" of the justice system did not extinguish the fire.

Now, church "experts" together with journalists servile to the Church and local politicians indoctrinated by the Church start a running battle against the Land of Peace, which in its malice over the years blatantly shows how small-minded the cassock wearers and their accomplices really are.

You have to stir up the fire of slander to keep it burning, this is what many a newspaper journalist thinks, who wants to enhance his image at the expense of his fellow human beings. In June 1993, the farmers at the land discovered a dump that their predecessors had created years before. They disposed of the waste properly and trimmed some bushes for this purpose. But what was written in the local newspaper *Main-Post*? Under the headline "Accord of Words and Deeds? – Biotope Cleared, Rubbish in Nature," journalist Tilman Toepfer writes that "an unauthorized clearing of a biotope is said to have occurred."

However, there could be no talk of a "biotope"; no one knew anything about it. And even if it had been a biotope – nothing was damaged. It was not until three days later that the newspaper's readers were informed of the true facts. In December 1993, when a Catholic professor of the University of Würzburg, while walking near the farm, was annoyed by free jumping and barking dogs (which were immediately whistled back) and wrote a nasty letter to the district office and the police, editor Toepfer made a "story" out of it again with the headline: "Incident with Free-running Dogs ... Just Dutiful or Aggressive?"

Tilman Toepfer is one of the journalists, who, to this day, use every occasion, no matter how small, to put himself in the limelight at the expense of the Original Christians in Universal Life. Above all, one can hardly do anything wrong for one's career – because to be against the "heretics" has always been part of "bon ton," especially in the Würzburg area. Tilman Toepfer is thus, virtually the prototype of a journalist who opportunistically ingratiates himself with the taste of the masses. And the masses are, as the Protestant theologian Professor Walter Nigg noted, one of the greatest enemies of prophecy. In his book "Prophetische Denker" (Prophetic Thinkers) Nigg writes:

The best known enemy of prophecy is the masses. … The masses are an amorphous entity. … Mass suggestion has a demoralizing effect on most people; they lose all good qualities the moment they immerse in the masses and become a fanatical herd of animals. The masses … are without a head and without a heart and can therefore easily be misused for all bad actions. … The masses also include the person of public opinion who, without his own conviction, adapts to all fashions and thus joins the army of hangers-on, who no longer has a face of his own and is not even aware of his immortal soul. … The sophisticated person of society, who is without contours and lives without norms, regards the prophet merely as an object of curiosity, which can be discussed in an interesting way over tea and fruit salad, if not even as a mere fantasist, who does not reckon with reality. ... The crowd is always the great enemy of the seers, an antagonism that always ends with the persecution of the prophets. ... (p. 123 f.)

A journalist like Toepfer thus makes himself the mouthpiece of the stirred up "masses," as Walter Nigg describes them, and of their xenophobic instincts, which he hardly counteracts as a journalist. Here, serious journalism is replaced by pure populism. Even a seemingly honest man, if he often plays with fire, will at some point become an intellectual arsonist.

Since Toepfer lives in Hettstadt and thus, near the farm *Terra Nova*, as it is now called by the inhabitants, Universal Life remains his preferred topic of incitement for years.
In no time at all, he knows how to turn everything that goes on there, no matter how worthwhile it is in terms of nature conservation, into something allegedly negative. In May 2001, for example, he sides with some hunters, especially from Hettstadt, who feel restricted in their freedom of sight and shooting by the newly created hedges.
Even the planting of woods, recognized as a measure to store climate-damaging emissions, is

presented rather negatively in the provincial *Main-Post*. In August 2001, Toepfer takes offence at the fences that were erected around the planted areas – strictly in accordance with official regulations – and makes them look huge in a picture. He describes as "oversized protective walls" the "Benjes hedges" piled up along some roadsides with dry branches and twigs, from which, after a few years, green hedges sprout as if by themselves.

In doing so, he once again makes himself the spokesman for the local hunting lobby, for whom such landscape-enriching measures limit the field of fire. There will be more about this lobby later.

The Covenant of God, of the Eternal Creator, with Nature and Animals

Undeterred by the constant bombardment of small minds, shortly before the turn of the millennium, Gabriele, the prophetess and emissary of God, laid the cornerstone there for the coming Kingdom of Peace, in order to let the commandment that is lived of love for God and neighbor, which also includes nature and the animals, become visible also externally. She founded the "Gabriele Foundation, the Saamlinic Work of Neighborly Love for Making Amends to Nature and Animals."

On the farm, as stated, some Original Christians under the guidance of Gabriele had begun to provide the plants, the animals, and also the soil and the life in the soil, with love and care.

Thus, within a few years, a previously totally bare, cleared-out agricultural desert was transformed into a flourishing oasis of life. It is the largest private biotope network in Germany: A network of wooded areas, hedges, tree islands, wetlands and stone biotopes also offers undisturbed habitats to free living animals and plants, where animals and plants of all kinds can roam or spread out undisturbed.

The "Gabriele Foundation" has – in addition to caring for needy and sick people – above all, made it its task to create habitats for animals, plants and minerals. The animals received in these habitats may live with their fellow species until the natural end of their lives and are lovingly cared for.

In a brochure about the foundation it states about this:
In the year 1999, God, the Eternal, made a covenant with the animals and with all of nature and thus, with Mother Earth. He, God, the Infinite, entrusted Mother Earth into the care of spirit beings and divine beings of nature. God has thus placed in the hands of spirit beings and divine beings of nature

the cleansing of the Earth, which has been contaminated and maltreated by humankind, as well as the establishment of a peaceful environment for a peaceful coexistence of all creatures. They will be responsible for the recovery and restoration of the Earth in His spirit until He can entrust the Earth to peaceable people. ... And God said ...: When spiritually-cosmically peaceable people inhabit the Earth, I will give the Earth to the people again, just as Jesus, the Christ, said in the Sermon on the Mount: Blessed are the meek, for they shall inherit the earth.

With this, God, the Eternal, continues with what the prophet of God Hosea had already announced: *And I will make for you a covenant on that day with the beasts of the field, the birds of the air, and the creeping things of the ground. And I will abolish the bow, the sword, and war from the land; and I will make you lie down in safety.* (Hos. 2:18)

While countless people not only from the surrounding area, but from all over the world are enthusiastic about the Land of Peace, while they learn to appreciate and love this place of peace and biodiversity, while daughter foundations of the *International Gabriele Foundation* in Africa are beginning to work according to this ingenious concept, all these activities are hardly noticed, let alone appreciated by the German media, but are almost exclusively commented on derisively and disparagingly. If church organizations had achieved anything even remotely and similarly grand, it would, of course, have been highly praised in the media!

The modern inquisitors and their assistants in the mass media and in politics now attacked on two fronts simultaneously: On the one hand, they continued to wage a running battle against the Land of Peace, for every blade of grass and every hedge, as it were. On the other hand, they fought on a trans-regional level with mendacious opinions and vilifications against all the activities of the followers of Jesus of Nazareth, with which they advocate for peace between human beings, nature and animals. For this is exactly what the Kingdom of Peace on this Earth contains.

Let us first turn to the events on a trans-regional level.

Original Christians Advocate for Peace

... I will abolish the bow, the sword, and war from the land; ... – these words of the prophet of God Hosea were not quoted by chance in the afore-mentioned brochure of the Gabriele Foundation. Already in 1991, the Original Christians publicly advocated peace among the people. They addressed the scandal of a war of aggression started by nations that call themselves "Christian." When in January 1991, a military coalition under the leadership of the USA began to bomb Iraq, the Original Christians protested with a series of Extra Editions, which they distributed on the streets in tens of thousands of copies. In these, they not only point out that Jesus of Nazareth was a pacifist who taught love of the enemy and condemned all violence. They not only asked: "Cain, where is your brother Abel?" They also reminded us that, not lastly, "Mother Earth" along with the animal world were suffering unspeakably from the war.

Especially after the turn of the millennium, Christ-friends increasingly work for peace between human beings and animals. With billboard campaigns they promote a vegetarian diet – in fact, not primarily for health reasons, but for ethical reasons. "Please, Please, Don't Eat Us," animals implore from billboards, or it is ascertained: "What Has Eyes, Intelligent People Do Not Eat" – while the eyes of chickens, pigs or cattle look directly at the observer. Occasionally, there is even an advertisement on television to encourage people to abstain from animal foods. To draw attention to the suffering of the animals, Original Christians regularly hold demonstrations with the motto: "Eat No Meat! Away with the Animal Ghetto Wardens! Down with the Slaughterhouses!" But they also take part in other demonstrations, which, for example, have the abolition of hunting as their goal or the protest against animal experiments or against so-called "Hubertus masses," during which pastors and priests "bless" animals shot by hunters.

Aren't Animals Part of Nature?

It seems that any attempt to change the consciousness of the population toward peaceableness is a thorn in the side of the cassock wearers. In many places,, where billboards appear, church representatives immediately speak out.
For example, in Münchberg (Upper Franconia), the billboard "You People Made Us Ill – Now You Eat Our Illness" triggers an immediate response and

the *Frankenpost* (June 8, 2006) reports an interview with the Lutheran pastor and sect commissioner Bernhard Wolf, who is allowed to pursue his inquisitorial work at the University of Bayreuth at the taxpayer's expense – in a specifically established "Research and Information Center for New Religious Beliefs."

What sounds harmless and idealistic in itself is for sect experts an ingenious strategy. "In the past, Universal Life focused on ecological issues, but recently, the sect has moved more in the direction of animal protection and is seeking to recruit members in this way," states Bernhard Wolf.

His attempt to discredit Universal Life is based on a misrepresentation, and thus, his whole argumentation amounts to nothing: Universal Life does not recruit members at all; it has no members. Anyone who attends the events is completely free to come and to go.

Incidentally, the Lutheran reveals the "blind spot" that his Church has in common with the Vatican Church: They pretend that animals, of all things, do not belong to the big "house" (Greek oikos) of ecology – as if "animal protection" and "ecology" were completely different issues.

Right from the beginning, Original Christians under the guidance of Gabriele have achieved something astounding, particularly in the area of ecology and the efforts for creation, for nature and animals – this cannot be denied, so the churches must somehow have to make it look bad in the eyes of the populace. Especially since with their dogmas that are contemptuous of nature, they themselves have laid the cornerstone for the brutality against the life, against God's creation, – and as before, still approve of it.

The Goal:
Discrimination and Ostracism

Thus, a group of "heretics" may not advocate for anything without immediately being accused of dishonest motives. Nor may the "heretics" participate anywhere – because then, there is immediately, the alleged "danger" they will "subvert" the actions of others.

Thus, the Lutheran sect commissioner, Thomas Gandow of Berlin, watches the participation of Original Christians in the anti-hunting demonstra-

---

Yesterday – Inquisitor:
Persecution all the way to murder

Today – Sect Commissioner/Sect Expert:
Persecution all the way to character assassination

tions in Berlin with "concern." The *ARD* program "Polylux" (October 21, 2002) does not report about the concerns and arguments of the hunting opponents, but exclusively about the "concerns" of the Church. Gandow's actual words:
I can only advise every animal protector who really wants to achieve something and wants to be taken seriously to detach himself from this campaign, which merely exploits the motives and feelings of animal protectors. ...

Yes, Original Christians appeal to the feelings of their fellow human beings, to sensitize them to the fact that animals are our fellow creatures, our little brothers and sisters, who have the same right to life as we do. What's the problem? There is none – again, it's just cheap propaganda.

With our thoughts, let's go back into the Middle Ages. A church representative warns the populace: "Do not make common cause with the heretics! Do not be seen with them! Otherwise, you'll get into trouble!" A well-behaved Catholic (or Protestant) is not where a "heretic" is – not even when it comes to working for the animals, which are shot down by the millions with the blessing of the mainstream churches.

You cannot go about things today like it was done during the Middle Ages, when you were not even allowed to give food or shelter to a heretic who was "banned by the Church" when you met him. But the modern inquisitors are apparently still striving for a kind of "apartheid," a greatest possible ostracism and banishment to a social ghetto. None of the reporters who take up this ecclesiastical slanderous ploy critically ask whether anyone has ever attempted religious proselytizing at the demonstrations, which are allegedly being "subverted." The churches are solely concerned with disturbing the activities of the Original Christian minority, wherever it appears.

The Church and the Meat Lobby: Together Against Vegetarians

Bear in mind again that here, there is incitement against people who are against killing, who promote life, peace and freedom, who advocate for nature and animals and who have created a unique, private biotope network system.
But they just have – and this is their "mortal sin" – the "wrong" prayer book. In the broadcasting laws of all German federal states it is clearly stipulated that no minorities may be discriminated against by the programs of public broadcasting stations. But "paper is known to be patient." This rule is not en-

forceable in our "constitutional state." The Original Christians have had to experience this.

In those years, similarly worded defamations were spread again and again, and Pastor Behnk also takes the same line, when in connection with Universal Life, he claims: "Obscure soul-catchers are trying more and more frequently to lure people through the esoteric and eco-scene. (*Bavarian Television*, "Unkraut," January 13, 2003).

It is not surprising that butchers also conveniently resort to church ammunition in order to take a stand against a television advertisement for vegetarian food. The German Butchers' Association simply claims in a press release that here "under the guise of the vegetarian way of life, a sect is being indirectly advertised." The fact is: A firm, *Lebe Gesund-Versand* which sells vegetarian food, commissioned the spot. (One has to stick to the facts – otherwise one could also say, for example, that "under the guise of meat consumption," the Vatican's large sect is indirectly being advertised when a Catholic butcher places an ad.)

The German Farmers' Association also play the same tune as the German Butchers' Association, when it apparently sees that the income of the farmers raising livestock for slaughter is being threatened. Therefore, all those willingly jump on the slander bandwagon of the churches who, in their occupation, and with the blessing of the churches, do business with animal suffering and the murder of animals anyway.

In a statement of March 6, 2003, the Farmers' Association speaks of a "sect milieu" (what does one want to imply by that?) and refers to Carla Bregenzer, a fanatical Lutheran SPD member of the Baden-Württemberg state parliament, who, in turn, calls on the ARD directors not to extend the advertising contract for this spot.

This decision was at first taken from the head directors of the TV station by the Regional Court of Würzburg, which allowed a complaint by the "Association Against Improper Practices in Commerce and Industry Cologne e.V." and forbade the spot. It was said that "the sequence of images triggers shock-like feelings of disgust and revulsion, and that this would affect competition and disadvantage the meat industry." Only after two years of litigation did the Bamberg Higher Regional Court overturn the decision.

In other cases, as well, Original Christians have to fight in court for the right to confront their fellow people with the accusing eyes of their fellow creatures, the animals. In Berlin, the public transportation companies suddenly back out of an already concluded advertising contract, according to which the poster "What Has Eyes, Responsible People Do Not Eat" should be hung in the subway. In court, representatives of the authorities claim that the Berlin Senate – at the instigation of the churches, of course – "warned" against Universal Life in 1997. (Chapter 11) After half a year, in October 2003, the Schöneberg District Court ruled that the contract must be upheld, stating that Universal Life is "not forbidden, and its activities are neither unconstitutional nor punishable."

But what kind of a country is it, in which such self-evident matters have to be taken to court time and again? Whereas it should be noted here that the last two court rulings mentioned are rather an exception. In numerous other cases, however, the judiciary was and is not prepared to go against the current of an ecclesiastically shaped "spirit of the times."

What is certain is that the Original Christians, in their publishing commitment for the animals, again and again had a spoke put in their wheel, be it through TV stations, newspaper editorial offices or lengthy legal proceedings, with which they had to fight for their rights.

A Running Battle Against the Land of Peace

The attacks were also directed against the Peaceful Land in development.

As the next local elections came in sight in the spring of 2002, Hettstadt's Mayor Eberhard Götz (SPD) is photographed in the *Main-Post* with demonstratively raised hands: He is against the fact that "hikers are no longer allowed to pass through entire areas of land" – a dig at the Original Christians, who, as stated, create Benjes hedges, plant tree islands and ensure reforestation on formerly barren agricultural land. Yet, the thoroughfare roads are still passable, since the numerous public pathways between the forestation areas remain, of course, open to all.

In the run-up of the local elections, Greußenheim's mayor (CSU) also loses courage to treat the Original Christians as all other citizens. At first, he offers the prospect of a plot of land in the village's industrial park to a delicatessen business – which is run by Original Christians and which, among other things, processes crops grown in Greußenheim. But then, in a citizens' meeting, agitators again appear on the scene and raise the well-known church suspicions. It is decided to carry out a "citizens' inquiry" about the impending purchase of the land – although such a thing is not even provided for in the Constitution: Either the local council decides on the sale of land, or there is a proper citizens' petition, that is, an official referendum.

Nevertheless, the mayor has the ominous inquiry carried out – although the delicatessen company had already withdrawn its purchase request, for as Original Christians, they refuse to become the object of a tribunal about their faith. Although the Catholic priest had agitated from the pulpit against the Original Christians, in the vote in mid-January 2002 (with a participation of just under 45%), about 26 percent were *in favor* of a sale. The Original Christians themselves had not taken part in the vote. According to journalist Toepfer in a commentary, the Greußenheimers had "raised their voice." He describes the church-influenced agitators as "concerned inquirers."

An "Original Christian" Hedge Is Cleared

When the Original Christian farmers plant an apple and olive orchard in February 2004, they thin out a hedge to make room, by carefully digging up some trees and bushes and replanting them elsewhere. When Tilman Toepfer gets wind of this, he writes in the *Main-Post* (Feb. 19, 2004) about a "clearing action" that contradicts the Sermon on the Mount, and mocks: "If you measure them by their words ... then they must still be deaf to the wailing of the little trees when they laid hands on them." The next day the *Main-Post* has to sheepishly concede that the alleged drama of the occurrence was fictitious.

Exactly one year later, it was the neighboring village of Hettstadt that actually carried out a brutal clearing operation. Several meters of hedges that had been planted by the Original Christians were ripped out by bulldozers, because they were on a few square meters that did not belong to the Original Christians. Actually, they couldn't help it, because the course of the path at this point had already been diverted from the boundaries of the property for decades – that is, already under the previous owner of the farm. The neighboring farmers had used a "shortcut," which then tacitly became an "established right." All attempts to exchange, acquire or lease the erroneously planted areas failed.

Incidentally, a staff member of the Lower Nature Conservation Authority of the Würzburg District Office had – according to *Main-Post* (February 16, 2005) – still tried to save the hedge by classifying it as "worthy of protection." But the department's lawyer decided differently. No wonder: The head of the District Office is District Administrator Waldemar Zorn, CSU politician and at times, church official, who had already driven Original Christian settlers out of "his" village at the beginning of the 1990s.

All this sounds like a provincial farce and is one, as well, but with a serious background: Every effort is made to zealously hinder every sign of life of an Original Christian "heretic" in our country, no matter how positive it may be – indeed, especially then.

A local boundary officer has nothing better to do than to check whether the "border distances" were adhered to when planting poplars to the left and right of the access road to the farm and to "complain" to the municipality about the partial non-compliance. The farmers then offer to donate the trees to the village.

But as a good Catholic, may one so simply accept a gift from "heretics"? When the "discussion" about it drags on for months, the Original Christians dig up their Original Christian poplars and replant them. A commotion was then caused, not because of the incomprehensible behavior of the village, but because of a sign that was temporarily put up in place of the replanted trees to inform passersby about the situation.

On the same access road, the operators of the farm also put up signs asking drivers to show consideration for animals and to drive slowly. These signs also had to be removed again, at the behest of the District Office.

One May Not Think Good of "Heretics"

The enemy image, which the churches circulated about the Original Christians, was maintained at all costs. Anyone who approaches Original Christians, who "fraternizes" with them by behaving normally, or even says that he likes something, is considered a "collaborator."

When at the beginning of 2004, the Hettstadt chapter of the German Friends of the Earth dared to simply find the biotope network system good, regardless of any considerations of faith, Mayor

Eberhard Götz (SPD) and Tilman Toepfer, a reporter living in Hettstadt, declared their resignation in "protest." And anyone who sells land to the Original Christian farm must to this day be aware that no one will join his table at the village inn and that people will change sides on the village street when they meet him.

The fact that the Peaceful Land is nevertheless constantly growing with the help of many supporters from Germany and abroad can only be described as a miracle under these circumstances. It is as if the church masterminds in the background are fighting doggedly for every square meter of land that is withdrawn from their influence, and on which peace-loving people show how the "sins" of a technocratic land consolidation of the past can be more than made up for in the shortest time.

The opponents of the Free Spirit try with all means to prevent people from recognizing the good and exemplary things that the Original Christians have especially created on the developing Peaceful Land under the guidance of Gabriele. That is why television teams are sent again and again to the Franconian province, in order to uphold the enemy image and the fairy tale of the "evil sect" with appropriate comments and pictures. **Twice** in

just a few years, it is the program *"Quer"* of the – how could it be otherwise – *Bavarian Television* that provides the necessary ricochets. The moderator "explains" the Catholic view of things to the viewers:
"If you live in Würzburg or in the immediate vicinity, you should be grateful. And why? Very simply: If the world ends, Würzburg and its surroundings will be spared. You don't believe that? But the followers of Universal Life say so. ..." (June 21, 2001) The fact that this is not true has been sufficiently explained. Nevertheless, the old false assertions are simply rehashed again and again.

The Inquisition Helpers May Appear on Television

Five years later the same moderator speaks as follows:
"The end of the world, by the way, has been prophesied time and again in the last centuries. So far it hasn't worked out. But what isn't yet, can still be. And there are always people who believe in an imminent end, despite all the disturbing facts – for instance, the sect Universal Life ..." (July 7, 2006).
Two reporters once again put Catholic neighbors in front of the camera as accomplices of the Inquisi-

tion. The hunter Norbert Gram from Hettstadt was allowed to complain that he had been disturbed while hunting. (How often he himself had disturbed the peace of the farm by shooting at night was not mentioned). Then a local village council was allowed to spread out maps to show which properties the "sect" had already bought. (As if it were disreputable or forbidden in our country to acquire land).

The First Victims Are the Animals

Let us now turn to the scene that was intended by a coterie of hunters, politicians, journalists and church representatives for a purposeful strike against the Peaceful Land of the Original Christians: hunting.
How can one destroy an area where peace between people, nature and animals is the priority? By shooting as many animals as possible there!

First of all, it is striking that in the immediate vicinity of the Farm *Terra Nova*, animals that were shot and wounded and died in agony are repeatedly found: a wild pig without a lower jaw; another with only three legs; a pregnant sow with a shot in the stomach and dead fetuses in the open belly; a fox without legs, a peacock that had lived on the farm and died from rat poison. ... Or that animal carcasses are obviously being used as bait. The Lower Hunting Authority granted the trigger-happy hunters special permission to shoot wild boar (with the exception of leading sows) even during the closed season. Numerous animals fled, shot and wounded, into the territory of the farm of Original Christians, where they perished.

In at least one case, an animal that had been shot was even tracked to the farm and then taken away – which normally constitutes a criminal offence of poaching.
This was, however, only the prelude to a much larger confrontation, because the corruption between hunting, politics and church is considerable ... .

Order to Shoot in the Kingdom of Peace?

In November 2004, a helicopter sent out especially for this purpose flew over the farm completely unannounced. Using a thermal-imaging camera, it supposedly spotted 120 wild boars around the farm. This did not take into account the fact that there were also grazing animals such as cows in the woods and pastures around the farm, many of which were frightened by the low-flying helicopter and fled in panic into the woods adjoining their pastures. However, with a thermal-imaging camera, one can hardly distinguish between cows and wild boars. Nor was it taken into account that during the nights prior to this helicopter operation, especially heavy gunfire was heard along the borders of the territory: perhaps in order to drive wild boars and other wild animals into a certain area?

The head of the Lower Hunting Authority in the Würzburg District Office (his superior: Waldemar Zorn), had in any case contrived the desired occasion. At the end of November 2004, he demanded that the game tenants responsible for the "hunting grounds" belonging to the farm shoot 18 wild pigs every month – and he backed up this demand with the threat of a monthly fine of 10,000 Euros in case of violation.

The reason for this measure of violence, however, was quite flimsy: There was increasing damage caused by wild pigs in the surrounding fields. Yet almost all of these fields belong to the farm itself, whose farmers had never complained about wild boar damage. The fields of other farmers were protected by electric fences, so that no damage could be claimed here, either.

In addition, the hunting authority claimed that there was the "danger of an epidemic"; swine fever was threatening. Yet there was no evidence of it in a wide radius. And it has long been known to experts that such animal epidemics – which incidentally, also include the notorious bird flu – do not originate in game populations, but in factory farming.

How much some of the local hunters, given the presence of peaceful followers of Jesus of Nazareth, feared for the practice of their bloody hobby was expressed in the statement of a hunter who, on July 18, 2004, in the hearing of an Original Christian, said: "I wish there would be swine fever."

"There Will Be No Shooting Under the Resurrection Cross!

The Original Christian farmers of the land defended themselves against this order to shoot, which had arrived shortly before Christmas – the timing is certainly no coincidence – by means of publicity and legal action.

In Extra Editions ("Under the Sign of the Resurrection Cross of the Original Christians, which Means Life, There Will Be No Shooting"), they informed the population of the surrounding villages about the background – because the local *Main-Post*, under the pen-leadership of Tilman Toepfer, had mainly spread the disinformation of the hunters. In court, they filed a complaint against the alleged "urgency" of the issued decision. In the first instance – one day before Christmas! – the Administrative Court of Würzburg dismissed the complaint against the immediate execution – with the cynical "reasoning" that the wildlife population would recover after the shooting, even if it might have been unnecessary.

Shortly after Christmas, another helicopter was sent out. January 2005 brought an unexpected turnaround. The Bavarian Administrative Court reversed the decision of the Würzburg Administrative Court: The immediate enforcement was suspended. The court simply did not understand why there should be a need for urgency, when there was no trace of an outbreak of swine fever anywhere.

But the hunting lobby did not give up so quickly. Right at the next Christmas season 2005, the hunting authority announced further helicopter flights to again determine the "wild pig population." According to the *Main-Post* (December 29, 2005), its director spoke of an "explosive increase of wild pigs"; the population had to be "reduced." When the police helicopter reached the area on January 12th – again unannounced, of course – it flew only briefly over the woods where the wild pigs were supposed to be, so as to then hover over the actual farm area all the longer. The cattle grazing on the adjacent pastures fled in wild panic and tore down a fence. "An attempt at intimidation," an observer of the scene judged, "a clear threatening gesture according to the motto: 'We'll get you yet.'"

Demonstration Against The "Massacre" Fraternity

To expose and thwart the plans of the hunters' clique, the Original Christian farmers decided to take an unusual step: They called on the population to join a demonstration in the center of Würzburg. One of the main demands was that the "Animal Massacre Fraternity" had to be stopped. The farmers requested to be placed under the authority of another District Office as long as the Catholic District Administrator Waldemar Zorn placed the interests of the hunters above those of the general public there. Furthermore, they again demanded the right to decide themselves regarding the practice or non-practice of hunting on their own land.

The demonstration on January 28, 2006 proved to be an impressive rally for the right to life of animals that are entrusted to human beings. More than a thousand people, including numerous animal friends from abroad (Austria, Switzerland, Italy, Slovenia, Croatia, etc.), marched through the city center with banners on which the main masterminds were named and an end to compulsory hunting was demanded. At the final rally on the Würzburg marketplace, numerous expressions of solidarity were read out from animal protection associations from all over the world, including North and South America, Africa, Australia and southern Europe.

The Incidents Increase

The importance of this international support became evident not only in the trial itself, in which the intended massacre of the wild boars could be prevented. Only a vigilant international public can also form a counterweight to the campaign, which is supposed to mark peace-loving people as outsiders in the tried and true manner. The politicians, journalists and church representatives who launch such a campaign, purport to merely wanting to "criticize." While they try to wash their hands in innocence, the first effects of their campaigns have already occurred.

In every population there are confused minds that are only too happy to take up the enemy images offered, in order to act out their neuroses and psychoses.

On July 20, 2002, for example, two figures in camouflage pants, boots and olive green T-shirts crept through the surroundings of the farm. The summoned police found camouflage make-up, a helmet and a functioning pistol in the car of the two "would-be Rambos" (*Main-Post*, February 14, 2003).

This is by no means the only incident of this kind. On December 21, 2003, about 300 nails, each three centimeters long, were found on the road leading to the farm.

In November 2005 – shortly after several derogatory articles by Tilman Toepfer in the *Main-Post* – a horse paddock belonging to people who had left the Church was destroyed; a road sign was torn out and placed on the access road to the farm in such a way that an accident could have happened if the sign had not been discovered in time.

At the end of December 2005, another horse paddock near the farm was devastated – this time, not one that belonged to an Original Christian, but who of the hooligans knows this so exactly, none of whom could be identified until now?

The incidents just mentioned are – it must be said at this point – only a small segment from the large number of violent effects that church defamations repeatedly produce. Death threats, insults on the street, graffiti, damage to property, smashed windows, arson – all these are events with which Original Christians have repeatedly been confronted for years.

Who Lacks the Willingness to Integrate?

To contain such incidents, the farmers at the Terra Nova land suggested to the village of Greußenheim that they be allowed to put up a traffic sign saying: "Residents Only from 10 p.m. to 6 a.m." This would have provided a means of combating the disturbance at night. But the village council refused this request. Original Christians are apparently not fellow citizens that a community would have to protect from hooligans and attacks.

Similar things occurred in numerous other cases. For example, at the end of 2009, the farmers wanted to set up an information board at the entry area for the numerous visitors to the Land of Peace – refused.
A visitors' parking area was refused, as well.
In 2006, the farmers wanted to erect a cross near there with the inscription: "Nip It in the Bud! Against Intolerance and Ostracism!" – rejected.
A trade show was planned in the industrial area of the municipality. The Original Christian farmers were also informed about it – but in the specific planning and implementation of the event they were no longer taken into account.
In 2010, they submitted an offer to the village to exchange land for the layout of a planned bicycle

path. It was rejected, although this option would have been more cost-effective for the village.

An offer by the farmers from the land to coordinate with the community on the consolidation of forestland was also rejected.

And then, in 2014, one of the local councilors complained that the inhabitants of the Terra Nova farm were not "integrating themselves in the village community." But what kind of willingness to integrate did the majority of the local councilors show? There are other examples of this. In many cases, the inhabitants of Terra Nova had to turn to higher authorities in order to laboriously achieve what every citizen is normally entitled to:

In 2002, the local council refused permission to drill a well in the area of the fruit orchards. The Würzburg District Office then issued the permit, contrary to the illegal refusal of the municipality.

The construction of an apple hall was also rejected several times by the village council. It was only the District Office that had to revoke the illegal rejection and grant the permit.

The permit for a Landhof Café (Farm Café) with farm shop was blocked by the municipality of Greußenheim between July 2010 and December 2011, before the Würzburg Administrative Court saw to law and order. When, despite this obstruction of law, the residents of Terra Nova invited the local councils to the newly opened café, they did not even receive a refusal. They are treated by most local councils as though they don't even exist. Is this the willingness of the local council to integrate?

In 2014, several applications for reforestation were submitted by the Terra Nova farm, which were unlawfully rejected by the local council. It was only the Department of Agriculture in Würzburg that granted permission.

Finally, in November 2014, the farmers wrote a letter to the mayor and all the local councilors in which they listed all these and more incidents. They wrote:

We are obviously being treated by the council as second-class citizens. This behavior often seems to us to be pure harassment, because we are not tied to a church, but follow Jesus of Nazareth. Are we really wanted in Greußenheim? We are neither Catholic nor Lutheran, but we seriously strive to put the teachings of Jesus of Nazareth into practice in everyday life. Thus, we are Original Christians in the following of Jesus of Nazareth. What is offensive about that?

Furthermore, the writers of the letter pointed out that the village is missing a great opportunity if it does not give up its intransigent stance:

Have you even noticed that the land of the International Gabriel Foundation represents the largest privately created biotope network in Germany, with a biodiversity that is unparalleled in all of Central Europe? A species diversity that at best, still exists in the Danube delta, as renown biologists confirm to us. ... Have you even noticed that the land of the International Gabriele Foundation and its subsidiary foundations in Africa ... is reported about daily by hundreds of TV stations around the world? Millions of people are interested in what is happening here. ... We are ready to cooperate fairly at any time.

Until now, there has been no answer to this letter.

The Purchase of a Woodland Is Denied

Another case shows that a farm, where people live in peace not only with each other, but also with nature and animals is not only a thorn in the side of some local hunters or priests and pastors, but rather, that supra-regional forces are at work here. It concerns a wooded area adjacent to the farm, which the farmers want to acquire and include in their care measures. This land is owned by the German state, which was initially quite willing to sell it – after all, the state needs money. But the consent is suddenly withdrawn; the decision is delayed. The Federal Property Administration, which is presented with an appropriate price offer, has no objections whatsoever, because it is obliged to sell properties wherever possible.

But the astonished Original Christians learn that in the end, not only the Federal Ministry of Finance – uncommon enough – but also the Federal Ministry of Family Affairs (!) was called in to make a simple woodland sale. The Ministry of Family Affairs – as if children were growing on the trees! The solution to the riddle: Decades before, officials influenced by the Church, had turned the Ministry of Family Affairs into a collection point of church propaganda against minorities of faith. And the Bavarian Ministry of Education and Cultural Affairs called in precisely this ministry.

After the responsible official in the Ministry of Finance initially agreed to a sale by telephone in July 2001, this was then succinctly rejected in October – without giving reasons. In some offices, dossiers of church sect commissioners are apparently still circulating, which should deprive the Original Christians of elementary civil rights.

The farmers then went to court in Berlin. However, the Berlin Regional Court at first instance, refused to view the refusal of the Ministry of Finance as discrimination. Rather, the court itself participated in the discrimination, declaring that the state could damage its public reputation by doing business with people like the plaintiffs.

The fact that this scandalous ruling was not a one-time slip-up became apparent in the second instance: This instance also did not want to acknowledge any arbitrary action by the state in the fact that a promise to sell had been revoked on grounds of faith.

The persons concerned now wanted to at least have access to the files, in order to find out what was circulating about them and be able to comment on it. However, access to the files was refused and they also had to fight in court over years for this right.

But even there the way was rocky: From time to time, it was suddenly stated that the files had been lost or destroyed. Later, they had allegedly been found again, but it was analogously said: You may look into certain files, but not into others. The "reasoning" that the authorities gave for this is revealing: Otherwise, people could no longer speak freely within the offices, if they had to assume that they could be prosecuted under criminal law due to the inspection of the files. ...

Didn't the officials thereby indirectly admit that they discuss things in the offices that are not in accordance with the law? And did the years of delaying tactics have the goal of letting the statute of limitations run out on possible crimes committed by libelers?

In any case, the inspection of the files that took place later showed that it was always the same church agitators at work.

A Giant Wind Turbine as a Threatening Gesture?

In 2014, a huge wind turbine, higher than the Cologne Cathedral, suddenly should be built directly in front of a high quality apple orchard. In this case, the permit was granted very quickly, but completely and unlawfully bypassed the farmers who operate this apple orchard. Yet, not only does such a huge plant pose the risk of casting off ice, but low-frequency sound can also affect the health of the workers – not to mention the danger to the lives of rare animal species, such as bats or red kites. The farmers take legal action against it, but the huge concrete tower is already standing.

On the supervisory board of the company that wants to build this monster, there is also a well-known politician: Monika Hohlmeier, the daughter of Franz Josef Strauss, whose eulogy was delivered by Cardinal Joseph Ratzinger. Already as state secretary in the Bavarian Ministry of Education, she had adopted the horror scenarios of the sect commissioners against the Original Christians and claimed that they, the Original Christians, would systematically seal themselves off from the outside world and pursue "economic and also political interests in a rather aggressive manner." (Chapter 9) Later, as Minister of Education (who is obliged to be ideologically neutral!), she had a "very negative" attitude toward the Universal Life school and stated that she works closely with the sect commissioners. The school, as she put it at the time, "is a thorn in our side."

The village of Hettstadt, on whose boundary the wind turbine is located, could have chosen any number of other locations in the vicinity. But the aristocratic owner of the large neighboring land placed the monster at the outermost edge of his extensive fields, disregarding all distance regulations – at a location that is most unsuitable from the point of view of the protection of people and nature – namely, directly on the border to the Land of Peace of the International Gabriele Foundation. However, the approval was carried out in such a slipshod and illegal way, that the farmers of the Land of Peace were able to prevent the start-up of the already completed tower through a lengthy last-minute legal process.

But the battle is not over: The operators applied for a new permit in 2017. And so it must be again said:

Everything, but absolutely everything that came and comes from the Kingdom of God to this Earth for a peaceful coexistence among people, as well as with nature and animals, is attacked by the cassock wearers and their accomplices to prevent it as much as possible.

Even if this has not succeeded and also will not succeed in the long run – the forces that rage against the Free Spirit, against the life and unity, try again and again.

"Enough Is Enough"

Gabriele's work in word and deed always takes place in selfless love for people, nature and animals, always for the life that is God in all things. Someone who is rooted in the negative cannot understand this, because he can speak, act and write only according to his momentary consciousness.

At the beginning of October 2003, a malicious article by the journalist Tilman Toepfer appears in the *Main-Post* with the headline "How Does the 'Prophetess' Celebrate Her 70th Birthday?" However, Toepfer uses this date only as an excuse to get off his chest the old well-known ecclesiastical, mendacious opinions, which are then served up again in the article.

As far as Gabriele is concerned, one can only say that she abhors any personality cult, and for her, that includes birthday celebrations, as well. Was this provocative article intended as a personal low blow? She, who brought the teachings from the Kingdom of God, the proposals and ideas, is presented again and again as an external "figurehead" – in order to be able to attack her all the more.

But anyone who knows Gabriele, knows that she **does not let herself be impressed by the me-**

dia superiority of the church-influenced witch hunters. She knows a higher power behind her that stands by her. She knows that the word comes from the heavens. It is God-Father and His Son, Christ, and the Cherub of divine Wisdom, who speak to her and through her. Otherwise, in view of the hopeless imbalance – according to human judgment – in the fight of David against Goliath, she should have lost her courage long since.

Instead, Gabriele takes up her pen again and publishes a statement with the headline:
Enough Is Enough – the Jug Has Gone to the Well Long Enough. This text bears witness to the clarity with which Gabriele analyzes the goings-on of the professional agitators from the mainstream churches.

Here are just a few excerpts:
Dear Original Christians, dear friends of Universal Life all over the world!
Many of you know that I have my 70th birthday behind me. For about 30 years, I have been serving the Eternal as His instrument. During these 30 years, He, the Almighty, has created a worldwide work of love for God and neighbor, a charismatic mark of value. ...

Through church indoctrination from the cradle to the grave, the church officials have led many of their believers away from the Eternal, the true God, and thus plunged them into externalization, which is substantiated by the image of many so-called church Christians today. ...

Jesus, the Christ, taught an inner religion, the religion of the heart, without ecclesiastical superiors, who put on airs as gods and put on the ecclesiastically "dignified" aureole shine like "Excellency," "Eminence," "Bishop," "Pastor," "Priest." The greatest mockery of the eternal God is the human "Holy" Father on Earth – although Jesus, the Christ, had bidden it differently, when He said, for example: ... "nor shall you call anyone on earth your Father, for only one is your Father, who is in heaven."

The Great Fill their Coffers, the Little People Have to Pay

Through externalization, the Church – which in time not only became obsessed with power, but also terrified its faithful with the cudgel of eternal damnation and thus brought them under its thumb – did and does just as Satan wants. Anyone who serves this Church and consults the ecclesiastical Excellencies and Eminences in matters of faith, ethics and morals, and offers them a place in the front ranks, is promoted and supported by the "venerable" alliance. The little people, the folk, may pay taxes so that the "great" can fill their coffers, thereby gaining more and more prestige and power. This global underhanded strategy – the ones are in charge, the others have to keep quiet and pay – has lasted for nearly 2000 years. Those who did not want to be servile were slandered, discriminated and thus muzzled, or they were killed.

Karlheinz Deschner summed up the whole hypocritical structure of a denominational totalitarian hierarchy of power and money. He wrote, and one may say this: "After intensely studying the history of Christianity, I know of no organization in antiquity, in the Middle Ages and during the present times, including and especially the 20th century, that at the same time is so long, so continuously and so terribly burdened with crime as is the Christian Church, particularly the Roman-Catholic Church."

If there is a God – do you believe, dear reader, that in the long run, God, the Father, the Creator of all beings and human beings, does not contradict this activity, this "official church morality"? He, the great Spirit, did it through Jesus of Nazareth, the greatest prophet of all times, who is the Redeemer of all souls and people. He did it through many enlightened men and women and through prophets. He gives His word again today, and this, already for 30 years. Through the prophetic word – for God does not have the human language – He enlightens the willing people and holds up a mirror to the church officials with blunt, clear, unambiguous words, before their counterfeiting eyes.

The Campaign of the Black Band

The true God, the Christ of God, His teaching of love, kindness and freedom is a thorn in the side of denominational forgers. Equipped with their influence on their own kind, on politicians, journalists and power-hungry followers, who hoped and hope for a little something, they crusaded and still crusade against the word of God, against Original Christians and, above all, against me, His instrument. The church authorities, whose highest commandment is power, reputation, assets, money and gold ownership, took for themselves denominational commissioners and also used other church-indoctrinated people for their negative activities, such as politicians, judges, journalists and all those who wanted and want to profit from the lie.

They found more than willing support for their malicious activities from people who had initially been attracted by the atmosphere of those companies whose responsible persons had made it their task to fulfill the commandments of God and the teachings of the Sermon on the Mount step by step. But because they wanted to cultivate other, indecent things there, they then left these businesses. ...

This is the world of today, but not the high teaching of Jesus of Nazareth, not His ethical-moral mark of value, which the great Spirit teaches in Universal Life.

For about 30 years, the church authorities have been crusading against the divine teaching in Universal Life in daily newspapers, via radio and television teams, with journalists and with the indulgence of the judges. ...

Universal Life – The Charismatic Mark of Value

How does the black band proceed? Denominationally indoctrinated "medieval" experts speak of a universal "economic empire" where people are "exploited" – as the "dropouts" say – and where donations are "converted into hard cash," where bosses lead a "totalitarian regime." It goes on to say that the work of the Eternal, of Universal Life, is a "totalitarian sect," and other accusations.

Enough is enough! The jug has gone to the well long enough. After 30 years of silence and setting things straight – which seldom showed any resonance – I now commission lawyers to call on the courts to get rid of the false allegations of a medieval regime.
Unfortunately, it must be said that judges, too, due to their indoctrination, applauded the hair-raising medieval procedure and the anecdotes that went with it, in order to cover up the structure of lies spread by journalists and by so-called "drop-outs" and further people servile to the Church, resulting in "expression of opinion."
Thereupon, it is said that one may say that Universal Life is an economic empire, that it is totalitarian, even dangerous, and that in the enterprises of Universal Life people are exploited, that Universal Life disenfranchises its followers, and that some few deprive others of their property and the like.

As already stated: All this and much more can be said because it was apostrophized by indoctrinated judges as expressions of opinion. But this "opinion making" is a lie; the lies are hidden in the guise of the term "expression of opinion."

Let it be clearly stated once again: Universal Life is a free work. It does not have a single business. Universal Life is based on the gifts of neighborly love. Therefore, it cannot practice totalitarian rule, because everyone remains free in his thinking and living. This is how it was from the beginning of the work of God, and this is how it has remained until today. The gifts, the donations, are used, according to the donor's wishes, to spread the word of God or for other purposes that promote the divine work. All statements to the contrary are lies against the work of the Eternal and against people who consider themselves Original Christians. In the approximately 30 years from the Homebringing Mission of Jesus Christ to Universal Life today, no person has enriched himself on the work of God. The statements about enrichment on the work of the Lord are projections onto Universal Life by church followers, because this is how it is done in the upper ranks of the church institutions. ...

As stated at the beginning, I have now turned 70 years old and would like to pass on the charismatic mark of value, the great gift of God to the people, without the dirty cloak of lies – just as the work of the Eternal has remained in truth, free and based on the word of God and neighborly love – as a legacy to true Original Christians. Universal Life is truly a charismatic, divine treasure of ineffable significance for the people who have learned and are learning to love God in Jesus, the Christ. As long as I live in the temporal, I will defend this heavenly treasure. God will stand by me.

I denounce the liars in the "garb" of character assassination. Lawyers will call upon worldly courts to expose the monstrosities, malice, and lies hidden behind the "expressions of opinion." I call upon all true Original Christians to support these steps. I repeat: Through lawyers, we call upon the courts. We do not want our rights to be pronounced – we want justice. Let us pray that there are still judges with clear minds, who do not fall under the characterization "obfuscation by indoctrination."

Dear Original Christians, dear friends of Universal Life all over the world, this was merely a small excerpt from nearly 30 years of lies, discrimination and medieval diatribes against men, women and children. ...

Linked in the love for God and neighbor,
Gabriele

Judges Under the Influence of the Church

As announced, representatives of Universal Life then commissioned lawyers who are not affiliated with Universal Life to try to get the *Main-Post*, as representative of other newspapers, to ban at least some of the most common mendacious distortions. However, after two years of litigation, this failed because, among other things, the Bamberg Higher Regional Court denied the Association of Universal Life the right to legal action. Translated into plain English: The judges took the position that the association Universal Life, which has only a limited number of members (it was founded only because a legal entity is required for certain legal procedures), could not speak for the community of faith, Universal Life, as a whole.

If you, dear reader, now shake your head and say to yourself: "I don't understand that!" – then you are right-on. It is easy to see that this is a far-fetched juristic excuse not to have to think about the substantive justification of the complaint. Incidentally, numerous courts between Hamburg and Passau see this differently and have not questioned the so-called "right to act."

Gabriele already indicated in her statement that many judges are prejudiced. Why was this action, nevertheless, carried out?

Because in such actions, it is not the ostensible victory that is decisive – what is decisive is the gain, which is often apparent only at second glance. This gain can, for example, consist in the fact that one or the other who hears or reads about such cases, thinks about whether an Original Christian minority isn't actually being given a raw deal – or that the journalists of the *Main-Post* and also their publisher at the time, the Holtzbrinck-Verlag, are confronted with their own behavior. Or in the fact that the judges' "escape reflex" is exposed.

In her book *"Die kirchliche und staatliche Gewalt und die Gerechtigkeit Gottes"* (The Power of Church and State and the Justice of God), Gabriele writes about this:

Through personal experience and analysis, many Original Christians came to the conclusion that only a small part of the judges baptized Catholic and Lutheran do not submit to the dictates of the Church. The impression arises that, unfortunately, there are few Catholic and Lutheran judges who have clearly and without influence – whether from the churches or from ministers and deputies shaped by Catholic and Lutheran influences – maintained their independent judgment, so that, according to the Church's wishes, they do not fob off the church denigrated, unloved, non-denominational plaintiff, with "expression of opinion is permitted," and thus, do not brand him and consequently expose him to further vilification and abuse. (p. 38)

Despite this unfavorable initial situation and limited chances of success, the followers of Jesus of Nazareth have, over the years, repeatedly exercised their rights as citizens and have tried in court to counteract the discrimination and ostracism by church officials and their accomplices.
For this reason, the media liked to call them "litigious" – even though they adhered exactly to the advice of Jesus of Nazareth, as it is handed down in the Bible of the churches:

If your brother sins against you, go and tell him his fault, between you and him alone. If he listens to you, you have gained your brother. But if he does not listen, take one or two others along with you, that every charge may be established by the evidence of two or three witnesses. If he refuses to listen to them, tell it to the community. And if he refuses to listen even to the community, let him be to you as a Gentile and a tax collector.
(Mt. 18: 15-17)

In this case the "community" is the state with its courts. Only that today, the state and its judges, as well, are often themselves like "Gentiles and tax collectors," because they let themselves be influenced and patronized by the churches.

Nevertheless, this step must be attempted – on the one hand, so that no one can say they knew nothing. And on the other hand, who knows if everything would not be much worse if the followers of Jesus of Nazareth had not at least gained a certain amount of respect here and there through the legal proceedings that they pursued?

Nor did Jesus of Nazareth simply let everything pass over him silently. He asked the high priest's officer, "Why do you strike me?"

Even if, as Gabriele writes in her book "The Power of Church and State and the Justice of God", the masses of people *have handed over their responsibility to the caste of priests* (p. 168) – today, more and more people all over the world are grasping what an inestimable gift God, the All-Kind-One, has given to us human beings, by sending Gabriele, the daughter from His heart chamber, the Seraph of divine Wisdom, to the Earth. Despite all the attacks of the adversaries of God against the work of the Lord and against the bearer of the word of God, Gabriele, who had to suffer greatly under this maliciousness all these years – the adversaries of God have lost this battle.

Christ Is the Victor

Even though hard times still lie ahead of humankind due to the effects of the eons-long turning away from God – Christ, the Co-Regent of the heavens, is the victor, for He is the peace, the way, the truth and the life. His teaching is simple – it is the love for God and neighbor, toward human beings, nature and animals – and He is with God, our eternal Father, the Free Spirit, God in us, who supports all those who turn to Him in their inner being.
Gabriele, the prophetess of God, His emissary in this our time, is the divine Wisdom, incarnated in the human being Gabriele, in order to work from the Kingdom of God, for God, the Eternal, here on Earth, and bring His message of love, of freedom and unity to all seeking people. God, the eternal Father of us all, does not want His human children to suffer, to remain rooted in the human work of the external religions, in dogmas and cult practices, even in the fear of an alleged eternal damnation. He wants us to find our way to Him, to the

Free Spirit – God in us – and through His prophetess Gabriele, He shows us the way back to our eternal homeland, to the heavens, from which we once left.

As never before in the history of humankind, Gabriele brings the all-encompassing truth from the Kingdom of God for all seeking people – about the great cosmic correlations, about the structure of the eternal creation of Being, about the unity of all life, about the meaning and purpose of life on Earth and the path of the soul into the eternal homeland – and especially the truth about God:

God is eternal love. He is the eternal One, always the same, unchangeable, the one God, who does not differentiate, but loves all His children equally – no soul is lost. Since the Fall, He works through His prophets, in whom high beings from the Kingdom of God are incarnated, in order to enlighten His human children, to warn them, to show them the way to a fulfilled life in love, freedom, unity and peace – and to bring us all home.

Gabriele bears all this and far more of love and wisdom in herself – and had to experience how the mainstream churches fired a constant barrage of inciting attacks against her and against the eternal word of love from the Kingdom of God; how, through character assassination campaigns of the mainstream churches, the eternal word of God, His message of freedom and love, has also been withheld today from many people – just as the caste of priests at all times tried to silence the prophetic word and prevent people from finding the Free Spirit – God in us.

The fact that Gabriele endured all this and, at the same time, was able to build up the great, worldwide work of the Christ of God is a superhuman achievement, which can be accomplished only by someone who lives in God and remains steadfastly loyal to Him out of selfless love.

In the meantime, more and more people see through the machinations of the priestly religions and turn to God in freedom, without officeholders, cults, ceremonies and the like.
Through Gabriele's untiring work to give people an understanding of the message of love for God and neighbor, millions of people all over the world today are finding their way to the near God, the Free Spirit – God in us – and to the Inner Path of love and peace in the Messianic, Sophianic Age.

Appendix

The author received several letters on this topic, excerpts of which are passed on here:

In a TV program I heard details about how politicians of almost all parties in Germany and also in my country of origin, Austria, took part in the witch hunt against the prophetess Gabriele and the movement of faith of the Original Christians in Universal Life; how they simply parroted what church representatives, so-called "experts," put out in the world in terms of opinions and assertions about her.

I was particularly outraged that even the stirring statement of Professor Lazarovits, a former concentration camp prisoner and Jewish fellow citizen from Hungary, apparently went unheard. He wrote from his own painful experience something that should actually be self-evident, but apparently is not so in the 21st century: that one should not treat people with hostility because of their religious convictions, denigrating them collectively: "Back then it was 'only' the Jews, today it is 'only' the 'sects' – what's the difference?" Politicians in particular should be vigilant in terms of human rights and justice in the country, and not immediately give in out of fear of "eternal hell" when they even just see a priest's robe from a distance.

Walter Weber

I was deeply impressed by the TV programs on the topic "The Persecution of the Prophetess of God and of the Followers of Jesus of Nazareth." I think the greatest scandal is that in the 20th and 21st centuries it was still possible that Gabriele could be so denigrated and ostracized, a woman who did nothing but good for the people and who brought so much help, hope and a true life perspective for many people – people who had distanced themselves from God, because they could not even begin with such a cruel church image of God. And this woman is then publicly denigrated, and not just by church representatives who are paid by their religious concerns to mock innocent people and spread malicious untruths about them. With them, one is used to that! No, also by the authorities, the politicians, the representatives of the media, who have a responsibility to respect the Constitution. The politicians are not above subsidizing these religious conglomerates with many billions a year, although they are stone rich. And for what? That they then cover people with mendacious slogans just because they believe differently? I find it incomprehensible that I have to support something like this with my tax money without being asked!

Elena dell'Eva

In Spain, the state church was abolished in 1978, in Germany as early as 1919, and yet I have the impression that it still exists here in Germany, and indeed, that it exists double: two state churches that, admittedly, do not call themselves that, but do have the state and the politicians totally under their thumb. Outwardly, the politicians act as if independent – but when it comes to discriminating against "heretics," almost all of them cower and hand over the stage to "modern" Inquisition. We had plenty of experience with that in Spain – but the perpetrators in the black cassocks seem to be back today, only with slightly different methods. In the book "Das Kettenopfer" (The Chain of Sacrifice) you can read that this has been going on for thousands of years: priests against prophets. The sad thing is that the ruling politicians have not been able to see through this until today – or do not want to see through it. What are they afraid of?

Itxaso Diego

Recommended Reading

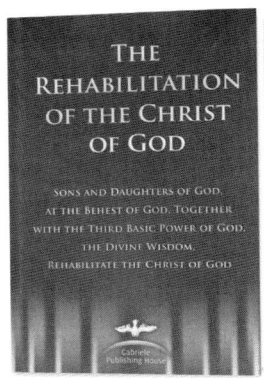

The Rehabilitation of the Christ of God

Martin Kübli, Dieter Potzel, Ulrich Seifert

Perhaps you are wondering: Why is a rehabilitation of Jesus, the Christ, necessary? What would ever have brought Him, the Son of God, the Eternal, into disrepute, or could even have done so to make a rehabilitation necessary? Did He ever say or do anything for which He could be accused or blamed for? But Jesus of Nazareth, the Christ of God, has been revered and respected for generations, all over the world, like no other man who ever lived!

Yes ... but ... The Christ of God was and is brought into discredit in the most ignominious way. This book exposes the fraudulent labeling with the name "Christian" and likewise, the infamous acts which were and are committed under the abuse of His name, with devastating consequences for humankind and for the entire Earth.

Learn more about: Violence, War and Crime under the guise of "Christian" – Church Dogmas – The Abysmal Depths of the Teachings of Martin Luther – The Disdain and Suppression of the Woman – The Clerical Abuse of Children – The Crimes against Creation ...

696 pp., HB, Order No. S 469en, ISBN: 978-3-89201-487-4

Vegetarians – Godless heretics?

What meat-eaters and vegetarians alike should know

Ulrich Seifert

Excessive consumption of meat is a very serious problem: For human beings it causes overweight problems, coronary heart diseases and other illnesses. It causes unspeakable torment to the animals in the factory farms and a horrible death in the slaughterhouses. What remains are clearcut rain forests, polluted land and waters – and a planet Earth, that is being driven directly into the climate disaster.

There's a war raging against the life on this planet, and the animals suffer terribly in the midst of it, as does the planet Earth. What shapes humankind's behavior and where do the ethical-moral values come from that we depend on for guidance in our lives?

Who got us into all this trouble? Whoever sharpens his sight find the profession that had already laid the cornerstone centuries ago for the brutal disdain of life – and continues to uphold this "tradition" until today ...

The author researched a fullness of hardly known correlations and facts. He appeals to the reader: "Do not look away! Look at what is being done to the animals!"

144 pp., SB, Order No. S 463en, ISBN: 978-1-890841-48-5

From Abraham to Gabriele

The Word of the Prophets Is Being Fulfilled

Martin Kübli

This book shows in condensed form the great span that underlies the works of the true prophets of God, but also the devastating effects of the being disregarded y the majority of people who have not followed the word of God. Starting with Abraham all the way to Gabriele, the prophetess and emissary of God in our time, the one Spirit, the All-Intelligence, has been working for the one plan,, which lies in the fulfillment of the prayer that Jesus taugt: "On Earth as it is in heaven."

This plan, throughout all the times of times, is behind the works of all true prophets of God, until this very day, for guiding back again to theKingdom of God the Fall-beings, which, in the very basis of their souls, are divine beings from the eternal homeland.

Like parls threaded on a string, the word of God is directed to us according to each individual's state of consciousness of the respective time and society, in an ever broder and more comprehensive scope, with ever more in-depth spiritual teachings. ...

82 pp., SB, Order No. S 465en, ISBN: 978-1-890941-34-8

We will be happy to send you our free catalog
Gabriele Publishing House,
Max-Braun-Str. 2, 97828 Marktheidenfeld, Germany
P. O. Box 2221, Deering, NH 03244, USA
www.gabriele-publishing-house.com
mail@gabriele-publishing-house.com
Toll-Free No. 001-844-576-0937